BUSINESS DRIVEN ACTION LEARNING

Business Driven Action Learning

Global Best Practices

Edited by
Yury Boshyk

1185655

First published 2000 by
MACMILLAN PRESS LTD
Houndmills, Basingstoke, Hampshire RG21 6XS
and London
Companies and representatives
throughout the world

ISBN 0–333–75240–6

University of Glamorgan
Prifysgol Morgannwg

Learning Resources Centre

A catalogue record for this book is available from the British Library.

This book is printed on paper suitable for recycling and made from fully managed and sustained forest sources.

10 9 8 7 6 5 4 3 2 1
09 08 07 06 05 04 03 02 01 00

Designed and formatted by
The Ascenders Partnership, Basingstoke
Illustrations by *Ascenders*

Printed and bound in Great Britain by
Creative Print & Design (Wales),
Ebbw Vale

Contents

PART I   Business Driven Action Learning: Multinational Company Experiences

PART II   **Facilitating and Enhancing Business-Driven Action Learning: Guidelines on Coodination and Teamwork**

Preface and Acknowledgements

THE idea for this book had its origins in 1995 with a meeting at IBM's Learning Center in Armonk, New York where Ron Bossert from Johnson & Johnson, Ron Hosta from IBM , Stephen Mercer from General Electric, and I, met to exchange practical advice and lessons learned from respective business focused action learning programmes. All agreed that what was needed was a wider forum at which practitioners from around the world could exchange experiences freely and constructively. As a consequence, in June 1996 the first Global Forum on Executive Development and Business Driven Action Learning was held and ever since, about one hundred multinational company representatives throughout the world gather annually, by invitation only, to discuss their approaches to business-driven action learning. Understandably, the majority of the articles in this book were originally presentations made at these forums.

This book is different from many others on executive development and action learning for at least three reasons. First because it is written primarily by practitioners from leading global companies and those who have worked extensively with them. Second, the breadth of the contributions is more international than other publications on this subject. And finally, most contributors are united in a common purpose – to tie behavioural and organizational learning and change to business results. Most companies in the book describe how they integrate executive development and action learning – business driven action learning – to develop executive leadership, foster teamwork and solve real business issues of strategic importance to their company.

Business driven action learning does not claim to be a new educational or management theory. In fact, it combines many of the most practical features of traditional and well known 'action learning' with the best of the rest in executive and organizational learning.

As we shall see in the introductory article, the house of action learning has many doors. In general, the classical or traditional variety as developed on the foundations of Reg Revans in the UK has flourished and is practised today most widely in the English-speaking and Nordic regions of the world. This approach concentrates on the individual and group or 'set' dimensions, and on the development of personal skills and business learning by and from the managers themselves. The business issues are not the central focus but are not excluded. In essence, development is the focal point and the business issues follow. Business driven action learning places the business issue or issues at the core and then develops the required learning around that core, but it also involves individual and team development and learning. Business driven action learning is not just 'project work' for the sake of projects and neither is it 'new' or 'invented' in the USA. Some companies have been using business driven action learning for many years. What is certain, however, is that more and more organizations and companies are beginning to adopt business driven action learning. Even in this volume alone, many companies are mentioned as having something to do with it, and many describe the connection in considerable detail. Recently, one of them, DuPont, has been recognized by the American Society of Training and Development as having a 'best practice' executive learning programme, 'Leadership for Growth'. But more on definitions, background and key features of business driven action learning in my introductory article.

This book is divided into two parts. After the introduction on definitions and elements of business driven action learning, contributors to Part I discuss their company experiences with business driven action learning. In Part II, practitioners discuss how to facilitate business driven action learning and the process of personal and team development during action learning, including the coaching role and interview phase 'country coordinator' role. For the reader's convenience I have also included a rather extensive list of recommended sources on business focused action learning.

In this volume we begin with a selection of some of the best practices among multinationals. Each contributor was asked to address a number of issues and questions: why action learning was initiated; to describe the actual programmes, objectives, content, selection of participants and so on; to share with us the business and developmental results, and if applicable the way in which these are measured; to comment on the success factors and the lessons learned from being involved in business driven action learning; and finally, to briefly mention what they and the company will be doing with business driven action learning in the future.

There is a wide variety of approaches to business driven or business focused action learning in these articles. For example, even within one company, General Electric, people sometimes refer to several approaches to action learning. Among these are Work Out and the Change Acceleration Process

(CAP) as well as the executive programmes like the Global Business Management Course (GBMC) and the Executive Development Course (EDC). Stephen Mercer focuses on the latter two rather than on the process approaches. The same can be said about duration of business driven action learning programmes. We see considerable differences. Some of these company programmes are of a short duration as in the case of DuPont, General Electric, IBM and Johnson & Johnson where the programmes are from three to four weeks in length. Others, especially the Europe-headquartered companies, prefer programmes that are longer and include project work while on the job, so to speak. DaimlerChrysler, Philips, Scancem, and Siemens use such an approach. And several of these include distance or 'distributed' learning throughout the programme. Some companies do not have formal learning programmes but projects, as in the case of Motorola, for example and many French multinationals – but in Motorola's case they involve facilitators during the project process.

Several companies in this volume describe programmes that do not fall into the usual definition of action learning or business driven action learning but they have used very innovative techniques that involve participants in learning and teamwork and can be used in business driven action learning. This is why I have included the Dow experience where they use 'learning maps' to outline their business process and stimulate discussion and a common understanding of the business and its values. The same can be said for Nigel Barrett's contribution on involving several company representatives to reflect of their experiences on several themes of concern for a consortium of companies. Some of the learning has also taken place in very dramatic circumstances as in the case of Boehringer Mannheim when the company went through an acquisition by Hoffman La Roche during their executive development programmes.

Some companies and individuals were interested in contributing but for a variety of reasons could not for this edition. Some of these will appear in an upcoming volume. I would like to thank the following for their interest and contributions: Gian Piero Bigando from Fiat, Mika Honjo from the Dentsu Institute for Human Studies, Grazyna Lesniak-Lebkowsa from the Warsaw School of Economics, Bonnie McIvor from Unilever, Thomas Sattelberger from Lufthansa; and the consultants, Chantal Fleuret, Morgan Gould, Brian Isaacson, Filippo Martino, Taebok Lee, Ake Reinholdsson, Alan Saunders, and Jan Fitzgerald Rycl. Others I would like to thanks for the time they gave and in some cases, the discussions during the preliminary interviews that I undertook with them. Among these were Janet McLaughlin from Corning and Garry DeRose, College of the Finger Lakes, Tom Hennebury and others from Nortel Networks, Paul Russell from Pepsico, Krystyna Weinstein from IFAL, Lennart Rohlin from the MiL Institute. I would also like to thank Kenneth Moore from

PriceWaterhouseCoopers, Lee Hofmann from DuPont, Ron Bossert, Stephen Mercer and all the contributors for their goodwill and enthusiasm for the publication.

My colleagues at the Theseus Institute, Ahmet Aykac, Francis Bidault, Nigel Freedman, and Ron Hosta were most supportive. Daniele Chauvel, Nicolas Rolland, Pamela Woodcock, and especially Claire Meneveau were always most helpful. Ruma Dutta was tenacious yet diplomatic in handling the coordinating role of so many contributors and in assisting in some of the editorial work. Stephen Rutt from the publisher was very thoughtful, professional and patient. To Nadia, Zara, Julia and Mutti as well as to my parents, I owe a debt that can never be truly expressed. They too have travelled on the long journey to publication and have lived through the many facets and dimensions involved in business driven action learning for themselves.

Business Driven Action Learning: the Key Elements

Yury Boshyk

BUSINESS driven action learning is a process and philosophy that can help change a company's strategy, and the behaviour of its people. In its most accomplished form it can provide breakthrough business results as well as highly rewarding personal and organizational learning and development. But, as with everything of professional value in life, it is both an art and a 'science'.

As a philosophy, business driven action learning is based on the belief and practice that learning should be tied to business realities, and that some of the best business solutions can and should come from fellow executives and employees. Many of the companies that utilize business driven action learning are those who also have a high respect for their people and who appreciate that learning often comes from the sharing of experiences in an open exchange, which in turn encourages reflection and practical application. One such company, Asea Brown Boveri (ABB), has predicated its approach on this foundation and has stated its belief that managers learn and develop 70 per cent on the job, 20 per cent through the influence of others, including their bosses, colleagues, and subordinates, and, 10 per cent through external courses and seminars.[1]

In today's world, business driven action learning is gaining greater currency because it is suited to the realities of today's business world and its demand that the development of people be of direct value to executives, and be measurable and relevant to business applications. At Johnson & Johnson, the world's largest healthcare products company, the business results of action learning have been measured as being often better than commissioned consulting reports and the leadership development better than anything ever done in the corporation.[2] For over twenty years, Heineken was one of several companies that participated in an action learning developmental programme. The former Chairman of the company, has stated that in his experience:

> Real progress in business is only achieved by corporations and individuals trying out creative ideas and making them work, by running into problems and solving

them, by pooling talent and scoring with it, and most of all ... by having fun and learning while doing. Business driven action learning is a superb vehicle for achieving this.[3]

And at General Electric for over ten years the business results from business driven action learning executive programmes have never been systematically measured because the return on the learning investment is evident to all, especially to the Executive Council and its CEO, Jack Welch.[4]

In some of the most successful companies, business driven action learning is seen as a necessity – as a strategic competitive advantage, for example at Siemens:

> The speed at which a corporation can learn and employ new knowledge is a decisive factor in competition. It is not enough to learn and to work. Learning and working must be integrated. Only then can a corporation be a learning organization. Action learning addresses this challenge very efficiently.[5]

Executives themselves are requesting more action learning from their companies. At NatWest, for example, a British financial institution, a survey of several hundred 'high potentials' between the ages of 25 and 33 indicated that the highest demand was for workplace-based action learning or project learning on real issues that related to the company's strategic and tactical agendas.[6] And when this learning and development is offered to young executives, they find the experience most gratifying and of benefit to many in the company, as in this example from DuPont:

> The project work is an excellent approach. Using a real-life business project really did enhance the learning and development and contribution back to the sponsoring business.[7]

Not surprisingly, therefore, some leading Western multinational companies have embraced business driven action learning and those adopting it are clearly on the increase.[8]

At this point it is important to distinguish business driven action learning from other varieties of action learning because the house of action learning has many doors, and hence definitions and approaches can vary. For this reason, a very brief summary might help explain the various 'schools' – albeit in a somewhat simplified way. In this context perhaps it is wise to recall the words of one commentator who stated that:

> Action learning is one of those blissfully simple, commonsensical ideas which has consistently been derided for being just that. While the essence of action learning is very simple, it is deceptively so. [10]

Contrary to some people's conceptions, action learning was not invented nor developed first in the United States. Today most people would equate action learning with Reg Revans who began to articulate and implement his approach in the 1930s in the United Kingdom. The essence of his approach and philosophy is that 'there can be no learning without action and no (sober and deliberate) action without learning'. Organizations and individuals cannot develop and flourish unless their rate of learning (L) is equal to, or greater than, the rate of change (C) being experienced: $L \geq C$. According to Revans, learning is composed of two elements: traditional instruction or Programmed knowledge (P), and Critical Reflection or Questioning insight (Q). The Learning equation is therefore: $L = P + Q$. Revans stated that managers confront what he called 'puzzles' and 'problems'. Experts can help with solutions to 'puzzles' but 'problems' have no right answers. In this area 'Q' can help. Managers learn best when they come together in action learning 'sets' or groups in voluntary association. In this way they learn and share their learning and understanding about the problems being addressed, about what is being learned about oneself, and about the process of 'learning to learn'. The last two are 'essential for the transfer of learning to other situations'.[11]

Over the years we have seen variations of this approach with the introduction of outside 'subject' specialists and with an orientation towards implementation. Various individuals and institutions could be included as propagators and supporters of this modified version of the 'traditionalist' or 'classical' Revans approach. Among the individuals we could mention are Alan Mumford, Mike Pedler, and Krystyna Weinstein, and various institutions. These include the Department of Management Learning in the Management School at Lancaster University, the Revans Centre for Action Learning and Research at University of Salford, and International Management Centres (IMC), sometimes known as the virtual action learning business school.[12] Some of these are in turn grouped around the International Foundation of Action Learning (IFAL), housed at Lancaster University with affiliates in Australia, Canada, and the United States. They seem to work primarily with lower middle and middle management although this is, of course, a generalisation. They also work with public sector managers in these countries.

Action-Reflection Learning

The emphasis on reflection is also very much part of 'traditional' action learning but one group or 'school' has emphasised this more than others. This is the 'action-reflection learning' approach practised by such institutions as the MiL Institute in Lund, Sweden and its US counterpart, Leadership in International Management Ltd (LIM). They in turn are involved with a circle of US-based educationalists, among them Victoria Marsick at Teacher's College, Columbia

University. They cooperate very closely with the 'traditionalists' and have trademarked, so to speak, the 'action-reflection learning' approach. In 1999 the first worldwide conference involving the 'traditionalists' and the 'reflectionists' was held after a period of unofficial isolation. The founder of MiL, Lennart Rohlin has an active group of supporters and practitioners primarily in the Nordic region of Europe and holds an annual conference. They came to emphasise reflection before the Kolb learning cycle (experience–reflection– abstraction–testing–back to experience) became popular, and they have also recently developed a philosophical foundation to their approach.[13]

What is Business Driven Action Learning?

Business driven action learning as practised in some of the best companies involves five key elements:

- the active involvement and support of senior executives;
- work on real business issues and the exploration of new strategic business opportunities;
- action research and learning focused on internal and external company experiences and thinking that can help resolve business issues;
- leadership development through teamwork and coaching;
- and the implementation of recommendations and follow up on business issues examined, and the organizational and individual learning that took place, thus enhancing positive business results and ensuring that learning is greater than the rate of change (L > C).

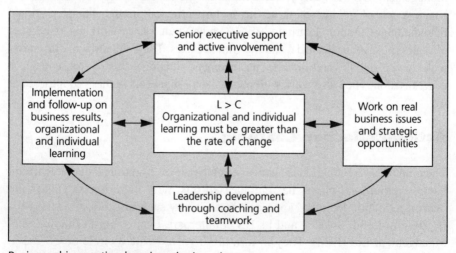

Business driven action learning: the key elements

Business driven action learning differs from the above-mentioned approaches because it has a very emphatic business focus not like the other varieties of action learning that stress the importance of the individual learner or that of the group or 'set'. But business driven action learning also integrates company-wide learning with individual executive development and teamwork. At the core of this approach is a real business issue or strategic opportunity as defined and sponsored by the most senior executives in the company. Also, due to the pace of change in the business world, the premise that organisational and individual learning must be *greater* than the rate of change (not just equal to and greater) is a fundamental starting point for business driven action learning. Action research and learning focuses on interviewing clients, customers, suppliers, subject experts, 'best practice' companies and others who can help with understanding the business issue. At the same time, individual coaching and teamwork facilitation is a key part of the leadership development. And finally, the implementation of business solutions as well as the leveraging of the organizational and individual learning require follow up and company wide cooperation.

Other differences from the 'traditionalists' and other varieties of action learning are most evident when discussing the component parts of executive development action learning programmes that are described in this volume. These will be evident to the reader but we can summarize these component parts as well as the learning methods used in business driven action learning in the following two figures.

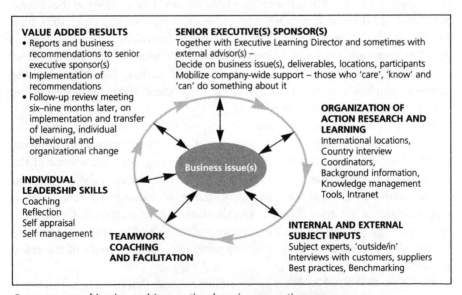

VALUE ADDED RESULTS
- Reports and business recommendations to senior executive sponsor(s)
- Implementation of recommendations
- Follow-up review meeting six–nine months later, on implementation and transfer of learning, individual behavioural and organizational change

SENIOR EXECUTIVE(S) SPONSOR(S)
Together with Executive Learning Director and sometimes with external advisor(s) –
Decide on business issue(s), deliverables, locations, participants
Mobilize company-wide support – those who 'care', 'know' and 'can' do something about it

ORGANIZATION OF ACTION RESEARCH AND LEARNING
International locations, Country interview Coordinators, Background information, Knowledge management Tools, Intranet

INDIVIDUAL LEADERSHIP SKILLS
Coaching
Reflection
Self appraisal
Self management

Business issue(s)

TEAMWORK COACHING AND FACILITATION

INTERNAL AND EXTERNAL SUBJECT INPUTS
Subject experts, 'outside/in'
Interviews with customers, suppliers
Best practices, Benchmarking

Components of business driven action learning executive programmes

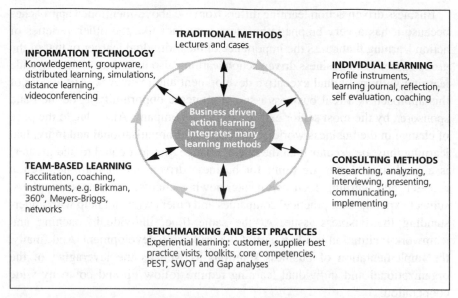

Learning methods used in business driven action learning programmes

Some 'Lessons Learned' and Concerns

Finally, a few words should be said about some 'lessons learned' and concerns relating to business driven action learning. We mentioned from the beginning that business driven action learning is both an 'art' and a 'science' because a particular and delicate clarity must be maintained on a variety of matters such as the balance between internal business consulting and leadership development; reflection and action; team and individual needs, and a host of other such issues. This is the responsibility of the learning facilitators and the senior executives who must always strive to be clear about harmonising the learning and business objectives.

It is very important that this thinking be done from the very beginning so as to deal better with a number of potential problems and opportunities. Problems could arise when expectations of senior executives do not match those of the participants, when the participant selection is viewed as being questionable, and when a business issue is too tactical in nature, to name but a few reasons. Opportunities could arise through consideration of such matters as how best to implement the proposed business recommendations and leverage and capture the learning generated in action learning programs, for the benefit of the entire organization.

We know that it takes courage, commitment and determination to launch business driven executive action learning programmes and that the rewards for a company and the individuals involved speak for themselves. While the participants in action learning do not have a collective voice in this volume, almost all the individual articles stress the very positive experiences of the learners and the satisfaction of those who sponsored and encouraged this learning and development. There is no doubt in the minds of the contributors, many of them initiators of business driven action learning, that the process was worth it despite the myriad of details and challenges. We hope that the articles in this volume will also encourage others either to launch business driven action learning within their own organizations or to appreciate better the action learning already taking place.

Notes

1. Arne Olsson of ABB, as cited in Kevin Barham and Claudia Heimer, *ABB, The Dancing Giant: Creating the Globally Connected Corporation*. London: Financial Times-Pitman, 1998, p. 336.
2. As stated by Dennis Longstreet, a Company Group Chairman, in an internal Johnson & Johnson video presentation on the company's Executive Development Programme, 1999.
3. Gerard van Schaik, President, European Foundation for Management Development, former Chairman of the Executive Board of Heineken. I am grateful to Gordon Lackie and Maarjte van Westerop for their assistance in providing this and other comments on action learning.
4. See the article on General Electric by Stephen Mercer in this volume .
5. Quotation by Professor Peter Pribilla, Head of Corporate Human Resources, Member of the Corporate Executive Committee, Siemens AG, as provided by Dr Matthias Bellmann, Siemens.
6. See Nigel Barrett's article in this volume.
7. Participant quotation on the DuPont Leadership for Growth Executive Development Programme, as provided by Vickie Legros, the programme director.
8. Albert A. Vicere and Robert M. Fulmer, *Leadership by Design: How Benchmark Companies Sustain Success Through Investment in Continuous Learning*. Boston: Harvard Business School Press, 1997; see also, Martine Plompen, *Unleashing the Power of Learning: Executive Development in Europe*. Brussels: European Foundation for Management Development, 1999.
9. See the very good overview and review of the literature by Alan Mumford in Mike Pedler, ed., *Action Learning in Practice*. Aldershot: Gower, 1997. Interview with Krystyna Weinstein, 12 May 1999.
10. Stuart Crainer, *Key Management Ideas*. London: Financial Times-Pitman, 1998, pp. 258–61.
11. As summarized in Mike Pedler, *Action Learning for Managers*. London: Lemos & Crane, 1996, pp. 20–2.
12. On IMC see the articles in Alan Mumford, ed., *Action Learning at Work*. Aldershot: Gower, 1997.
13. Presentation by Lennart Rohlin at the Third Theseus International Conference on Strategic Executive Development and Action Learning, June 1998. Lennart Rohlin, Per-Hugo Skarvad and Sven Ake Nilsson, *Strategic Leadership in the Learning Society*. Lund: MiL Publishers, 1998.

PART
I

Business Driven
Action Learning

Multinational Company Experiences

DaimlerChrysler: Global Leadership Development Using Action-Oriented and Distance Learning Approaches

Wolfgang Braun

LEARNING has become, more than ever before, a key differentiator in the selection of tomorrow's leaders. Management, today, has to survive in more complex, cross border business environments by finding and applying new business solutions rapidly. To learn better and faster than the competition is the main objective of corporate management programmes which help companies deliver to the market in a short time and provide innovative business solutions for a globalizing enterprise. 'Work smarter not harder' is the main challenge for future managers who aim to be 'proactive instead of reactive'.

Action-Oriented Learning combines new learning techniques with actual business assignments, involving teamwork to come up with state of art solutions for improving internal business processes. It closes the gap between theory and practice and transforms business operations. Action Oriented Learning has been applied for more than two years by more than a hundred managers at Daimler Benz and now this will no doubt continue at DaimlerChrysler. It has already brought in visible improvements and has demonstrated success in the global business transformation exercise. Distance Learning links places of competence with places for business action using videoconference and group computing technologies.

Management Responsibilities in the Global Business Environment

The pressures on today's business leaders have become very complex. New issues and problems require radically new approaches. If a business wants to be successful it must grow. Substantial growth for traditional corporations is achieved either through expansion of the existing business portfolio, i.e. launching new products or services, or by going global, i.e. entering new markets or market segments. Additionally, national boundaries are melting into free trade zones. As a result, local brands increasingly tend to become global brands, multidomestic products address different cultures and international communication channels and modern information technologies enable a business to operate easily on a global scale.

These changes have had a severe impact on a company's competitive position in the business domain. If one wishes to remain a business leader, one has to confront cross-cultural requirements and increasingly complex business situations. Despite this, companies show a reluctance to change. One major reason is identified as follows: 'If the obsession with next year's performance becomes a struggle, to what extent is the organization overwhelmed by strategic initiatives or … a victim of the numbers game?' With reference to the unintended consequences of industry leadership, the symptoms can be summarized as:

- Restructuring of the resource base, though denominator management (cost cutting) is inherently self limiting.
- Even if the revenue stream is prolonged there is no growth.
- Executives do not see the need for change.
- There is an unwillingness to make change happen.
- There is an inability to act effectively.

To attack these symptoms and to achieve prosperous change, a leader must bring about a sense of urgency for change as well as a change vision among all in the organization. He should be able to guide the organization and understand its capacity for change. Additionally, he should list actionable first steps in supporting the structure and processes that would steer his teams towards value creation.

Managers who ignore productivity gains from information technology and who are reluctant to change their outdated management paradigms resist the process of global business transformation. Their traditional experiences are limited to hard skills acquired in a rational and less complex business world. These managers must adapt an open minded attitude towards change and respect the unavoidable business globalization challenges. They have to appreciate the tremendous opportunities and recognise available skills and competencies within the organization.

We have started the Transnational Development process by selecting a group of high potential managers. We have empowered them to lead well into the next century, using a refined method of Action Learning. This method was applied to enable the organization to transform itself substantially and to defend our ability to remain better and faster than the competition.

Understanding the Business Dynamics to Define a Human Resource Oriented Strategy

> 'To achieve leadership, a company must reinvent the business, ... to sustain leadership, a company must reinvent itself.'
>
> (Change Associates International)

In a global business, learning from the past is no longer adequate. To be successful in the future we have to find new ways of preparing our leaders by extending their skills and competencies. We compared our decision-making processes with the common business obstacles stated by Change Associates International, which are as follows:

- Top management spends more time on internal negotiations than on customers and competitors.
- Top management concentrates its efforts on leveraging existing competencies instead of acquiring new ones.
- Top management focuses on exploiting existing opportunities instead of creating new opportunities.

And, as they would in most multinational corporations, we acknowledged that these obstacles could lead to major management deficiencies, with the corporation's dominant concern being managing the current business rather than defining future business.

To escape this short-sighted approach to management, we implemented Action Oriented Learning which forced us to focus on the future by addressing the following issues:

- Fundamental assumptions about what the customer values.
- Fundamental assumptions about what the company needs to do well to provide value.
- Fundamental assumptions about how value can be created in the future.

We used the results to train managers to develop a common way of thinking about strategy. We then applied Action Learning to implement our strategies. This enabled us to define a strategic process based on two main building blocks – by asking every element in the company to (1) develop an internally consistent value chain, focusing on core competencies that create meaningful value, and (2) distinguish competencies from assets, thus charting a road map for subsequent management actions. Ultimately, Action Learning breaks down the global business strategy into manageable operational actions at three levels:

- Actions designed to win in the present, based on current success factors.
- Actions designed to take advantage of discontinuities.
- Actions designed to build capabilities for the future.

The goal is to achieve value creation for the company as an integrated system of activities. This became our business model for the whole organization.

Analysing Learning and Learning Assumptions within the Organization

Why is the tenet 'Change or be changed', or the phrase 'life-long learning', so critical to the employability of a manager? Change stems from increased competition or customer demand in world-wide markets and through the global transformation of your business processes. To understand the type and dimension of change, we used the following frame:

Timing of change (reference: Tushmann / Nadler)[1]

Reactive	Shareholder value, Year 2000 conversion	Euro conversion, US Gaap Implementation
Anticipatory	Customer orientation, Process optimization	Globalization ie Asia Strategy, Mergers and Acquisitions

Incremental   Strategic

Scope of change

To keep the competitive advantage of our globally leading company, trained managers were assigned to activities in the quadrant of anticipatory/strategic change, to ensure that the changes in the business processes were 'proactive' rather than 'reactive'. This strategy converted our traditional culture into an innovative company culture, driven by leaders who encouraged their teams to act as learning organizations. The fundamental question for leadership development in a highly dynamic business environment now becomes: can we learn from the past or must we learn anew for the future?

To answer this question we made an assessment of how long the knowledge provided during training could be applied to current business assignments and found that there was a half-time attached to acquired knowledge. The erosion of knowledge is thus represented by an asymptotic curve declining over time.

Let us take the example of a two-year MBA executive programme. At the conclusion of the programme, only 50 per cent of the knowledge acquired is applicable to current business problems. Four years later, only 25 per cent of the knowledge is relevant, after six years 12.5 per cent, after eight years 6.25 per cent and finally after 14 years less than one per cent of the knowledge remains relevant and applicable to business assignments. If we apply the economic value of the possession of knowledge to a business organisation, we may claim that any knowledge leverage below 30 per cent has no employability value to a company. Based on this assessment, an MBA degree would no longer be marketable three years after graduation.

The conclusion from this must be that managers have to respond with continuous knowledge updates. To stay up-to-date as a manager and to improve the value of employability, a manager would need to refresh his knowledge inventory frequently. This fact makes learning a must in order to survive in the future business environment.

If we shift from the receiving end of training to the delivery of training, we can identify learning traps as well. Taking a closer look at how we run training, we had to conclude that nothing had changed dramatically in the last hundred years of learning. To better illustrate the traditional learning concept, we use the following training efficiency table.

Type of learning	Percentage of applicable knowledge
Hearing	5
Reading	10
Seeing	20
Doing	40
Self learning	80

Measuring our former executive education programmes using this table, we discovered that most of these programmes were limited to an efficiency factor of 20 per cent. This translates into a learning benefit of a mere half day out of a five-day training seminar. And the more senior the programme, the more remote the training location – thus adding travel time and making executive seminars longer and less effective.

From a financial perspective, our reading of this phenomena is validated thus: if you were to invest a total sum of US$20 000 for a five-day executive training, plus travel time and expenses then you would be gaining less than five per cent of the training investment in terms of cost savings on the job. Furthermore, most executive trainings still concentrate on rational or functional business topics (hard skills), whereas new demands in management training, including the demands of going global, require more of an emphasis on soft skills which are almost impossible to teach in the classroom. A functional management development approach cannot adequately solve actual business problems, in the light of the learning gaps and strategic challenges outlined above.

Globalization has introduced change in a wide range of work processes within a company. Keeping 'up to date' with the growing flood of information on global business transformation causes an information overflow for most managers. With business change coming in ever shorter cycles, 'on the job' learning becomes a must for survival. Considering this vital need for information as well as experience, designers of executive seminars have to be skilled in information engineering.

Some managers argue that the way they learned in the past is still the appropriate way to learn in the future. Their attitude cannot be ignored. But neither can the excitement of learning with new technologies (e.g. the world-wide web and multimedia – which provide very individual and active ways of learning).

Identifying participants' need for knowledge as well as their skills and competencies requirements gives the first insights into the knowledge engineering process. The second insight comes from an observation of training demands: application of the organization's 'knowledge inventory' helps to identify the gap between management development content and skill and competency needs. As a test for the knowledge inventory analysis we have been using the Myers Briggs Type Indicator (MBTI) test. The MBTI test results are placed in the following knowledge inventory framework to obtain a structured view on learning requirements. 'To work smarter not harder' became an Action Learning slogan with demands for better information delivery.

Functional Knowledge Requirements ('Knowledge Inventory')

Don't know	(3) *Marketing* Value of a brand, Product portfolio positioning and pricing strategies	(4) *Strategy* New market entry strategies, Mergers and Acquisitions
Know	(1) *Finance* Shareholder value, new accounting standards *Production* Quality management	(2) *Organisation/HR* Innovation and knowledge management, management of multicultural teams
	Know	Don't know

Business change requirements

Through strategic thinking, we gained an understanding of the deficiencies in an organization's functional and change management requirements. That analysis provided an answer for the upper left quadrant (3) or the 'you know what you should know' factor. Using a market and competition analysis we were able to plot the 'you know what you need to know' factor for business transformation in quadrant (2). The upper right quadrant, (4), conveys either the biggest business risks or greatest business opportunities. These risks often emerge when companies are going global, when business leaders are confronted with challenges they have never faced before. The business opportunities unlock the knowledge potential – 'if we knew what we know we would be the most innovative enterprise' – thus transforming best practice procedures obtained from industry benchmarks and radically affecting the application of tested management concepts fom business schools.

We conducted a survey among managers who had attended executive development trainings to find out how much they had actually learnt from the trainings. We found out that up to 80 per cent of what they were taught was from the 'knows what he knows' quadrant, i.e. quadrant (1).

Today we avoid these time-wasting training refreshers, by interviewing seminar participants weeks before to identify their seminar expectations and contributions. Their answers help keep quadrant (1) learning to a minimum and save us time and effort in training preparation. Since we were now able to concentrate on quadrants (2), (3) and (4), using more of the Action Learning techniques, we were able to exchange experiences with colleagues and address current business issues. By eliminating redundant training content, based on the findings in the interviews, we managed to close the gap between theory and practice.

The involvement of participants in defining the agenda for learning is a crucial element in Action Learning methodology. Time saved on teaching can now be dedicated to transforming best practice procedures across the learning teams.

As a result of Action Learning:

- Time spent on training was already producing business results for those who presented their business problems.
- Attendees were taking full advantage of the available knowledge and experience, as in a learning organisation.
- Participants benefited by seeing their knowledge applied in different ways, thus sharpening their skills for the business environment.
- Participants became more involved, as they were involved in finding the solution to actual business problems.

Analysing Managers' Skills and Competencies for Leadership Development

As a supplemental test to the Myers Briggs Type Indicator, we used the Learning Style Inventory (Firo-B test) to identify the learning types of the individuals attending the Action Learning programmes. The results from the tests enabled the trainer to apply the appropriate learning techniques and to build work teams capable of generating innovative solutions.

The optimal mix of workteam members (profile description) includes four types:

Activist	*Reflector*
Having an experience	Reviewing the experience
Theorist	*Pragmatist*
Concluding from experience	Planning the next steps

Firo-B Type Indicator

In our former training we seldom saw an immediate improvement in performance. With Action Learning, we changed from a sequential event 'off the job' (where the manager leaves his work environment and returns as enlightened leader) to the more natural approach, i.e. hosting the training in a live business environment, or conceptually converting business units into training centres. Leadership development is now tightly integrated with 'on the job' problem solving which builds upon existing skills and competence in education, experience, strategy, team responsibilities, team structure, career planning, coaching requirements and business assignments of the executives' work environment.

It is not always easy to convince executives to host Action-Oriented programmes in their work environments and to propose programmes tied into existing strategic initiatives, performance assessments, measurable returns, large scale exercises for teams, shorter and more focused programmes or action learning projects involving international audiences and global exposure.

Furthermore, Action Learning requires intimate business knowledge, as well as thorough preparation on the part of the business school faculty responsible for delivering on-site trainings.

The integration of suppliers, customers or joint venture partners in an Action Learning environment allows complete business solutions to emerge. The role of business schools has shifted from presenting business concepts derived from rigorous research to the live examinations of business processes, producing solutions that can be applied immediately, and results measured in terms of business growth and value added.

The job of the Human Resource function is now driven by more local business strategies. In order to align local actions with corporate strategy, the Corporate University has to address remote business operations and deliver best practice expertise on site.

The preparation of management development objectives, knowledge inventory collections and learning style examinations prior to the seminars is designed to be cost and time effective. 'On the job' integration demands additional precautions on timing and schedules. The partnering business school is remotely linked to the local training location via videoconference so that the training stays consistent across business units.

Action and Distance Learning approaches were executed in form of a modular Transnational Development Process and satisfied all participants. Participants showed higher levels of commitment as they were involved in designing the training content at a very early stage. During interview preparations, attendees spontaneously came up with business assignments for study. On a variety of international issues, we were able to bring cross-national, geographically distributed resources together in 'virtual work teams' and come up with solutions in real time.

Videoconference systems and workgroup computing platforms on the internet allowed us to work with the business school as well as with remote work teams.

Action Projects have been successful in:

- Analysing licence agreements.
- Improving the success rate of new business proposals (the business development process).
- Providing value-based investment scenarios.
- Core competence and competition analysis.
- Analysing the value chain (component production strategy).

Action and Distance Learning Approach for Global Leadership Development

The real dilemma in Global Leadership Development seems to be: 'If you tell me what your job will be in five years, I can provide excellent leadership development seminars.' Not many people are able to foresee future responsibilities, and, if they could, they would not search for the appropriate help in preparing for that future. The new role of leadership development is to make intelligent assumptions about the future of business and to provide business simulations.

Business Simulation is a key element in Action Learning. It teaches leaders how to deal with new and unknown problems, and it changes business units into concurrent learning teams that combine 'off the job' and 'on the job' training. But participants also came up with new methods of training and examined their optimal learning style as well as the power of learning teams in the organization. Using a selected group of high-potential managers, the firm can now build on a 'change' network for business transformation. In addition, the concept of Action and Distance learning has been used to form a transnational development process and to build up a cross-border, cross-cultural change manager network.

The Change Manager network is based on the hypothesis that three to five per cent of leaders are sufficient to change a whole organization. These leaders, coming from all parts of the organization and from different business functions, can be trained within a three to five year timeframe. Careful selection of leaders is key, to ensure good distribution across the company. These leaders form the Change Management network and may be directed by the board members.

A three module concept was developed for transnational management development. An open Global Leadership Programme was selected for top management. This is offered by an international business school. It is a four to six week open programme, including field trips and leadership development training. The result of the Global Leadership Programme is the development of a real business strategy for each participant. These strategies can be divided into strategic projects which can then be delegated to middle management. The top manager becomes a sponsor for the strategic initiatives and coaches middle management in driving the change process. Middle managers chosen to manage the strategic projects are then invited into a customised Executive Leadership Programme, on the lines of the Global Leadership Programme.

The Executive Leadership Programme thus identifies high potential general managers with a need to prepare for global business operations.

An innovative approach was needed for the last module, targeted towards the first management levels, where the number of managers to be trained was in the hundreds. Sending these target groups to open programmes would have meant a major training investment as well as a loss of work capacity for the organization. An Executive MBA programme was chosen for these management levels, with a modified MBA course curriculum that could directly address business transformation topics relevant to the company. Selected lectures were delivered to company premises via videoconference from the USA. This allowed managers to attend a part time MBA programme one evening a week for a full year, absorbing concepts and information covered in the Executive Leadership Programme as well as in the Global Leadership Programme. This third module is called the Advanced Degree Programme and includes project assignments derived from strategic projects in the Executive Leadership Programme. Participants of the Executive Leadership Programme act as mentors for the project teams of the Advanced Degree Programme.

All three modules are supported by core faculty members of the business school and are coordinated by the HR Development function. The link between faculty and the Change Manager network is done via the internet, enabling coordination and communication across all modules.

The management development concept is also tightly integrated into the firm's management appraisal and succession planning systems. Management development is seen as an investment for high potential managers selected on the basis of the firm's skills and competency dimensions. It is paramount that developed resources are spread through the worldwide body of the organization in a 'change network', filling key corporate positions with 'change managers'.

This pragmatic approach enables intensive global learning and provides an innovative approach to international business problems. The transnational development programme outlined above was established for global leadership development and serves equally well for innovation and knowledge transfer within the organization. All selected 'change managers' have been excited about the speed and relevance of learning.

In closing, I believe that this concept serves well as a key element in a learning organization and can address the needs for leadership development as part of a global business transformation strategy.

CHAPTER 2

Sustaining Change and Accelerating Growth through Business-Focused Learning

Pierre Guillon, Robert Kasprzyk and Jeannine Sorge

Introduction

OVER one hundred years ago, Herbert H. Dow founded The Dow Chemical Company in Midland, Michigan, USA. With its global headquarters in Midland, Dow has 115 manufacturing sites in 37 countries. Dow has grown steadily over the years, from a small midwestern company to the global company we are today. Dow is the fifth largest chemical company in the world with annual sales of more than \$20 bn. Dow supplies chemistry-based solutions to customers in more than 160 countries around the world in a variety of industry sectors including automotive, appliances, aeronautics, electronics, home furnishings, construction, health care, food services and recreation. Our workforce, numbering more than 40 000, mirrors this level of breadth and diversity.

For many years, Dow's growth was driven by our ability to transplant our production, process technology and our large, integrated operations to any country in the world, where the employees who built them felt they were part of the larger Dow family. In addition to geographic growth, we also grew through the development of new and better solutions for our customers using our commitment to cutting-edge science. This dedication to innovation and process technology, coupled with our talented people, forms the core of our competitive advantage, and will fuel our continued growth into the next century.

Dow Recognizes the Need to Change: Creating Our Strategic Blueprint

As economies, businesses and our customers became global, we understood that we had entered a new age. For the chemical industry, this new age is at the same time both a serious challenge to our survival and a new world for opportunity.

A challenge, because it has confronted us with new low-cost competitors in developing countries, fuelled customer and consumer expectations of ever-higher quality and ever-lower prices, and heightened the battle for investment capital. But it is also a tremendous opportunity, because of new markets and new consumer demand.

To respond to the marketplace and the changes taking place around us, our change journey started in 1992 with massive re-engineering of our critical global work processes that impact on what we do. We had been institutionalizing our approach to quality and re-engineering and improving our work processes for several years, but now we had to take stronger action. In 1993 Dow's leadership established and communicated our Strategic Blueprint as the road map for Dow's transformation to achieving our vision and mission 'to be the best at applying chemistry ... to be the most productive, best value-growth chemical company in the world.' The Blueprint, modelled on the corporate Dow diamond logo, sets out four critical and interrelated themes: competitive standard, productivity, value growth and culture. Dow's leadership has made implementing the Strategic Blueprint its driving force. The Blueprint was our guide to create our future in times of great change and was an anchor for the many changes Dow expected for the next few years.

To understand Dow is to understand the elements of our Blueprint (see Figure 2.2).

- Competitive Standard is our approach to the active management of Dow's business portfolio, with business accountability for strategy and profit and loss results, business alignment to meet customer needs, and an external focus to understand customers, competitors and market trends.
- Productivity in the Blueprint requires us to leverage best practices around the world, optimize our chemical process and production integration to enhance asset efficiency and to continually review and re-engineer work processes to achieve top-tier performance versus external benchmarks.
- Value Growth in the Blueprint represents our desire to grow existing businesses, leverage leading product and market positions, commercialize new products and services to create new business opportunities, and expand geographically to capture emerging market opportunities.
- Culture representing the desire in our Blueprint to restructure the organization and processes to encourage the desired attributes of our organization, connect business success with personal success, create a learning organization through a special emphasis on training and development and modify HR policies to match strategy and the global business structure.

PURPOSE

Provide superior solutions for our customers and society through science and good thinking.

VISION

To be the best at applying chemistry to benefit customers, employees, shareholders and society.

MISSION

To be the most productive, best value-growth chemical company in the world.

CORE VALUES

Fundamental to our success are the values we believe in and practice.

People are the source of our success. We treat one another with respect, promote teamwork, and encourage personal freedom and growth. Leadership and excellence in performance are sought and rewarded.

Customers are the reason we exist. They receive our strongest commitment to meet their needs.

Our **Products** and **Services** reflect dedication to quality, innovation and value.

Our **Conduct** demonstrates integrity and commitment to ethics, safety, health and the environment.

THE DOW CHEMICAL COMPANY

Figure 2.1 Dow Chemical *Purpose, Vision, Mission* and *Core Values* statement

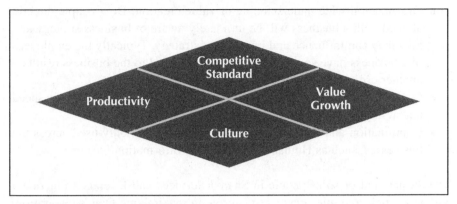

Figure 2.2 Dow's Strategic Blueprint

Each of these elements provides Dow with the necessary direction for success in the future. Developing and implementing Dow's Blueprint for creating the future has been the context for all actions since 1993.

Dow Restructures to Create Global Business Units

Reacting to the Blueprint strategy, a major initiative touching all of the Blueprint themes, and the most far-reaching change, has been the organizational changes making Dow's new Global Business Model a reality. The new model combines small company speed, flexibility, entrepreneurial spirit and customer focus with big company technical and financial strength and global presence. We are uniquely structured to emphasize customer service and quality while maintaining productivity and keeping our costs low by avoiding unnecessary duplication and leveraging our strengths across the businesses.

Today Dow is structured around 14 unique Global Business Units from adhesives, sealants and coatings, to hydocarbons and energy, to polysterene to Dow AgroSciences. Each is a discrete economic and organizational entity that creates and implements distinct, global business strategies. Many people in functional and geographic jobs are now part of these businesses; activities and resources are prioritized and focused on value-creating, customer-driven needs.

There is a simple premise guiding Dow's Global Business Model: by having the vast majority of people directly reporting into a business, they become much more knowledgeable and focused on the market trends and customer needs facing that business. By roughly doubling the number of people directly accountable to a Business – from less than 40 per cent in 1996 – Dow stands to make dramatic gains in:

- Organization-wide understanding of value creation; Dow people directly aligned with a business will be intimately aware of business strategy and how they can influence and impact that strategy. Typically the employees of a business have some portion of their pay tied to the business results – another critical aspect of linking performance with results.
- Our overall ability to focus on the business agenda and respond, with speed and agility to customer needs.
- Coordination and sharing of services that are commonly used across the businesses, such as Human Resources and Information Systems.

The 20 per cent or so of people in Shared Services and leveraged functional and geographic activities play a critical role in maximizing Dow's integration. They share their skills and expertise across the organization to ensure the implementation of best practices around the world and, therefore, are integral to ensuring that Dow's business model is optimized.

Human Resources as a Shared Service: One Example of a Leveraged Function in the New Global Business Model

As one of the leveraged, or shared, services at Dow, Human Resources realized that its challenge in the new organization was to provide globally effective, cost-competitive services that satisfied our clients, the Global Business Units and other functional clients. With this in mind, Human Resources re-engineering began in 1995, with three key objectives:

- Re-engineer the Dow Human Resources function globally.
- Globally standardized processes with smaller organization.
- Move toward first quartile performance and partnership with the businesses.

Dow HR began to look externally in order to establish benchmark metrics against which we could measure ourselves and determine where improvements needed to occur and, equally importantly, find best practices that could be leverages inside Dow. To meet this need, Dow took the lead in building and nurturing a consortium of companies that were interested in obtaining comparable measurements and best practices.

After a series of personal visits to Human Resources departments of companies, including chemical industry and other premier companies having global operations and who were also interested in benchmarking metrics and sharing best practices, the consortium was initiated. To protect confidentiality and ensure a globally standard process for data collection, Dow retained the services of the Saratoga group to develop the surveys, collect, analyze and report the data.

After collecting the responses from the different companies, Saratoga provided the ability to assess quickly where Dow HR rated when compared with the other companies in the consortium. The data provided the ability to assess our competencies against those considered 'best in the world'. With the results of the studies, we designed globally consistent processes reflecting what we learned as best practices in the sharing of the consortium to enable us to provide flawless delivery of our services at competitive costs and measurable satisfaction levels. Beyond the metrics collected it was clear that the value of the consortium was also in sharing and discussing best practices with each other.

The benchmarking and best practices discussion around leadership development also revealed our need to change our current practices. Our approach to leadership development at that time was not as strategic as other best practices companies, so the HR Committee (HRC), composed of the seven most senior leaders in the organization including the CEO, was determined to move forward with a new approach to leadership development. We had regional and unconnected approaches to general leadership development and many of our programmes were not reflecting the changes the company was making. While our leadership development for future leaders was well established with university partnerships and consortiums providing excellent results and feedback from the participants on general business management classroom experiences, it was available only for a small percentage of the audience affecting all Dow employees. It was clear that to fully realize the benefits of the Global Business Team model, we would have to align all leaders on the key strategic themes and provide a solid background for future decisions. What was needed for Dow leaders was a specific intervention that would help all of our leaders be able to articulate the direction and strategy of the company clearly and with conviction. The discussions and data provided by the benchmarking gave Human Resources the ability to address the changes the HRC wanted to make. We were convinced an alignment and communication exercise was needed to ground everyone on the overall strategy and thoughts about the business direction. What form and process the exercise would take would be decided on through a partnership with the HRC and with Human Resources.

The Changing Role of Leadership at Dow

Keeping pace with the changes we've described above is a fundamental responsibility of every Dow employee. The nature of business today demands that we – as individuals and as an organization – accumulate, assimilate, process and deliver information at incredible speed. In days gone by, 'experienced' meant that a person had gained a certain level of knowledge and expertise over time. Today, that is not always the case. That same experience can quickly become outdated, unless it is continually renewed and refreshed. Today's experienced people understand the importance of lifelong learning and realize that it is our most powerful offensive asset in the competitive marketplace.

No longer is leadership confined to traditional roles as supervisors, deploying command and control techniques, or managers, distributing work assignments. Dow's leaders today must take on the role of coach, mentor and teacher. One of their fundamental responsibilities is to articulate the strategy, teach our values, and energize Dow people to think creatively, take informed risks, stretch themselves to reach new heights of achievement, and provide career development guidance. Our senior leaders realized that for everyone in the company to understand 'the big picture', to comprehend the forces of change in our industry, and to realize the impact their development actions have on our customers, we would need a revolutionary new approach for continuous learning. In this context, the idea of a special network of leaders was considered.

Leadership Development Network is Created

To help leaders carry out their important new roles, Dow created the Leadership Development Network (LDN) which consists of approximately 3000 Dow people in critical roles for the corporation, including people leadership. The members of the LDN meet once per year to participate in an interactive learning experience – facilitated by selected Dow senior leaders – focused on understanding critical issues facing Dow. The attendees are then charged with creating a 'shared vision' with all Dow employees by replicating the learning experience world-wide, assuring the company direction reaches everyone. By promoting face-to face dialogue, debate and discussion, the LDN is fostering a continuous learning environment. Many different techniques for accomplishing a leadership learning event were discussed, but the research suggested that adults learn best when they are engaged and conduct a dialogue with one another.

In order to stimulate discussion and promote understanding of Dow's direction, Dow worked with Root Learning, Inc., a company specializing in development of a unique process for communication and learning. We worked closely with Root Learning to develop customized, interactive 'Learning Maps®' to graphically depict Dow's issues. This interactive Learning Map process is designed to promote dialogue around the complex environment that we operate in and to help participants discuss and understand how – and why – we are responding to the challenges.

Learning Maps Explained

The Learning Map methodology is a highly interactive learning process, and very different from the traditional training and education programmes we have used in the past. We learn best when we are interested and when we are having fun. The Learning Map process creates conditions in which people can learn easily and come rapidly to their own conclusions.

The learning method developed by Root Learning challenges people to discuss and deal with key business issues and no longer permits the participant to be a passive member of the organization. Moreover, the participants must engage in discussion without being told the 'answers'. They learn by coming to their own conclusions, guided by the questions and information in the dialogue and on the visual. Based on these principles, Dow's Executive Committee determined we would use this methodology as the driver of a learning programme aimed at Dow's critical issues.

Implementing the Leadership Development Network Quickly

The LDN workshop was delivered to all 3000 participants over six weeks in two-day sessions, with approximately 50 participants per session in five global locations: one each in Europe, Pacific and Latin America, and two in North America. Every effort was made to make sure the teams were a mix of people from different geographic areas, functions and businesses. The initial 3000 were then asked, in turn, to teach and dialogue on the same messages to the rest of Dow's population, reaching all 40 000 employees using exactly the same tools. The component of applying what the leaders attending the LDN learned immediately to real situations of communication and teaching in their own organizations was a critical design strategy for LDN. This component of 'learning as you are doing' was key to the alignment of the organization around the overall business strategy. The LDN attendees completed this action within five months of the initial session. Many businesses within Dow used the workshops as a component of their global business meetings to help inform and align the organization they were leading. Speed and quality of the dialogue was critical. We were also able to leverage this unique approach to learning to impact the cultural attributes we expect from our leaders. They were responsible and accountable for delivering these learning sessions consistently around the world.

Dow's Seven Maps

In year one of the LDN Workshop (1997) Dow focused on fundamental background issues that provided a solid foundation for change and alignment.

- Map 1: *Global Chemical Industry – Dynamic Change and Opportunity*, focused on the overall industry dynamics, the rate of change in the world, expectations of our customers and new geographic markets. This was the foundation of our business map. Every leader and employee should understand the basics of the business we are in (see Figure 2.3).
- Map 2: *Creating our Future: Our Strategy*, provided a discussion on our new global business structure. Moving from our past organizational model to the new global business structure required an understanding of how Dow responded to the changes in the world in our business. This map provided a solid background on the roles which the global business units, shared services (HR, IT, Controllers etc.) and the corporate leadership team have in making Dow a success.
- Map 3: *Economic Profit – Value Creation*, provided a deeper understanding of our metric – Economic Profit – that is a key measure of our success. Understanding the terms and the basics of investing, cash flow, economic profit, where Dow's spending is, what Dow's capital costs are, what Dow's total shareholder return has been, how can we become a better place to invest in, all contribute to a better grounding in the basics of business that all employees must understand to be effective in their roles (see Figure 2.4).
- Map 4: A *Great Performance*, explained the role Dow leaders and people play in the effort to be the best. This map focused on reviewing the changes in expectations of leaders, of employees, and of the corporation given the changes in the business environment, the strategy, and the way we look at measuring our success.

In 1998 our second year of the Leadership Development Network, we continued our learning with:

- Map 5: *Purpose, Values Culture – Dow's Road to Success*, allowed us to revisit our company purpose and values.
- Map 6: *Creating Long-Term Shareholder Value – The Dow Scorecard*, provided an introduction to the new corporate scorecard measures.
- Map 7: *Accelerating Value Growth – Productivity AND Growth*, stimulated discussion about our drive for growth and the gains made through our productivity efforts.

As we implemented the Learning Map methodology several key themes around learning became clear:

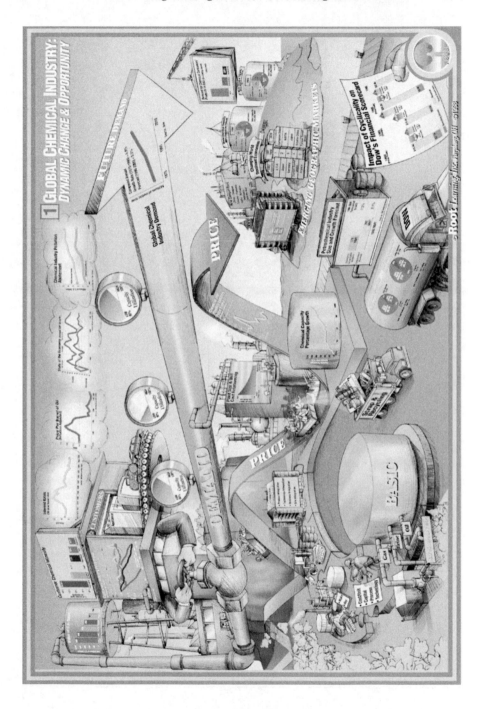

Figure 2.3   Global Chemical Industry – Dynamic Change and Opportunity

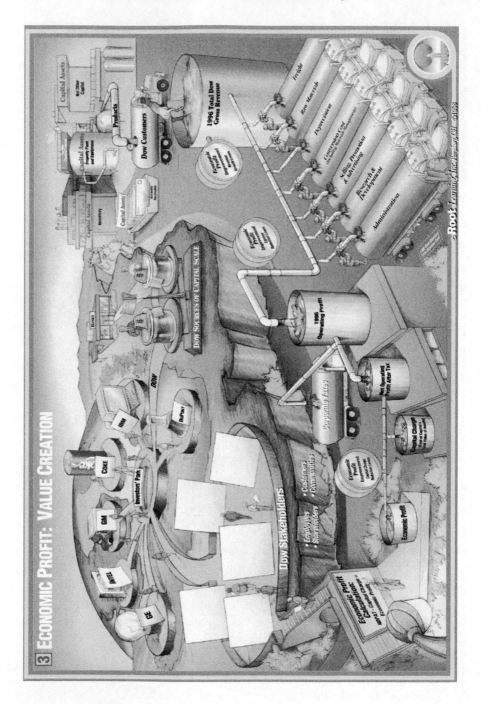

Figure 2.4 Economic Profit: Value Creation

Visualization of Complex Business Systems

It has been said that if a picture is worth a thousand words, a metaphor is worth a thousand pictures. The visual metaphor used in the map pictorial is the focal point of the discussion. It creates a mental framework that allows all employees to speak about the same issues at the same time with the same words. For the Dow experience, we observed employees relating themselves to the pictures and describing their roles as we discussed the questions. This approach worked across cultures, background, nationalities. Everyone was engaged equally in the discussion. The dialogue at all levels was rich and provided the first true engagement of all employees around the business of Dow.

Data Connections

Within the visual, key pieces of data are linked to create learning. Data allows dialogue to occur around facts, not just opinions. Since we are very analytical by nature, this aspect of the maps was very well accepted and appreciated. Data also provided no hiding behind anecdotes.

Dialogue and Discovery

Learning is a matter of asking the right questions, not simply giving the right answers. Dialogue questions not only lead the group through the learning process, but allow the group to create a forum for exploring critical business issues with people throughout an organization, from the factory floor to senior management. Dow's senior leaders engaged in the facilitation of the sessions provided the focal point for the dialogue and questions. The LDN sessions and the employee workshops that followed provided the leader with tools, processes and messages to align and connect with employees in a manner that was not previously done.

Learning Tools

Card decks and game pieces introduce additional information into the learning process and increase the interactive nature of the experience. The learning peripherals also harness one of the most effective ways people learn – by making mistakes. Engaging everyone in this process was a safe and effective way to get deeper understanding of the direction by seeing all the pieces that go into the decisions. And since it was designed like a game, it was fun!

Group Interaction

The Learning Map visual is ideally experienced in a group of six to ten people. This is the optimal group size to ensure that enough ideas are brought to the table while allowing everyone to be involved or engaged.

This approach to learning requires participants to summarize key business issues in their own language, encouraging them to embrace the need for change and more quickly connect the changes in their daily work to organizational goals and priorities.

Results

We employed several methods of measuring our success, but the most satisfying data came from Dow's Global Employee Opinion Survey, administered once per year to a statistically representative sample of Dow people. In the year since the LDN and subsequent employee sessions were held, several distinct improvements in employee perceptions were noted:

- Employees reported greater understanding of company direction by showing an improvement of 15 percentage points (41 to 56).
- Employees showed an improvement of ten percentage points in their ability to see a clear link between their work and the company's objectives (62 to 72)
- Employees showed a nine percentage point improvement in Dow's effort to keep employees informed (53 to 62).
- Employees reported a nine percentage point increase in satisfaction with the information they receive from management on what is going on with Dow.
- Employees reported an increase of four percentage points in understanding how their personal goals were aligned with the business they work with (74 to 78).
- An employee communications focus group showed that employees who participated in the learning event had *three times higher buy-in* to corporate strategy.

We continue to build on the success of LDN through *The Digest: The Leadership Development Newsletter*, published on-line, providing leaders with regular insights into company direction, external trends and the competitive environment that bridge the gap from event to event, and by integrating the Blueprint messages in global employee communications strategies. In addition, LDN materials are used to quickly educate and orient new employees to the company strategy and direction. We also have used these tools successfully with analysts, customers and suppliers.

Lessons Learned

In the two years since our decision to pursue this direction for leadership development, we can say that our learnings almost directly correlate with the original project objectives.

First, organizations must have a vision. However, we must emphasize that having a corporate vision is not enough. The leadership of the company must be able to articulate it throughout the organization. Unique tools, communication methods and engaging employees in these exercises provides the understanding of the business which in turn provides the foundation of alignment. We cannot expect employees and leaders to lead unless we give them sufficient understanding of the path we have chosen to take.

Key to the success of any leadership development initiative is the involvement of senior leadership. The most effective method is for leaders to develop leaders. A quote from Ralph Waldo Emerson says it perfectly 'What you do thunders above your head so loudly, I cannot hear the words you speak.' Without the involvement and ownership of the Human Resource Committee and the senior leader facilitators, LDN would not have been successful. Leaders and employees have 'heard the thunder' and its consistent with the words being spoken at Dow around our strategy. Employees have commented on the openness and candor in the workshops which is a direct result of the synergy of the tools and strong supportive, involved, and concerned leadership.

Third, we strongly advocate a unique approach to learning in order to differentiate the messages from those that are routine. LDN provided something unique and different for both the leaders and the employees as they discussed the business of Dow. Its unconventional nature also provided an avenue to continue challenging our culture and the way we typically get things done.

In order to compel substantive discussions of what needs to change, you must provide reliable and consistent data. This is very effective in eliminating anecdotal discussions, and allows you to move to action plans. Without the data, everyone's conclusions are correct. The data helped to provide a better context for the debates and dialogue which ultimately ends with a decision. While people may disagree with the ultimate decision, the value of the discussion can lead to a better understanding of the complexity of decisions and the need to have everyone align with the direction of the company.

A strong partnership with professional communications support is also key to a successful programme. Having a team with diverse membership ensures that a wide variety of solutions will be entertained and discussed. Ownership by the Executive Leaders (in our case the HRC) is the key to success. Without this ownership, the sessions would not have been effective or as powerful as an alignment tool.

Finally, it is imperative that all involved in a project of this magnitude understand their roles clearly. It is up to the programme director to set and manage expectations of all participants.

What's Next?

LDN '98 is already in full swing, but will this be the method we continue to use to educate our leadership and employees? This type of learning event fits with our current culture and is providing our leaders with the valuable skills and information they need to bring Dow into the next century, and to develop the leaders that will see us celebrate our second century in 2097. We believe that to effectively continue the learning for our organization, we must continue to provide alternatives for our leaders to continuously learn and apply their learning to the situations of their work The continuation of the LDN series is creating an environment of employees who are aligned and motivated, which has a direct impact on our customers, and ultimately long-term shareholder value. The LDN series provides a solid background and base to build on for further development of our leaders and employees. The overall approach Dow has taken to redesign its organization, the activities carried out to measure and learn from best practice companies, and the approach to the development of its leaders and employees create an organization able to respond effectively to our customers and the business environment of the future. We are well on our way to achieving our mission to be the most productive, best value-growth chemical company in the world.

CHAPTER 3

DuPont: Business Driven Action Learning to Shift Company Direction

Victoria M. LeGros and Paula S. Topolosky

DUPONT is the largest US chemical company and a leader in science and technology in a range of disciplines including high-performance materials, specialty chemicals, pharmaceuticals and biotechnology. The company has 83 000 employees and operates 200 manufacturing and processing facilities in 40 countries worldwide. Sales are approximately $25 bn.

With established major market positions in North America and Europe, the company is expanding its presence in Asia Pacific and South America. The company aims to grow in businesses with differentiated market positions such as Corian®, Lycra®, and Tyvek®, while maintaining its foundation businesses such as nylon and specialty chemicals. At the same time, DuPont is becoming a major player in life sciences and is rapidly building competencies in biotechnology-derived products in agriculture, materials and pharmaceuticals.

After 197 years of continuous operations, the company has, in the past few years, achieved one of its greatest transformations – liberating value through productivity and efficiency improvement, while reorganizing to speed decision-making and implementation. The aim now is to create value by at least doubling the rate of revenue growth, while maintaining emphasis on productivity improvement. This shift in corporate direction from 'value liberation' (cost cutting) to 'value creation' (growth) created the need to align and mobilize senior managers and to strengthen capability to lead for profitable growth.

Action Learning through Project Teams

Leadership for Growth (LFG) is a learning and developmental three-week session (outline attached) that combines classroom work, personal/team coaching and activity-based learning through company projects.[1] Target audience is top 400 employees across the company. Participants are selected by the vice-presidents of corporate business units and functions.

29

The design incorporates both traditional and innovative learning methods including classroom interactions, topical break-out groups and action learning projects. Typical 'class' size is 30–35 participants from around the world and five coaches. Five projects are selected for each session, each of which has a team of six or seven team members and one coach. To-date, all programmes have been held in the USA.

Project nomination and selection begins several months prior to the beginning of a session. Projects are solicited by the CEO, with nominations coming from businesses and functions throughout the company (see Questions for Project Sponsors, below). LFG graduates are strong supporters of the programme and are often involved in identifying projects within their business arenas. The primary criterion for project selection is its potential to impact growth efforts throughout the company. The initial submission is typically a one-paragraph write up of project intent that includes an identified sponsor. After all submissions are received, the Office of the Chief Executive gives final approval of the five projects for each session.

Many of the projects are looking for 'how' and 'with what products' should DuPont expand growth. In some cases this involves new technology that's just been discovered. In others it could mean application of old technology or products into new markets. Some project issues have been under debate for some time, and sponsors are happy to get a fresh perspective from senior leaders within the company. One sponsor told us he particularly valued the objectivity of people with no knowledge of the problem and 'no axe to grind'.

One example was the question of whether DuPont should enter a market where patent was expiring for a competitive product. At first this looked like a simple yes/no question. It had people on both sides of the fence within the sponsoring organization. However, the team was also asked to consider strategic relationships that could be built to strengthen the case for market entry, as well as document a route to market.

A project can be strategic or tactical in nature, as long as it is related to growth, has potential for significant impact and can be accomplished by the team in the time given. Again, upfront agreement with project sponsors is critical to develop project focus and define scope.

Three interrelated processes are critical factors in successful project design and delivery:

- Sponsorship.
- Project development.
- Team selection.

Sponsorship

Project sponsorship typically resides with senior leadership, usually at the vice-president level. High profile support contributes to both the importance and potential impact of the team's results. However, because the implementation of team feedback is most likely at lower levels in the business, it is critical to identify an 'operational sponsor' soon after high level support is achieved. After an initial meeting to define the project scope, most of the project development work occurs with the operational sponsor.

Buy-in from the operational sponsor is imperative to a successful experience for all. It is important that this person fully identifies and understands the value that his/her business can realize from the perspective of this high level project team. Not only will the sponsor help to develop the project, he/she will also interact very closely with the team before, during and after the three-week session.

Experience has shown that the quality of team results are directly related to how well the sponsor actively engages, supports and energizes the team. In essence, while not involved in the entire programme, the sponsor is an adjunct participant in the session. As one recent team observed prior to their project presentation: 'Our sponsor was pacing like an expectant father. He was more nervous than we were!'

Project Development

A programme manager of Leadership for Growth resides within the Organization Development group of corporate HR. This person provides centralized efforts on project development, participant communications, facility planning and outside speaker coordination.

After the CEO solicits projects from the VPs, all subsequent communications occur through the programme manager. This person answers any questions potential sponsors may have and, if requested, assists in writing the submissions. He/she then consolidates the submissions, sends them to the Office of the Chief Executive (OCE) for final selection and approval. Sponsors are then notified and the first meeting is scheduled.

Prior to the first meeting, sponsors are sent a list of questions (attached) that become the discussion points for the meeting and, eventually, the executive summary of the project. The intent is to identify and focus on what new information the project team can deliver in the three week time frame, and ask why the sponsoring organization hasn't been able to get this information in the past. Usually it is the perspective of high level, objective new thinking that is most important to sponsors. The project teams are positioned as value-adding internal (but external to the business) consultants.

The first meeting provides enough information to create a first-draft executive overview of the project. Once the sponsor sees his/her ideas on paper, they usually continue the process of narrowing the scope of the project to focus on deliverable results. The executive overview typically goes through several iterations before the sponsor and programme manager feel totally comfortable with it. Discussions concerning supporting documentation begin and the project briefing books begin to take shape. Of particular importance are the external resources that the team may tap to formulate their feedback. Sponsors are encouraged to identify what outside perspectives would help the team: previous teams have met with suppliers, customers, trade associations.

Each team member receives a project briefing book that includes all the information gathered from the sponsor. The books are sent to the team participants two–three weeks prior to the beginning of the session, giving them time to become familiar with the project deliverables and to read the background information enclosed. Typical information includes: executive summary; schedule and logistics; project background; key contacts; business background; potential markets; internet searches and project literature.

Team Selection

After the executive summaries are finalized (about ten weeks before a programme begins), the project sponsors are videotaped giving a ten-minute 'sales pitch' on why the participants want to work on their projects. The challenges and deliverables are discussed as well as the sponsor's desire for new perspectives and creative thinking. The use of props and other media are encouraged and provide interest to the project story. Because participants are located all over the globe, the video has been an effective communication tool for sponsors and participants alike.

The clips of all sponsors are edited onto one tape and a copy is sent to each participant along with a project preference sheet. Participants are instructed to view the tape, make notes on what does/does not appeal to them and then rank their interest in the five projects. They are instructed to eliminate those projects from their own businesses as well as any they may know something about. Experience has shown that the less one knows about a project, the greater the participant's development as well as the team's feedback to the business.

The preference sheets are faxed back to the programme manager who begins the process of selecting participants for the five teams. The programme manager has personnel data on each participant and uses this information to make the teams as diverse as possible, while trying to accommodate individual preferences. Diversity in geography, culture, EEO status (gender, race and ethnicity) and functional/business expertise are all considerations in configuring the team rosters. Participants are then notified on their team, teammates, coach and asked to begin making travel plans, if needed, for their project work.

The project briefing books are distributed and very often the sponsor begins communications with the teams. Coaches begin to discuss individual learning objectives and everyone looks forward to the first face-to-face encounter on day one of the session. The selection of these objectives is voluntary and left up to the individual. The coach raises the subject with the team and invites them to discuss any objectives privately with the coach or publicly with the team. Most opt to open up to the team and this usually enhances the learning experience.

Participants arrive at Leadership for Growth sessions anxious to begin project work and teams begin meeting in the afternoon on day one. At this point team members have had minimal contact with one another, and usually begin by discussing team processes and identifying learning objectives. But, in part, because these are senior level people, it is typical to see them drive to formulate 'the answer' early on. They eventually realize that each member may have independent right answers that need to be reconciled for successful project completion. The process is further complicated by the fact that they view the project as 'real work' but they are continually pulled back to the classroom for group experiences and meetings with stakeholders and outside speakers.

The role of the coach emerges as week one progresses. This is a difficult but important role, one that helps integrate the classroom learning with project team development. The coaches are not encouraged to become team members, but rather observers that mirror team activity and behaviour. They wait to be 'invited' by the team to provide coaching and feedback. (For a description of the role of the coach see below). Decision making frameworks from the plenary sessions are re-introduced as potential tools for reconciling project recommendations. Opportunities for one-on-one coaching and 360 degree feedback discussion with the coach are made available. At the end of week one, the teams meet with their sponsors to clarify issues or questions that have surfaced and reaffirm project deliverables.

Week two is devoted entirely to project work. If meetings and interviews with outside resources are recommended by the sponsor, they are organized by the programme manager of LFG and the sponsor and scheduled during this week. Teams and coaches travel to meet these resources wherever they reside and this travel provides an opportune time for team interaction and bonding. The team becomes a safe environment for self-exploration and honest feedback, things seldom possible in the daily work lives of these senior leaders.

Week three brings all participants together again for plenary meetings with executive vice-presidents and outside stakeholders. With project work foremost in their minds, participants are usually reluctant to return to these sessions and week three becomes a dilemma of how to do both. At this point they are figuring out how best to leverage their learning from external resources and focus on the specific recommendations and deliverables that their sponsor expects.

Recommendations from the project teams are reviewed on the last day of the programme. These meetings are attended by sponsors, key vice-presidents, and others responsible for implementation of the recommendations. Teams frequently share the process they used to formulate the recommendations, often discussing the tools (typically ones they've been exposed to in plenary session) which they employed and the input received from their external resources.

To-date, 159 participants have attended Leadership for Growth and 26 project teams have been commissioned. Follow up meetings with project sponsors indicate strong acceptance and implementation of team recommendations. Approximately half of the teams have interactions with the sponsoring organizations long after the sessions are over, continuing their roles as business consultants.[2] Several of the teams maintain the personal relationships they initially formed on the projects by scheduling periodic get-togethers. The words 'friends for life' have been quoted to describe these relationships. While other teams may not have structured encounters, most indicate a sense of being networked across the company, with trusted alliances to consult with as business issues arise in their day-to-day work.

We find it very difficult to quantify project returns. One year after recommendations are given to sponsors, we meet with them to determine how valuable the team feedback has proven to be over time. Generally the sponsors are very enthusiastic about the team's process and grasp of knowledge in such a short time frame. Implementation of feedback varies from full to none. One business recently set up a web site and business process directly related to project team feedback. In another case, a change in orientation nullified the value of team recommendations. It is important to keep in mind (and this our CEO reinforces) that the primary value of the projects is developmental and to provide new thinking on business issues. It is wonderful if the new insight is accepted and acted on by the sponsor. What is more important is to create a culture where businesses ask for help, seek new insights and share knowledge across the many businesses within DuPont.

Action Learning for First Line Supervisors

Having successfully incorporated action learning into executive development, plans are underway to apply similar learning processes throughout all levels of leadership in DuPont.[3] At the end of 1997, a corporate-wide effort was initiated to develop first line leaders, or supervisors, because of the potential impact of their behaviours on levels of employee satisfaction and productivity. Formal and informal assessments involving over 400 employees at various levels in the organization were conducted to identify development needs. Core Modules were designed to address knowledge and skills gaps and to provide the participants with a common frame of reference. The Core Modules are:

- Transitioning to leadership.
- Evaluating and appraising performance.
- Taking corrective action.
- Creating a productive work environment.

Action learning was chosen to extend the learning experience beyond the Core Modules and to provide an opportunity for the supervisors to practice and learn additional knowledge and skills while working on current organizational problems.

The action learning experiences are known in this programme as Leader Labs. Because efforts have been focused on the roll-out of the Core Modules, implementation of the Leader Labs has been slow. The following describes the plans for the design and development of the labs and identifies some of the problems that have been experienced in the initial phases of the programme.

Leader Lab: Design and Development

A list of 30 topic areas was prepared using output from the needs assessment. These topics were intended to integrate multiple knowledge and skills, to provide focus for the learning teams and their managers, to help organize possible learning materials, and to refer to learning experiences in the Core Modules. Topics included:

1. Dealing with resistance to change.
2. Stepping up to the challenges of the new workplace.
3. Making the work environment more productive and safe.
4. Giving praise and criticism.
5. Advancing in the system.
6. Leading people that are different from you.
7. Handling tough messages and situations.
8. Managing dilemmas.
9. Dealing with poor performers.
10. Doing things without resources.
11. Inspiring commitment and exceptional performance.
12. Time management/balance.
13. Increasing communications impact.
14. Managing within the law.

15. Selling your ideas.
16. Operating in a third party world.
17. Managing group dynamics.
18. Leveraging diversity.
19. Thinking and acting creatively to solve problems.
20. Overcoming paralysis: making things happen.
21. Growing people and a business.
22. Learning how to speak business.
23. Dealing with emotions.
24. Thinking systemically and long-term.
25. Learning to balance the 'scorecard'.
26. Enhancing customer focus.
27. Challenging the status quo.
28. Launching organization-wide initiatives.
29. Building better teams and networks.
30. Improving project management.

Following their participation in the Core Modules, participants are encouraged to self-select into learning teams of approximately six–eight individuals.[4] The composition of the teams varies depending on site or business needs and the number of participants that have completed the Core Modules, the only prerequisite for participation.[5] It is recommended that the participants not be expert in the areas selected for the learning experience to enhance individual as well as learning team experiences. Working with Human Resource managers, and site and business leadership, topics for the Leader Labs are selected based on business priorities and potential business impact. These are offered to the teams as possible areas for learning. Helped by trained learning coaches, teams are expected to identify a specific problem area and to submit a proposal describing the nature of the problem, strategies and resources required to resolve the problem, and assumptions about the impact which problem resolution might have on the business and on the work environment.[6]

Once accepted by leadership, the teams meet to establish roles and plans to resolve and implement solutions to the problem. At a more formal meeting, the team presents the results to leadership, logs the results of the efforts, communicates the results throughout the business or site, and prepares for the next problem. Time invested in the learning experience varies depending on the problem and the experience of the participants with the learning process. Participants progress through levels of labs that begin with smaller projects – usually contained to a single work site – to more complex issues that may involve multi-business unit/multi-site and even multi-regions. The process for tracking and disseminating the knowledge acquired during the Leader Labs is still under development.

Following the completion of a series of Leader Labs, a target designated by leadership, supervisors are expected to engage in a 360 degree assessment of their leadership skills. The assessment tool varies, being based on different instruments used within the business units. Each participant will meet with his or her own leadership to discuss the outcomes of the assessment and to prepare a long-term plan for targeted individual development. This plan might include completion of additional mandatory training or a curriculum designated by the business to address cultural or technical needs, mentoring or individualized coaching, or assignments designed to strengthen or acquire specific knowledge or skills. The intent is that each participant will later be developed to coach others through similar learning experiences.

Implementation Issues

Perhaps the biggest hurdle in the implementation of action learning is the misconception that Leader Labs are traditional workshops. As such, the expectations from both participants and their managers are that there is a single topic, a technical expert or facilitator, sets of learning materials, and designated timing for the learning event. The fact that the labs may vary depending on the problem and the participants makes it extremely difficult to secure commitment to the learning process. Rather that looking at the labs as a way to enhance the investment in the development that took place in the Core Modules, there is a tendency to question why additional time and resources need to be invested beyond the initial training experience.

The organizational levels of the participants in this programme have been both a help and a hindrance. Coming from the lower leadership ranks, the participants are closer to the real problems. However, they generally lack knowledge of business and systems thinking. In addition, the participants do not have access to the same resources as many participants in executive development programmes. They frequently have limited access to technology and travel, experience difficulty in gaining access to internal and external resources, and have extremely limited authority in executing plans or establishing priorities.

The learning process is inhibited by the lack of experience with either self-directed or collaborative learning. The participants are typically those who are selected for more technical or traditional training programmes where information is presented by a technical expert. An additional problem has been to identify and train coaches to assist in the learning experience. If the coach candidate search is successful, those selected are often already over-extended or are unable to commit to on-going sessions.

The selection of the topic area for the learning experience has been difficult.

In order to be energized, participants prefer issues that are within their span of authority or areas where they are already the technical expert. This results in challenges that are either too overwhelming but with significant impact, or too small a challenge with little or no organizational impact but with perceived personal significance. Corporate initiatives or 'buzzwords' often influence the selection of topic. In these cases, it is assumed that there is already corporate sponsorship and political correctness. However, these projects often result in duplication of efforts without lack of integration or connection. They also intimidate recognized experts rather than flatter them since the learning might threaten their status and expertise.

Metrics for evaluating the success of the programme also present a few challenges. Typically the value for the experience is assessed on the learning outcomes, the relationship and networking of the participants, the overall increase of knowledge and skills and the transfer of learning back to the organization. In organizations that have experienced several rounds of downsizings and budget cuts, the tendency is to only acknowledge those actions that impact the business bottom line and focus only on the utilization or implementation of recommendations. Since all projects are not always successful as they are measured by these standards, it is often a struggle to get continued participation in multiple sessions or adequate resources to maintain the learning system. Continuous marketing is required to define roles, track and communicate organizational benefits, and to keep participants and coaches passionate about learning.[7]

Though still in the very early stages, it is hoped that the use of action learning in supervisory development as Leader Labs will eventually prove a wise investment. To use work itself as a primary vehicle for personal and organizational growth should enable the corporation to manage knowledge better and, as such, be value-adding to any business unit.

Appendix 1: Leadership for Growth – Three Week Overview

Week one	Monday	Tuesday	Wednesday	Thursday	Friday
a.m.	Introductions Dupont transformation story	Leadership and dilemmas Inquiry/advocacy Ladder of inference	Dialogue	Scenario planning/ Systems thinking	Project teams/ sponsor meetings
p.m.	360° feedback Project teams	Project teams	Scenario planning/ Systems thinking	Creating value for shareholders	(Cont.)

Week two	Monday	Tuesday	Wednesday	Thursday	Friday
	←		Project work all week		→

Week three	Monday	Tuesday	Wednesday	Thursday	Friday
a.m.	Project updates Growth stories: a panel discussion	Creating value for customers	Creating value for all stake-holders (e.g: Nylon/India story)	Project teams	Project presentations • Time slot A • Time slot B Celebratory lunch
p.m.	Project teams	Project teams	Project teams	(cont.)	Project team debrief Plenary debrief

Appendix 2: Leadership for Growth: Questions for Project Sponsors

- What is the background for this project?

- What piece of information can the project team provide that would be of most value to you? Why don't you have this information now?

- What questions do you have that you'd like the team to answer? What are the challenges in getting these answers? In making subsequent decisions?

- How will you measure the success of the project team?
  - immediately following the teams' recommendations
  - six months from now
  - one year from now

- What is the critical information you can provide to the team? What critical information will the team need to identify/generate? Examples:
  - business/strategic plans
  - marketing plans
  - competitive information
  - financial results and plans
  - benchmarking data

- Who are the key people within the business/function that the team should meet with? Who will be responsible for scheduling people to meet with the project team?
  - marketing   - legal
  - financial   - sourcing
  - manufacturing   - any other

- Since developing solutions that meet all of our stakeholder needs is a critical aspect of Leadership for Growth, how can you help the project team access to these stakeholders? Who will be responsible for scheduling those interactions?

- What key people /organizations outside DuPont should the team engage? Can you help schedule those conversations/meetings now? Examples:
  - customers   - trade associations
  - suppliers   - government agencies
  - competitors

Appendix 3: Leadership for Growth: Coach

Role

Work with participants one-to-one to help interpret their 360 degree data and create relevant development goals; provide observations and insights to individuals on progress toward goals.

Observe the work of a project team throughout the session; provide observations and insights on work processes, team and individual behaviour as appropriate; make suggestions or introduce tools to help in these areas as appropriate.

Through appropriate suggestions or interventions, help participants apply what they are learning in the plenary sessions to their team assignments.

Help facilitate various activities and breakouts during the session.

Characteristics

Experience in working with executives; able to build credibility and trust with them.

Adept at interpreting individual feedback data and helping create meaningful development work consistent with it.

Keen observation skills (non-judgmental), skilled at 'seeing' what's going on beneath the surface.

Fluent in best practices related to group work processes and team formation; familiar with a number of tools to help teams work through process and team issues.

Skilled group facilitator but willing and able not to control team process; comfortable being an invisible observer much of the time and allowing the team to learn from mistakes rather than preventing the team from making mistakes.

Knows how to create a learning environment; is able to talk about behaviour and behaviour change with teams and individuals in a way that creates energy for learning and growth.

CHAPTER 4

General Electric's Executive Action Learning Programmes

Stephen Mercer

TRAINING and development magazines for the past several years have been featuring articles on an executive education process known as Action Learning. Management 'gurus' from academia and consulting have been boasting about their success in achieving new levels of leadership development with their 'new action learning programmes'. In fact, the concept is over fifty years old, and many companies have been using it successfully for years. The methods used to conduct action learning programmes are not particularly complex, however the most impactful programmes – those that not only develop the participants' leadership and business skills, but also deliver tangible results to the company – require a significant commitment of senior management sponsorship and involvement, as well as a thorough yet flexible planning and implementation process.

To help demystify this process, this chapter will provide a set of guidelines and tools to help you successfully introduce the action learning process to your company. It does not purport to be the only way to do these programmes, but it is an approach that has been used successfully by the General Electric Company for over ten years.

The process is described in five parts, the first of which includes the rationale for this process, and the background of its development at GE to help you sell the concept internally to your management.

- Programmme design/rationale/background.
- Selection of projects.
- Selection of participants.
- Conducting the programmme.
- Follow-up.

How is an Action Learning Experience Designed and Conducted?

Programme Design/Rationale/Background

The typical executive education programme of the past has been an academic based classroom experience which may have been completely conducted on a university campus, at a conference centre, or at a corporate education facility. In GE's case, all the executive programmes were conducted in their entirety at our Management Development Institute in Crotonville, New York. The decision to introduce the action learning concept involved a shift from an 'in class' focus to a 'field' focus – at least half of the educational experience would take place outside the classroom in the form of planning, gathering data, and analysing a problem at a business location or in another country. In fact, this was only one of a number of shifts in educational design strategy that resulted from the action learning decision.

The emphasis of the learning shifted from individual development to a combination of individual and team development, and to learning through team interaction. This concept had been in place to some extent in the form of case study teams and business simulation teams; however, the experience was now to be heightened through the imposition of the tension, time pressure, and performance pressure inherent in the solution of a live business problem and the preparation and presentation of a report to management. Further, the teams would be providing each member with continual feedback on their performance and contribution to the team objectives.

Learning shifted from passive to active. In the classroom the transfer of information depended upon the ability of the individual to process what he or she heard from the faculty and fellow participants, relate it to personal experiences, and decide how to apply the learning to his or her own business. In the field, the participant would apply the knowledge gained during the academic portion of the programme, integrating it with the cumulative experience of his or her own business life, and exchanging the result with the other team members in a coordinated effort to solve a business issue. This would be a 'learning by doing' experience, designed to make a more profound and lasting impression on the participant – one that could be further applied on the job upon return to his or her own business. Programme design shifted away from the paradigm of case studies of past business situations 'as a basis for class discussion, rather than to illustrate either effective or ineffective handling of an administrative situation' and moved to analysis of a real, unfolding, current situation in which the class would come face to face with the business leaders, their teams, and their customers and have to justify and defend a finding of 'effective or ineffective' to the actual people involved.

The design also shifted from a model that had sometimes been described as 'booking acts', in which programme flow was often influenced by the availability of 'star' faculty, to a model in which a tight programme sequence and flow was needed, to build toward the project objectives. This necessitated developing a group of core faculty with schedule flexibility and the ability to work together and coordinate their material with each other to present a seamless, integrated academic portion of the programme to the participants.

The faculty teaching mode also shifted from one of imparting cognitive knowledge to the participants to more of a coaching role. Faculty members worked with teams as they developed their project approaches, coached them on team process skills, critiqued their draft project reports, and in some cases accompanied them on project data gathering visits.

As more experience was gained in the action learning approach, a shift was finally made from domestic US-based programmes to global programmes. First this involved projects outside the US, then academic portions and projects in Europe and Asia, and finally movement of the entire programme to Europe or Asia to create a cultural immersion of the participants. These programmes have done as much to educate participants about the history, culture, politics, and customs of the countries they have visited as they have to educate them about business practices and issues. Participants' minds have been opened to cultural diversity at its most basic level – dealing with language problems, eating exotic foods, sleeping in unaccustomed accommodations. As one participant stated: 'I will never read a newspaper the same way again.'

Finally there has been a shift away from a general business focus for each programme to a 'theme' where it makes sense to do so. Thus there is a thread that runs through the programme – a spine, so to speak, upon which both the academic areas and the project can both hang in a coherent manner. For example, the themes of some classes have included:

- Emerging Eastern European markets.
- Newly industrialized economies.
- Japan as a market and a partner.

The cumulative result of these design strategy shifts has been a set of design principles or criteria applied to each programme:

- Mixture of academics and practice.
- Global scope.
- Cross-cultural contact or immersion.

- Market focus.
- Personal leadership effectiveness.
- Team building, process, effectiveness.
- Best practices transfer.
- Projects are not a task force – they are a learning experience.

This last point bears elaboration. In many instances, action learning projects are simply a substitute for a business task force or a consulting engagement. The job is done, the report is made, and everyone goes their separate ways. For maximum effectiveness, projects must be selected that involve a beneficial learning experience for the participants, as well as a tangible result for the project sponsor. The project selection process described later must assure this outcome.

The response to these design strategy shifts and the resulting design criteria has created an environment in which no two programmes are alike. Whereas in the old 'academic' environment, the general subject matter and even the day plans would be quite similar from session to session, the new action learning environment requires a virtually new design for every session. The framework for a four week programme would look something like the following: see also Figure 4.1 on the following page.

Week 1: Programme introduction
    Global environment
    Leadership effectiveness survey
    Team building
    Academic sessions related to current business issues and course theme
Week 2: Continue thematic academic sessions
    Team and project process
    Project briefing
    Project planning and coaching
Week 3: Field data gathering
Week 4: Report preparation
    Report rehearsal/coaching
    Report presentation
    Feedback session

The feedback sessions are an important element of the entire experience. Feedback is provided by the business sponsor regarding the quality of the analysis and recommendations. A framework is provided to the project teams for use for personal feedback and team process feedback during the field data gathering, report preparation, and post presentation phases of the class. Participants are encouraged to use the class as a laboratory to practice

SUNDAY	MONDAY	TUESDAY	WEDNESDAY	THURSDAY	FRIDAY	SATURDAY
23 February *Brussels* • Arrival in Brussels • Programme introduction	**24 February** *Brussels* • Global Business Environment • GE in Europe	**25 February** *Brussels* • Euro Business • Best Euro Companies • Innovation Leaders	**26 February** *Brussels* • European Union and Euro Currency Ministry visits Visit Report-outs	**27 February** *Brussels* • The Other Europe – Central/Eastern – VW in Czech/Russia • GE in Central/Eastern Europe	**28 February** *Brussels* • The Other Europe – Mediterranean – North Africa –Turkey To *Normandy, France*	**1 March** *Normandy* • Leadeship and Strategy Normandy Staff Ride
2 March *Normandy* • Normandy Staff Ride Utah/Omaha To *Paris* (Airport hotel)	**3 March** • Depart to Nordic countries – *Norway, Sweden, Denmark, Finland* (one team/country) • Company visits	**4 March** *Nordic countries* Company visits	**5 March** To *FLORENCE* • Visit debriefs Project preliminary briefings Growth Project	**6 March** *Florence* • Project background • Project briefings	**7 March** *Florence* • Project briefing • Project planning	**8 March** *Florence* • Project planning or Free time
9 March To interviews	**10 March**	**11 Marc h**	**12 March** Interviews (worldwide)	**13 March**	**14 March**	**15 March** Return to *Crotonville*
16 March *Crotonville* • Project report preparation	**17 March** *Crotonville* • Report preparation • Report rehearsal	**18 March** *Crotonville* • Video conference • Report modification • Graduation dinner	**19 March** *Crotonville* • Free time • CEC briefing • Return home	**20 March**	**21 March**	**22 March**

Figure 4.1 Programme schedule – an example

techniques learned in class, and behaviour changes deemed desirable in their leadership effectlveness surveys and team building sessions. They can receive ongoing feedback from the other team members and use the class time to integrate the new techniques and modified behaviours into their leadership style.

Selection of Business Projects

A key element of the success of an action learning experience is the nature of the business projects selected for the class to work on. As previously noted, the project must provide a learning experience for the participants, as well as a tangible result for the sponsoring business. If a project was selected that did not provide some learning opportunity for the participants the programme would be considered a failure no matter how enlightencd thc class rcports might be. Thus projects are avoided which simply involved data gathering and analysis with no decision element, or which involve simple confirmation of existing decisions. Instead, projects are sought which involve a strategic decision, an organisational recommendation, or in many cases, a marketing issue. Further, all projects must involve outside-the-company information gathering. Thus projects must include interaction with suppliers, customers, industry experts, and partners, in addition to people within the business and the company.

In order to accomplish this, the action learning programme managers need to have a network with the businesses. Each project needs a high level business sponsor who will assure access by the class to the necessary people within the organisation and who will also assure that access is obtained to customers and suppliers. This is not necessarily an easy network to develop. It may require a high level member of your executive development team to personally embark on a series of visits to the senior vice presidents in charge of each major business in order to sell them the concept. This must be done with CEO backing. The objective is to get three businesses to 'get the ball rolling' by sponsoring projects in a pilot action learning session. Once this session is completed, and the results are picked up by the informal communication network, it will not be difficult to get projects for subsequent courses. There should then be boundaryless contacts between course programme managers and senior management at the businesses to develop projects. Businesses volunteer projects. Participants return to their businesses and are catalysts for the subsequent sponsorship of projects. The CEO suggests projects.

The criteria for the selection of a project include:

- Involves a strategic issue.
- Involves cross-functional issues.
- Externally focused – not a purely internal issue.

- Market focused.
- Requires interaction with customers/suppliers.
- Is a live issue – not a hypothetical one.
- Is a real-time issue requiring early resolution.
- Requires a decision.

Further, it is desirable that the project involve global issues or have some element of cultural diversity or cross-cultural issues.

Once a problem is selected as a project for the programme, a meeting is held with the business to begin framing a problem statement. The problem statement is a clear, concise description of the background of the problem, the business view of what some of the key issues and alternatives are, and a set of deliverables. The deliverables are a critical element of the problem statement as they describe the business expectations for what they will learn at the final report session at the end of the programme. The problem statement usually is two or three pages in length, and may have a page or two of supplementary information. Preparation of the problem statement is an iterative process and may require several visits or phone conversations with the business, as well as several transmissions of drafts and redrafts.

Once the problem statement is agreed upon, there are two additional preparatory tasks for the class. First, a set of interviewees must be developed. This will include people within the business and the company who have knowledge of, or influence on, the issue being studied. More importantly, it will include an outside perspective on the issue through interviews with customers, suppliers, partners, academic experts, industry experts, and any others who might shed light on the problem. A detailed interview schedule needs to be set up, since the project teams will only have one week to ten days to conduct their interviews, data gathering and analysis. Some time in the schedule is normally left open for teams to develop and include some of their own interview ideas.

Second, a briefing book needs to be prepared. This book contains all the relevant background and available data on the issue. Normally the briefing book consists of existing presentations, organization charts, studies, and raw information about the business and the problem. No attempt at prior analysis of this information is made. The teams work with it 'as received' from the business. One of the goals of the project is to experience the need to cut through to the relevant information, and discard the irrelevant. In addition, an objective of the project development process is to minimize the administrative burden on the business. Using existing data with no 'massaging' helps accomplish that objective.

Selection of Participants

The selection of participants for the course at GE is an integrated process between the businesses, Corporate Human Resources, and the Management Development Institute. The final decision, however, rests with the businesses. They are considered to be the best qualified to make the final choice of attendees and priority for attendance.

The process begins with an initial allocation of seats in each class to each of the businesses, based on the proportion of Executive employees in the businesses. Each of the businesses then makes a preliminary selection of candidates for the class. The list of candidates is then scrutinized during the Annual Manpower Review process, which, at GE, is an annual, company-wide process for evaluating all professional employees, identifying high potential talent, deciding on succession plans, and identifying key individuals for educational programmes. This process involves both the businesses and the Corporate Human Resources staff. Once this process is completed, a list of eligible participants for each Executive Education programme is communicated to the Management Development Institute. For the top Executive Development Course, the highest level programme offered, the CEO approves the candidate list.

Upon receipt by the Programme Manager, the list of candidates is coordinated with each business. Factors considered include:

- Theme of the course.
- Development needs of each individual.
- Business mix of the class.
- Functional mix of the class.
- Operations vs. staff mix.

The objective is to put the right mix of people in each class, and focus on the operations side of the business. Thus if a candidate were slated for an offshore assignment in the future, it might be recommended that that person attend a session conducted offshore. If another candidate had spent most of his or her career in Europe, it might be recommended that they attend a session in the US or Asia. Once all the discussions are over, the class mix should include representation from all businesses and all functional areas and a good representation from outside the US.

A priority list of backups is constructed with each business from their list of candidates. In the event of a cancellation, the business will thus retain its slot in the programme, and their next eligible candidate will be moved in. Prior to this approach being instituted, a 'first come – first served' approach was used to fill vacancies created by a cancellation. This sometimes resulted in a business losing all its representation in a class if it had too many cancellations The 'reserved by business' approach helps assure adequate representation by each business in each class. Of course if a business does not have enough qualified candidates, its seats are given to other businesses to fill the session.

Efforts should be made to enhance the international mix of classes by actively seeking more participation by Europeans and Asian branches of the businesses. In this manner, a greater appreciation of the growing cultural diversity of the company can be developed.

The objective is to be thorough and meticulous in the identification and development of critical talent through an integrated process. It is on this basis that individuals and their development needs are recognized.

One final note, and an 'Iron Law' we used in the assignment of participants to projects: You *cannot* work on a project sponsored by your own business. This was one of the most controversial aspects of our programme, but it was also one of the most powerful positive attributes. It allowed us to get some very creative 'out of the box' recommendations from people who did not have business 'blinkers' or the need to be distracted by irrelevant minutia.

Conducting a Programme

The actual conducting of a programme is best illustrated by an example. We will use the Global Business Management Course conducted in Europe in 1990. The theme of that programme was 'Emerging Eastern European Markets'. The class spent one week in the US and one week in Switzerland on the academic portion. The project portion was conducted in three Eastern European countries, with final reports presented in Switzerland to the Senior Vice President, International.

The programme was conducted with the assistance of an International business school in Switzerland. Several meetings were held to agree on the content of the academic portion. A faculty advisor was assigned to work with the BMC programme manager to design and conduct the class. To accomplish the project portion, the class would be divided into six teams. Two teams would travel to Czechoslovakia, two to the German Democratic Republic (GDR), and two to Yugoslavia. Their assignment would be to analyze the political and economic situation in each country, talk to a cross section of companies in each country, and prepare a report with their assessment of the nature of the opportunities, if any, for GE in their assigned country. In order to prepare for the project portion, the BMC programme manager and the faculty advisor made several trips to each country to develop relationships with academic organizations, governmental agencies, and business organizations who could help to set up the necessary meetings and visits. Companies were selected for visits to provide a broad picture of the economy, cover the full range of GE business interests, and include potential customers, suppliers, and partners for GE.

Once the final class roster had been selected, the participants were given a general idea of the nature of the project and asked to express a preference for the country they wished to be assigned to analyze. The programme manager then selected the project teams to provide a mix of businesses and functions while attempting to honour the participants' preferences to the best extent possible. Pre-course readings and information on assigned countries were sent to each participant, as was visa and travel information.

The first week of the course was held at the GE Management Development Institute, at Crotonville, New York. The issues covered during the first week included:

- Operating in a global environment.
- Leadership challenge (outdoor team building programme).
- Business ethics.
- Management style and effective teamwork.
- Leadership effectiveness feedback.
- Productivity best practices.

In addition, the teams received a preliminary project briefing, and each team received a country briefing covering the history, geography, customs, and language of their assigned country. Executive guest speakers included the Chairman and two Senior Vice Presidents of the corporation.

On Saturday afternoon, the class travelled to Switzerland, arriving Sunday morning. On Sunday afternoon, an orientation was held to prepare the class for the academic programme in Switzerland. The issues covered during this second week included:

- Techniques of country analysis.
- World competitiveness.
- Country assessment exercise.
- International political and social trends.
- Europe, and Eastern Europe.
- International economic trends.
- International trade and finance.
- Japan as a global competitor.
- Dealing with cultural diversity.
- Industry analysis.

In addition, each team had a country briefing and dinner meeting with a representative from the country they would be visiting. On Saturday morning, an Eastern Europe Business Leaders panel discussion and question/answer session was held.

On Sunday, the class was divided into teams and travelled to their assigned countries, where an informal orientation dinner was held for each group. The next day or so was spent interacting with academic and government experts in each country on a variety of topics covering politics, finance, economy, social structure, business environment, market structure, historical perspective, and other areas. Most of the week was spent in company visits and interviews in businesses and factories throughout each country. The project teams had met to prepare interview guides based on hypotheses and information gathering strategies they had developed in informal meetings during the first and second weeks of the course. Each project team was subdivided into mini-teams to provide an ability to visit more companies in each country. Each mini-team was provided with an interpreter. Team members communicated with each other by telephone each evening to exchange information, revise hypotheses, and modify questionnaires. A total of 42 companies were visited in each country over the course of the week.

On Saturday and Sunday after the third week, each team met to prepare their report. This is an intense time in which all their leadership skills and learnings must be brought to bear. A group of peers, which has been scattered around a strange country gathering information from a variety of companies, must now work as a cohesive team to synthesize all they have learned into a concise, focused, high-impact presentation which can be defended in front of the Senior Vice President International and his staff. This requires constructive give-and-take, and the ability to reach a consensus not on the lowest common denominator, or a mediocre middle ground, but on a powerful set of conclusions and recommendations based on the best thinking of everyone on the team. On Sunday evening, the reports were faxed to Switzerland where typists were available to put them in presentation form. The teams took two well-earned days off to relax and enjoy the cultural experiences of the countries in which they had been working. Mid-week, the teams returned to Switzerland. Each team had an opportunity to make final adjustments to their report. One day was then spent in dry runs and critiques with a senior faculty consultant. On the final day of the programme, the reports were presented to the Senior Vice President International and his staff. The report format permitted ample time for dialogue and question/answer sessions with each team, during which their alternatives, conclusions, and recommendations were tested and defended. A feedback session followed, during which the Senior Vice President and staff provided constructive comments to the teams. Finally, each team met privately for a feedback session in which each member received comments from all members of his or her team regarding their overall performance and contribution to the team over the entire programme.

Feedback is also provided to the BMC (Business Management Course) programme manager throughout the course. Written comments are solicited from the participants to determine the value and relevance of each major segment of the course, as well as the effectiveness of the instruction. Coaching is available to each team during the entire programme, utilizing the programme manager and faculty. A key objective is to have each participant reflect constantly on what is being learned and how it can be applied back on the job.

Follow Up

Programme follow up may occur in a variety of ways. A key issue to consider is that immediate implementation by the business of the team recommendations is not necessarily a criteria of success. Human nature being what it is, it is sometimes difficult for a business to acknowledge that a team of people, none of whom has knowledge of the business being studied, can, in a period of two weeks, develop a set of creative recommendations to solve an existing business problem. It is interesting to note that on several occasions recommendations were rejected, only to reappear several months later as a 'new idea' from within the business.

Nevertheless, various aspects of the programme can be subject to follow-up:

- Leadership surveys can be retaken after six to nine months to determine if behavioural change has occurred.
- Business leaders who sponsored projects can be interviewed to determine the extent to which projects have been implemented.
- Class reunions have been held after a year or so, in which class members have been invited back to hear presentations from the sponsoring business regarding progress made following the project completion.
- Follow up projects have been done based on ideas generated during some sessions.
- Surveys have been conducted of sponsoring businesses to determine the extent of value received from a project.
- A newly instituted 'tracking survey' has been established in which a sample of participants is contacted every six months to monitor their progress in the company and determine the extent to which they are using what they learned.
- Participants' managers are contacted to determine the extent of behavioural change.

The Bottom Line

Measurement of the return on investment of executive education is difficult, and approaches have been the subject of vigorous debate.

GE has concluded that Action Learning programmes are the way to go for Executive Education. GE has been doing Action Learning programmes for over ten years, and the CEO and Business Presidents are convinced that they work. Participants look forward to the challenge and consistently report that they have learned from the process. There is almost no way you can fail to learn if the programme encourages, and is built on, interactions with customers and other external constituencies. If you are going global, the cultural immersion can't be beaten as a learning experience. With regard to the projects, businesses report that even in cases where the team recommendations may be weak, the fact of the businesses' participation in the project always serves as a catalyst to action on the part of the business and this ultimately results in forward progress towards a solution.

At the end of the day, the 'Commodity Futures' analogy may be the most appropriate. When you speculate in commodities, you are likely to lose money on 90 per cent of your trades, but you expect to 'win big' on 10 per cent of them. Measuring Action Learning projects may be a similar exercise. Perhaps 90 per cent can't be measured precisely, or any real results proven. But on 10 per cent you can win big.

Examples:

- GE's Capital India resulted from a BMC project done against the wishes of the GE Capital CEO.
- GE's growth strategy in the mid-90s emerged from a one line recommendation from a BMC class.
- GE's Six Sigma Quality initiative was cemented by an analysis and recommendation by an EDC class.

As GE's CEO often said when asked about the return on investment for our Executive Education programmes: 'Take a look at the stock price'.

Then he would smile.

CHAPTER 5

Heineken, Shell et al: Twenty Years of Consortium Action Learning – The BOSNO Programme

Gordon L. Lackie

STARTED more than 20 years ago, the BOSNO programme is still appropriate today. Whilst the principles upon which it is based have never gone out of fashion, the current trend towards 'hands-on' experiential learning has stimulated new interest in the BOSNO approach.

In 1975, five large Dutch companies – all perceived as leaders in Management Development – realized that by learning together they could extend the horizons of their managers. However, they were unwilling to sacrifice a close integration of their training with their own company practices. Thus, BOSNO was born – a Management Development training programme, executed in a consortium framework, and based upon action learning.

The name 'BOSNO' is an acronym in the Dutch language for: 'company integrated training on the basis of co-operating Dutch organizations'. The five founders were: Shell, Heineken, Heidemij, Hoogovens, and Philips. The companies decided to run the programme themselves since they believed, from the beginning, that no external training institutes could meet their requirements. The current member organizations, who together form the 'BOSNO Foundation', are:

Koninklijke Ahold NV – foodstuffs
Ballast Nedam NV – construction
Digital Equipment BV – info technology
DSM NV – chemicals
NV Electriciteitsbedrijf ZH – electricity
Heineken Nederland Beheer BV – drinks
Koninklijke Hoogovens NV – steel
Koninklijke Nedlloyd NV – transportation
Politie – police
Stork NV – engineering
Wolters Kluwer – publishing.

Method

The BOSNO programme is oriented to daily practice by means of action learning. Reginald Revans, Senior Professor at the Manchester Business School, first used the expression 'action learning' in 1938. He devoted most of his life as a teacher to contesting traditional Management Education, and the academic theories to which it was associated. His ideas played an important role in BOSNO's choice of methods.

Revans concentrated on the talents and the motivation of managers; the key was their working method. He believed that people only begin to learn from – and with – each other, when they discover that no one has a full answer to a question, but that they must find the solution. Central in this, is the 'job' that must be done, and why those who receive the assignment must utilize their knowledge and skills – not simply taking an 'off the shelf' solution. Here, personal growth, and delivering a good piece of work to the organization, go hand in hand.

Revans' method gives form to learning from and with each other, and mutual stimulation. Within the BOSNO consortium programme, this is true for the individual company teams, and equally so for their co-operation with the teams from other companies. This combination of action learning and consortium training has been, and continues to be, a great Management Development success. To date, more than 600 managers, from 18 organizations, have completed the BOSNO programme.

Target Group

BOSNO's target group is the member organizations' continuity workers – the 'backbone of the management'; it is not their 'high flyers' (for which there are other, more cost-effective, training programmes). Promotion is not a specific goal of BOSNO participation, although it is often an indirect consequence.

Programme

Every year, the BOSNO Foundation organizes a new training programme; it starts in October and runs until the following May. Each member organization may decide whether or not to enter a team. If there are more than five teams, two BOSNO programmes are run in parallel. The programme's main objective is management development; its two major elements are (a) the action learning assignments, and (b) the plenary sessions.

Assignments

During the eight month programme, every participating team undertakes an action learning assignment. BOSNO's fundamental philosophy is 'learning by doing'; the assignment is the vehicle for this. Learning from practice is paramount, and it runs in parallel with the personal development of the participants. The aim is to achieve a balance between the time devoted to fulfilling the assignment and the attention devoted towards individual development.

The objectives, in the context of the assignments, are:

- To involve the participants in an unfamiliar (for them) management problem, preferably with strategic or policy aspects;
- To require a solution to the assignment, which is (a) implementable and (b) of genuine value to the Assignor;
- To ensure confrontation by other corporate cultures, using detailed company comparisons;
- To facilitate making use of, and learning from, each other's practical experience ('cross stimulation');
- In some cases, also to involve team members in the implementation of their recommendations.

Completing a 'real' assignment requires team working, with colleagues who mostly have never previously worked together, and usually have very varied experience. There is no defined structure. Who takes the lead, or is there no leader? Who makes a project plan? Who takes which task? Shall we set up an investigation with interviews, and who knows how to do it? By these means, participants experience the effectiveness of the teamwork, and are obliged to think of the best solution. However, if the team member wishes, he (or she) can learn much about himself, as well as his own organization. Insight into how his top management works can also have a major effect upon his own working and motivation.

Finally, a participant must excel in time management, since his daily work continues and may not suffer from BOSNO. Not easy, if the team meets for half a day or more every week in order to complete their assignment.

Plenary Sessions

A programme includes five 3-day plenary sessions, based in a high quality conference centre. The majority of a plenary session is devoted to invited speakers, progress reporting, exchanging ideas and experience, and various management development exercises (e.g. intervision). Most plenary sessions include a short visit to one of the participating companies.

The plenary sessions are highly interactive, with much emphasis placed upon working in mixed (inter-company) groups. Processing the offered material in small mixed groups has played a greater role in recent years than previously. It is based upon the active involvement of the participants: 'how does this material:

- Relate to our assignment?
- Fit with our corporate culture?
- To what other ideas does it lead us?'

The speakers invited early in a programme are chosen mostly for their ability to provide specific 'input' to the assignments. Later in the programme, when the assignments are almost complete, the speakers address more general or new management topics. In addition to professional speakers from traditional sources (e.g. consulting companies, business schools, training institutes), directors from BOSNO member organizations are also often invited to contribute. For example, they describe their personal experience of something unusual or successful in their company.

Company comparisons are also an important element of the plenary sessions, not as a primary objective, but as a tool for extending horizons and cross stimulation. Both lead to changes in an individual's approach and insight into leadership styles.

Roles

The allocation of roles is as follows:

Member Organizations

All member organizations, including those which are not participating in the current programme, must be willing to provide assistance – realistic, and relevant to the assignments – to other teams. (Criteria for BOSNO membership include that 'all information shall be treated confidentially, and that no conflict of commercial interests shall exist between participating organizations').

BOSNO Board of Management

The Board of Management comprises one representative (usually, the Human Resources Director) from each member organization. Together, they monitor the quality of the programmes; individually, they ensure that the conditions for learning, within their own organization, are optimum. Each year, the Board chooses a central theme upon which the assignment of each team must be based. This 'umbrella' theme must be sufficiently broad to enable every project Assignor to specify an acceptable assignment. Having a common theme in all assignments facilitates inter-team comparisons, progress reporting, data gathering and sharing, idea and experience exchange, etc., and the selection of guest speakers.

This theme is, as far as possible, based upon recent developments in Organizational theory. For example, in this current year, the central theme is 'The Mobilization of Collective Intelligence – One Step Further than Knowledge Management'. (BOSNO will act as the Dutch pioneers in exploring this new concept).

Participant and his Team

A participant can be either a line manager or a staff specialist; typically, in the HAY function evaluation system, his (or her) function has between 750–850 points. He has about 10–15 years work experience, and his age is between 35–45 years. By preference, he will have no specialist knowledge nor experience in the area of his assignment. Before starting BOSNO, he will have formulated his personal learning objectives, consistent with existing career plan, in conjunction with his direct superior and his Team Coach. These learning objectives are a vital tool in his personal development.

Experience has taught that a five member project team produces the greatest learning effect. If possible, they should all be from the same hierarchical (management) level; however, forming a team of participants with widely different backgrounds and experience adds an extra dimension.

The Participants' Superior

The direct superior of the participant agrees the participant's personal learning objectives; he (or she) also agrees the amount of time that may be allocated to BOSNO. (The participant holds the initiative in respect of these agreements.) Finally, the superior supports his participant by keeping himself informed about the progress of the assignment.

Project Assignor

Each participating team has its own project Assignor, who should be a member of his company's top management. He (or she) specifies the assignment for his team and – to a limited extent – cooperates in its execution. For example, he can facilitate access to background information or to top management colleagues. By means of regular discussions, the Assignor monitors the current progress of his assignment and the success of the learning process.

Team Coach

Every participating organization provides its own Team Coach, who:

- Assists in the formation of his organization's multi-disciplinary team (including intake interviews);
- Assists the formulation of his participants' personal learning objectives;
- Itemizes the learning needs of his team and, together with the Programme Manager, translates these – when possible – into plenary programme elements;
- Organizes training sub-programmes on topics not covered in the plenary sessions, e.g. oriented to personal attitudes and skills;
- Facilitates the learning process, by every means available.

Note that the Team Coach concentrates upon the learning 'process'; he is forbidden to contribute to the 'content' of the assignment!

Finally, the Team Coach ensures that his team does not devote too much of the limited time available to the execution of their assignment – at the expense of their personal development.

This has always been the tendency in BOSNO, since the assignment results are always more tangible than those in the personal development.

Programme Manager

The Programme Manager is accountable to the BOSNO Board of Management for the 'learning' which results from the plenary sessions. He, in close co-operation with the Team Coaches, designs and organizes the plenary sessions, briefs the speakers, etc. He is ultimately responsible for the financial result of each programme. The Programme Manager's workload has become so great that it is now undertaken by an external consultant. Previously, it was fulfilled as an additional task by the most experienced Team Coach.

Costs and Time Required

The current annual subscription for an organization's membership of the BOSNO Foundation is Fl 2500 (EUR 1125); the participation fee per team member is Fl 6000 (EUR 2700). The main cost items are the plenary sessions (speakers and accommodation), the BOSNO Secretariat, managing the BOSNO

Intranet, and the Programme Manager's fee. The financial objective is to break-even every year, whilst maintaining a modest financial reserve against contingencies.

The five plenary sessions occupy 15 days; in addition, the experience is that most teams also meet for about one day per two weeks in order to complete their assignment. Thus it is assumed that BOSNO will occupy a total of about 30–35 working days per participant, spread over eight months. Throughout the period, each participant remains responsible for the execution of his normal function.

The Benefits

In order to measure the benefits of the BOSNO programme, there are many formal as well as informal evaluations. At the highest level, there is a formal, plenary discussion every year between all participants and two Members of the BOSNO Board. At another level, there is the team member's annual appraisal discussion, during which both parties will evaluate his participation.

Working on one's own development, executing the assignment, and involvement in the plenary sessions, all offer a large learning benefit – and make action learning so attractive.

Additionally, a participant in BOSNO:

- Gets involved with real problems, and hence with his organization's daily practices;
- Increases his insight into his own and other organizations, including their corporate cultures;
- Comes in contact with senior management, perhaps for the first time;
- Learns in the context of a team, and from one's own and other's practical experience;
- Increases his personal effectiveness, e.g. working under time pressure;
- Establishes and maintains new networks, within and outside his own organization;
- Maintains, in parallel, his normal work situation.

Example

A recent BOSNO programme is outlined, as an illustration.

For the programme 1996–97, the BOSNO Board chose 'Forms of Growth' as the central theme. Ballast Nedam (one of the five participating organizations) developed this theme into an assignment with the title 'How do we go from here?' One of Ballast Nedam's Executive Board of Management asked his team of five managers and specialists, drawn from five different subsidiaries, to critically examine the group's current strategic goals. They should also determine to what extent these were dependent upon the group's existing capability to innovate. (Note: the full assignment comprised more than 600 words.)

The Ballast Nedam Team started by discussing their assignment in detail with their Assignor. They then entered into, and actually signed, a 'contract' with their Assignor – a written agreement on what (precisely) could be realistically delivered in May 1997, taking into account the limited man-hours available.

In November 1996, all five Assignors attended the second plenary session, and each explained, in the presence of all other participants, the reasons why his assignment was important to him and his organization.

During the execution of the assignment, i.e. for seven–eight months, the Ballast Nedam Team (and their Team Coach) met for one afternoon and evening per two weeks. In addition, the team initiated about six meetings with their Assignor, at which they discussed overall progress, and reviewed priorities.

Also early in the project, the Team Coach assisted each team member in the formulation of his personal learning goals. Theoretically, these were 'personally confidential', but in reality the team were enthusiastic to discuss the progress being achieved for a few minutes at the end of most team meetings. Examples of these personal learning goals were improving situational leadership, and other interpersonal skills.

However, the team struggled with one fundamental problem, namely the absence of a predefined team structure. In any Ballast Nedam construction project, normally everyone knows and accepts his position in the hierarchy; however, this is not the case in a new BOSNO team. It led to some frustration, wasted effort and lost time.

In the execution of the assignment, a key decision by the team was to interview 28 directors whose opinion they respected, about half from within Ballast Nedam. The interviews reaped a double harvest; first, they provided good data. Second, and perhaps more important, the interviews enabled the team to promote themselves – at a very high level – both as individuals and as members of a hand picked (BOSNO) team working on an important assignment.

In May 1997, the Assignors returned to the final plenary session to formally receive their teams' recommendations, and to give their initial reactions. The Ballast Nedam Team proposed a process of 'forward integration'; in other words, Ballast Nedam should become involved at an earlier stage of construction projects. The Assignor liked the recommendation, which was supported by convincing argument.

Now, two years later, the former Assignor is CEO of Ballast Nedam.

Reporting directly to him is a small staff department (led by a former member of the BOSNO team) which is dedicated to implementing forward integration throughout Ballast Nedam within the next five years. Of the other four members of the BOSNO team, two have also been promoted, but one has joined a competitor. The members maintain their contacts with their colleagues from the other organizations, and still meet as a team, informally over dinner, every few months.

The value of BOSNO has never been seriously questioned nor doubted within Ballast Nedam. Starting in 1979, Ballast Nedam has participated in 15 programmes, thereby training 75 managers. BOSNO is well known and respected; word-of-mouth recommendation between colleagues means that managers are keen to be selected.

Lessons Learnt

The BOSNO formula is a complex structure; even if only one element is weak, the whole framework might collapse. In the author's experience, the following five mistakes occur most frequently:

- A team member is selected for the wrong reasons, e.g. he is a 'problem child', or he is 'between jobs';
- An assignment is too theoretical; hence, it is demotivating and reduces the possibility of implementable recommendations;
- The role of the Team Coach is underestimated; e.g. it is assumed that any member of the personnel department will suffice;
- The amount of time required by BOSNO is understated, later leading to conflicts, especially between a team member and his immediate superior;
- The team become so enthusiastic about their assignment that they neglect their personal learning goals.

The cost of participating, in financial terms, is extremely low; however, BOSNO demands an enormous amount of time, and from everyone involved. For some, too many hours are devoted to training only five managers per year. It is almost entirely for that reason, not any other form of dissatisfaction, that previous member organizations have resigned.

Advice

The BOSNO Foundation no longer sees itself as an exclusive club, with membership 'by invitation only'. The Board is proud of its programme, and now welcomes every opportunity to share its considerable knowledge and experience with non-members located either in The Netherlands or abroad. Suitably qualified organizations which are either interested in joining BOSNO, or starting a similar programme in their own country, are invited to contact the BOSNO Secretariat.

Conclusion

In the past 20 years, BOSNO has survived many revolutions in Management Development theory, and has seen many management experts and their 'ultimate solutions' pass by. BOSNO has always been up-to-date because the 'action learning by doing' was based upon current problems and current practices. Many small changes to the 'golden' BOSNO formula have been tested, and the best incorporated; however, the main characteristics have remained unaltered.

A small 'alternative' BOSNO was run last year, in parallel to the traditional BOSNO programme; the individual participants undertook a 'mixed team' assignment within another member company. This experiment is especially interesting because it shifted some attention from the execution of the assignment towards the personal development of the participant – an attractive idea!

There are many other examples of recent innovation. First: much of the communication and information exchange between team members, and between teams, now takes place via the BOSNO Intranet. Second: lengthy, written assignment Reports are being replaced by, for example, multi-media presentations, videos, and CD-ROMs.

Although the foundations for this exceptionally successful programme were laid more than 20 years ago, BOSNO has always been capable of meeting the current need. Now, the time frame in which we live requires us to extend our horizons by 'looking over the fence at our neighbours' just as much as it did in the past. By this means, we are better qualified to anticipate change, enabling us not only to survive it but also to benefit from it.

CHAPTER 6

Hoffman La Roche and Boehringer Mannheim – Mission Impossible?: Management Development During a Takeover

Wolfgang Kissel

THE EXECUTIVE Management Programme (EMP) reviewed here was a development programme for managers in the Boehringer Mannheim (BM) organization. The overall idea for this programme was to support the goal of the CEO Gerry Moeller to build Boehringer Mannheim as one company. After years of turmoil in the company the 1995 appointed CEO gave the organization his six principles.

Short-term:	SWAT (Sell what's available today)	Cash
Mid-term:	Products	Markets
Long-term:	Patents	People

The HR department was expected to translate these six principles into all its development activities and so into the EMP.

Aims and Structure of the EMP

The target group was middle management, which was defined by the second and third level below the BM Executive Committee.

The major goals of this programme, which was jointly implemented with The Cranfield School of Management, UK, were:

- To give people a broader picture of the business, strategy and culture of the company.
- To provide tools to enhance business and leadership performance.
- To build up an international network to exchange experience and knowledge across functional and national borders.
- To build an attitude of 'how to contribute'.
- To support middle managers in self-development.

The programme itself was structured in several modules, which focused on:

- Strategy and finance;
- Organizational and individual change;
- Business simulation to experience the whole business process and consequences of decision-making;
- Globalization and working/negotiating across cultures.

To put this into practice a variety of methods were applied, like lectures, group work, computer-based training, business simulation, learning contracts and audio tapes to familiarize the participants with the scope of the programme.

The Executive Management Programme had a strong implementation focus and therefore should enable the participants to apply the learning to make a difference in their daily work. The programme was also understood to be an investment in people from whom top management expected a return.

The Executive Management Programme started in June 1997 and three programmes were completed. Sixty-four managers from 21 countries have participated, geographically and functionally balanced.

In terms of 'Action Learning' the programme wasn't planned like that. But the focus on implementation was intended to ensure the company and the participants that everything presented in the programme could be transferred into daily work. The EMP's structure could be described as having three different levels whereby people would get to know where the rest of the world was going, what were the future trends, and what we had to do to be prepared.

The second level was to ask top management to come into the programme and discuss with the participants how the company might fit into these global developments, how the company should position itself to be successful in this environment.

The third level was that people were asked to think and plan in such a way that they could undertake further learning immediately in their daily work. So we always asked this question in the lectures and discussions 'what does it mean to me? Given what I have heard, what can I do to transfer it into my daily work tomorrow?' People were really put under pressure thereby because they weren't used to that approach. At the end, though there were a lot of examples of participants implementing their learning in their daily work (we come to that later).

From the point of view of strategic impact on the company, we didn't have big strategic projects to be worked on and then implemented. The strategic impact of the programme could be seen in that for the first time people came together on a broad base, to discuss the understanding of the company's strategy and how it should be implemented and mirrored in work. Because this was the first time, it was really new to our company that wherever people were working, e.g. in the

USA, in Indonesia or in Germany, it was possible to create a common foundation and understanding of what the company really wanted. Most of the participants hadn't met before and found out that they were the same company, they had the same goals and had to work to make the company's strategy happen wherever they were. To create this common basis, even if people are working independently, was the strategic goal of the programme and should have had strategic impact on the company.

Acquisition News – The Effect

We were just about to start when Hoffmann La Roche, the Swiss based pharmaceuticals giant, announced the acquisition of Boehringer Mannheim. As soon as the announcement about the acquisition was made, the situation totally turned around and came to us as a Mission Impossible. A situation had arisen where the whole organization at all levels was pushed into changed attitudes, feelings and behaviours.

For example, we had started the programme when the acquisition was announced; immediately there was a discussion about stopping the EMP. We decided that we shouldn't, that we should go on with it.

The second thing was that attitudes, especially in middle management, changed when we tried to involve more of the managers who had a supervisory role towards these participants.

Throughout the acquisition phase, people started to think on their own, to think about their survival. So in the end only the CEO and a few from Senior Management put effort into this Management Development Programme.

The worst side to this was a growing lack of interest. Participants remained very involved, but a lot of other people in the company weren't interested anymore and if we had stopped it would not had been an issue with them.

The good side was that we had a lot of freedom in what we were doing. We had planned to have at least ten programmes. We had had approval for the first one, so we did it. We asked for approval for the second one and got approval though with a mixed reception. We didn't have official approval for the third one. We just did it because we had a lot of people on our waiting list and thought that it was important to do it in that phase. So we did it and we think that it was pretty successful. But the whole situation surrounding the acquisition made it appear more and more as a Mission Impossible for us.

With time, the attitudes and behaviours of the participants also changed. When people talk about big changes, a famous description which is always used is the transition curve. We and the participants have experienced every stage of a transition curve in a live event.

Participants who were very relaxed throughout the programme all of a sudden felt observed, and started to question parts of the programme such as self-development. To us from HR it was intimated that people could not be sure about confidentiality anymore and some were afraid that HR could interfere with the process about who could stay or had to leave. (From the beginning HR was never involved in this acquisition, which was a line management task only.)

All this put us in a very difficult situation. We also had to fight for our survival and we didn't know how we were being regarded.

What helped us a lot in this situation was the commitment of the CEO and a few other managers. For example the CEO always participated in the first module of the programme. The merger was announced two weeks before the programme actually started with the participants. The CEO was planned to come to the first module to give his speech about the direction of the company and how the programme fitted into the strategic goals of the company. But he couldn't say too much because he was not in the driver's seat anymore. He came, and knew that people were hungry for information and everyone thought that if the CEO was coming, he would be telling them how their future would look. So he came into a very uncomfortable situation. He stood in front of them and said: 'I am not able to give you more information about our future but let's talk about how you feel. I'll tell you how I feel'.

He did that three times. In this phase, over nine months before closing, whenever one of these programmes started, he came, knowing that everyone thought that he could tell them about the future.

A lot of people would have said that they had no time or that it didn't make sense any more, but he didn't give up. He was really committed to the programme up to the very last day, which helped a lot.

So let's summarize so far. We had planned and started a broadly based middle manager development programme with clear goals. When the acquisition of BM was announced the focus and priorities of people in the organization changed totally, especially over the time between the announcement and closing, some nine months. With growing uncertainty the completion of the programme began to look to us like Mission Impossible. The good point about this was that people from all over the world came and exchanged views at the programme. So the acquisition dominated the programme, in every discussion and lecture. We discussed the implications of an acquisition, how people could adapt and how they could prepare themselves. People could see that wherever their colleagues were coming from, the situation was the same for everybody. They had the same problems, and they could say to themselves: 'You're not alone'. Over time, as things became clearer, people on the programme became more relaxed, even people who had decided, or were asked, to leave the company. We could see that we were on the way up the transition curve. So, over the whole programme we could really see how the mood in the company was developing as we discussed with the participants. We had a good overview of the mood throughout the organization.

To monitor the relevance of the programme we put an evaluation process into practice. Initially the expectations of the participants and their direct managers were ascertained and applied to fine-tuning the programme. Furthermore after each module and at the end of each programme the participants were asked to give detailed feedback about the programme's relevance. On the basis of this feedback the EMP was under an ongoing development to raise customization. The satisfaction scores have risen continuously from 70 per cent to 85 per cent of participants who perceived the programme as highly relevant. When we ended the EMP we had a learning conference where the participants of all the three programmes had to report how they had transferred and applied their learning to their daily work.

The Learning Conference

Incidentally, the original idea for the learning conference came from the expectation of top management that development activities as an investment in people should show a return. So in addition to the evaluation process we held a learning conference. It was held four to six months after the last programme had ended. So participants had time to implement their learning on the job. Everybody was asked to be prepared to report about their implementation to the Head of the new Division Roche Diagnostics, to their colleagues and to us. So we put them into different workshop groups where participants reported to each other about their successes, the blockages they had experienced and what they did to overcome them, as well as their mistakes. Then they consulted each other on how to make improvements. The results of the workshops and a summary about their implementations were then reported to the audience where the Head of the Division and the 'CFO' of the Division also participated. As an acceleration for further learning and an outlook on the future a concept of knowledge management was introduced by the responsible person in the company. Here also we had workshops where people were asked to discuss what knowledge management could mean for them and how they could combine it with learning. The exchange of experiences throughout the conference should undoubtedly enhance and encourage the implementation of practical learning in the future.

In workshops the participants worked out what their benefits from the programme were and what they had implemented so far. The most common benefits to all working groups were described as:

- Enhanced capability to manage change organizationally and personally.
- Overall improved understanding of finance and of the business process as a whole.
- Increased knowledge of working with different cultures.

Implementing the Learning

During the ongoing evaluation of the programme we received feedback which told us that because of the acquisition people didn't see many opportunities for implementation. Surprisingly, at the Learning Conference every participant was able to report at least one example which he or she had implemented in their daily work. Here's a selection of the most impressive ones.

- One manager checked the business relevance of all decisions made in his department. This check up led to clearer discussions about what decisions had to be made and why they should be made. As a result a better overall financial performance could be observed .
- In one country a manager focused his organization on managing change and team building, especially during the transition phase of the Roche/ Boehringer Mannheim integration. The result was that the employees remained motivated, experienced people were retained, customer relations were unchanged and the biggest customer could be retained during this time of uncertainty.
- In another case a manager applied subsequently what she had learned about different national and organizational cultures and how to negotiate effectively. The increased efficiency and the higher level of professionalism in negotiations lead to a measurable cost saving of more than SF 1m in one case.
- In another country some of the analytical and strategy planning tools from the programme were applied to support the strategic switch of the Diabetes Care business from a hospital focus to a consumer focus. This resulted in a halt to an ongoing erosion of market share in that country and so also stopped the growth of the major competitor in that business.
- One manager trained the planning skills of project team leaders in his organization and encouraged them to increase cooperation with experts in other parts of the organization. The result was that development time in a major project was shortened by about three years.

The managers also discussed and consulted each other in the areas where implementation was blocked. They also discussed future activities to apply even more successfully the learning from the Executive Management Programme.

As a further result we could say that the EMP, which started as a programme intended to create a common base and understanding about the company's strategy, and how middle managers could actively contribute to its implementation, turned into action learning in terms of a live-action example of a merger and acquisition. Whereas the programme wasn't really what one would call action learning, the context was action learning for sure. We think that we could say so, because people became much more focused on the impact of the acquisition and so were more focused and clear too about the transfer of learning.

Conclusion

The conclusion for us is that, looking back, we didn't achieve what we had planned but what was experienced by us as Mission Impossible turned out to be an opportunity for participating managers to handle the impact of an acquisition on themselves in a more confident way. Another conclusion is that keeping development programmes running in such a specific phase of a company's life could support the organization and its people where management might not expect it.

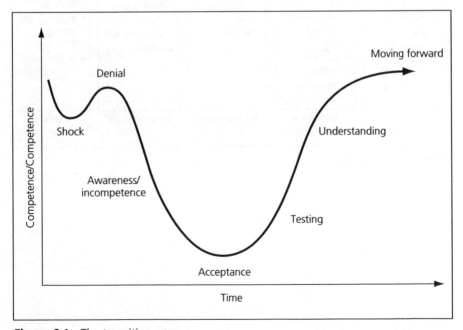

Figure 6.1 The transition curve   Cranfield University – School of Management

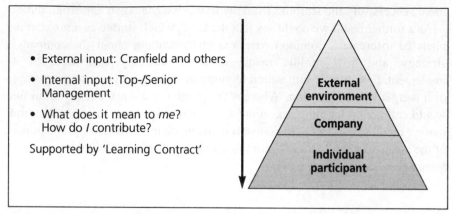

Figure 6.2   Structure of modules

Module I	Module II	Module III	Module IV	Module V
• Uncertainty in business • Strategic management • Competitiveness • Self development • Action planning	• Organizational change • Behave like a public company • Change and the individual (MBTI, 360°) • Team and coaching • Change process in our company	• Business simulation • Decision making • Cross functional tasks • Teamwork	• Reports • Managing information • Working across cultures • Negotiation skills • Action planning	• Presentation of learning results • Managing creativity • Workshops and learning partnerships • Implications for our company
Strategy/ finance	**Manager as individual**	**Business process**	**Cross-cultural/IT**	**Extended learning**

Figure 6.3   Programme outline

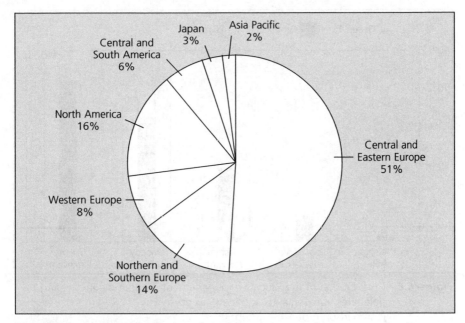

Figure 6.4 Regional distribution of participants

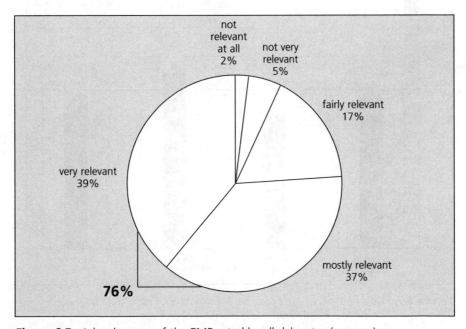

Figure 6.5 Job relevance of the EMP rated by all delegates (average)

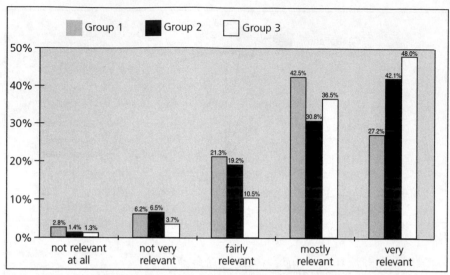

Figure 6.6 Contribution of the Executive Management Programme in meeting
delegates' job demands and learning objectives
(comparison group 1 – group 3)

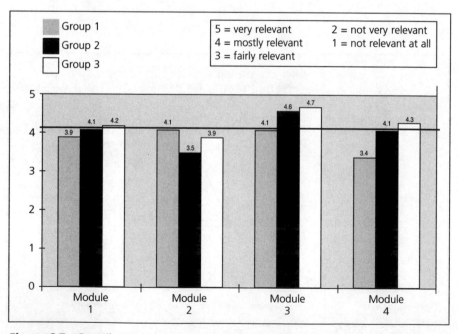

Figure 6.7 Contribution of the Executive Management Programme in meeting
delegates' job demands and learning objectives
(average ratings for each module)

Objectives:	• Exchanging learning implementation results and experiences among participants
	• Setting standards and values for our future by top managers
	• Acceleration and encouraging of further learning transfer
	• Making the learning conference a real learning event

Figure 6.8   Learning Conference (25–26 June 1998)

For participants:	• getting new ideas and practical advice on how to implement learning successfully in their own area of responsibility
	• getting in touch with top management and being informed on their views, strategies and objectives
	• receiving expert input/new methods on topics which are important for the future of our company.
	• networking
For top managers:	• getting clarity on what has been achieved by the Executive Management Programme
	• communicating their views/being challenged by people.
For the organization:	• use of experience available to accelerate learning transfer processes.

Figure 6.9   Benefits of the Learning Conference (25–26 June 1998)

CHAPTER 7

IBM: Using Business-Driven Action Learning in a Turnaround

Ron Hosta

THE year 1993 was very noteworthy for IBM. It was the first time in the approximate 75-year history of IBM that we brought in an outside Chief Executive Officer (CEO). Lou Gerstner was appointed the head of IBM, as CEO, and he came to us from RJR Nabisco. In addition, he brought in a few members of his senior team, and this was another very significant change in IBM. Up to that time, all promotions were from within and you can imagine the shock waves that reverberated through the system. It was about the time when Lou Gerstner came in that I joined executive development and was asked to head up the Global Executive Development Programme. The first year that we started to map out the programmes, the new head of Human Resources, Gerry Czarnecki, put a stop to all current programmes that had been going on for a year. We were allowed to re-examine everything that was happening in order to come up with an entirely new design. That in effect was quite a monumental thing for IBM, to bring everything to a halt and reconsider all our programmes.

The Global Executive Development Programme

My specific responsibility was the Global Executive Development Programme, and right from the start we decided that the best way to learn, to go about changing the culture, to help in the turnaround was to get the whole team on board through a business action learning programme. We really became enamoured with the fact that this could be a win-win in both instances. We would be solving some strategic initiatives for the business and at the same time learning while doing. Business driven action learning became, therefore, the crux of the entire programme.

Target Group

First of all, in terms of the participants, we decided that we wanted to initially target newly named executives, that is those just appointed to their positions within the past year. We wanted these young people off on the right foot.

The second level of participant selection was done by business units and by geographic allocation. We felt it was extremely essential that in every session of the Global Executive Development Programme we would have a global complement of individuals.

Another thing that was added in retrospect, after the first programme, was that we also decided to allocate the slots not only by geography but also by functions, so that neither marketing nor finance or any of the other functional responsibilities of a typical organisation would dominate any class.

We had twenty-four people per programme. We broke the group up into three teams of eight. The reason being that, according to the experts, the perfect-sized team is seven plus or minus two, so we just started the programmes with eight people per team in three teams.

The pool we had to draw on was the IBM executive population, a population of about 1500 out of 235 000 worldwide. It is so hard to categorize what an executive is, everyone has a different pecking order! But basically, Director, General Manager and above, appointments to that level. A typical participant would be the head of Marketing, of a marketing business unit such as large systems, or global services or mid-range, or PC, and so on. Most people who came to the class really ran a business unit and did have profit responsibility. The average age of the group was probably in the mid to late 30s, and most people had been with the company for a long time because it was just in 1993 that we started hiring from the outside to bring people into executive positions. During the last part of the time that I was associated with the programme, we began to see new executives who were hired from the outside start attending the programme.

The selection was done by the heads of the HR community working with different functional representatives in each geography. For example, my contacts were the head of HR in Europe, which covered of course all of Europe, Middle-East and Africa, the head of HR in Japan, which basically covered Japan, and then the head of HR for the rest of the Asian nations, which would take into account Korea, Indonesia, the Philippines, and so on; the head of HR for Latin America, which would include all of Latin America plus Mexico; the HR representative in Canada, and the HR representative in the US. They would select the people that they would send to the class.

Programme Objectives

The terms of the overall programme objectives that we wished to cover, were firstly, to enhance the shared values and understanding of IBM's strategic directions. Second, a big purpose of the programme was to build global networks and facilitate IBM teamwork.

This was very key to us because we realized that we were moving into a very global economy with different geographies having to work together, across borders, to bring a solution to the customer. We expected and hoped that the attendees would start to build the worldwide network of people that they could contact with whom they would feel comfortable exchanging ideas.

The third programme objective was, through business action learning, to develop their ability to think strategically and globally.

Most people get appointed to an executive position and earn their stripes in an operational role. Obviously, they get recognised for solving a key operational problem and then start moving up in the executive ranks where the operational part of the role is of course significantly diminished and the strategic and 'people' part of the role starts to become more important.

Finally, we also wanted to foster leadership of organizational change and performance. We were going through a huge transformation, we knew that the culture of IBM had to change, and we were hoping that these people would in effect become the change agents in the new IBM. On their return from the programme, they would begin to be the agents of Lou Gerstner in starting to transform the company into the image that he felt that it needed in order to get back on the track of success and profitability.

One has to remember the state of IBM at the time the programmes began, that is, in 1993. The company was literally facing bankruptcy. By the end of 1993, we went from approximately 425 000 people worldwide to approximately 225 000. That number, by the end of 1998, when I had retired, has subsequently risen to about 245 000. As huge as that reduction may seem, it was not as significant as the downsizing of some other companies. Because, obviously, you wanted to keep your high performing units, units that were able to compete in the new world, so the selection process was done by business area. Also of course, several headquarters (in terms of the old organization) were eliminated.

We went from a country organization to a regional organization. The typical headquarters that existed in every country we operated in were essentially eliminated. So that there was only one headquarters for all of Latin America rather than an IBM Argentina headquarters, a single IBM Europe headquarters rather than a single IBM Germany headquarters, IBM France headquarters, and so on.

IBM had lost billions of dollars. And the stock price for people who measure a company by its shareholder value, went from a high of $175 in 1987 to a low, of $42 in September 1993. The company was in serious trouble, facing very serious problems. Actually, facing survival problems. The company was truly on the so-called 'burning platform'.

Lou Gerstner's team hoped that the Global Executive Development Programme could help revive and get IBM on the right track again. What was impressive was the amount of effort and time that they were willing to dedicate to the Global Executive Development Programme, which certainly made my job a lot easier.

We ran approximately six of these programmes a year. So, in my four-year tenure (because, as I mentioned before, the first year we were in total redesign). I ran twenty-four of these programmes and Lou Gerstner missed one of the twenty-four. That was at a time when he had needed immediate eye surgery, and he sent a senior vice-president to the group to apologise. The commitment was there.

One of the objectives was to foster performance and leadership. And we had a model in mind. The model was really a three tiered thrust that Lou Gerstner introduced at the time. We modelled a lot of what we were thinking of doing on the initiatives being taken by Jack Welch and his team at General Electric.

How did we go about fostering the leadership? The one thing that I admire about the great leaders is that they are able to look at something very clearly and synthesize what appears to be a tremendously complex situation into a very simple format that everyone can get behind and start marching to.

We were all struggling with the myriad of problems that we had in HR, as you can imagine, with people going through the significant lay-offs and restructuring the company, its total organization, and so on. But Lou Gerstner just came out and said: 'Here is what I want my leaders to do'. And it was simply 'win', 'execute', and 'team'. Those three words just became cast in stone and that was the charge.

We had to win in the marketplace, we had to earn our stripes in the marketplace. Of course, behind that, he meant that you really had to become customer-driven in order to win. We had lost a little on that. I suppose a little arrogance sets in when you own 75 per cent of the marketplace for most of your history, and you actually think that you can start dictating to the customer. Lou Gerstner came in and said: 'No, in order to win, you have to be totally customer-driven'.

The second thing that he wanted, was that people had to execute. We were great people in terms of formulating processes and strategies, but the execution left a lot to be desired. Lou Gerstner said that we had to spruce up accountability and people had to execute.

The best way to achieve all of the above is through teamwork. So, he was really hard on people, especially in the new environment, forming global teams, not a country team, not a 'team Germany', or a 'team USA', but a truly global team that would come up with solutions to solve worldwide customer problems.

Which, by the way, very much reinforced his first decision upon coming on board, which was very significant at the time and I feel I should mention. We were well on our way to totally splitting up the company under the former CEO. We even had the names! A new name for the storage division, the printer division, the computer division, and so on. The paperwork was done, the letter-heads were made, the Presidents of those divisions were all appointed, and so on.

And Lou Gerstner came in and said: 'No, the strength of IBM is in its whole, and that is the best way that we can bring a worldwide total solution to our customers'. That was probably his first most profound move when he came on board, so that is a little more background on the type of change that we had to encounter in 1993.

Programme Design

We wanted to achieve all of the programme objectives through working on a strategic business issue – business action learning – not case study action learning of an event that happened in the past to some company, these case studies are everywhere. We wanted to work on a real IBM strategic issue. And the way that that came about, which again goes back to the type of support that I had from Lou Gerstner, is that he sent out to all of his senior executives a letter stating that he expected their total participation in the overall Global Executive Programme, and that they also introduced a strategic initiative.

Let me describe who I had these strategic initiatives from. Lou Gerstner had organized the company where his inner circle was ten people, called the CEC, Corporate Executive Committee. Underneath the ten people, were 42 more people; the ten were also in this group, so that is 32 more people. This was called the Worldwide Management Committee.

So the way that he ran the company was really with a group of 42 people, all Executives in IBM. It was from one of these 42 people that I would receive the strategic business issue.

What was that strategic business issue? The directions to these executives were really quite simple. It had to be a strategic issue that was currently keeping them awake at night, hence it was real, not something that they had already solved. They may have been thinking of it for a while, but it certainly had not reached the bottom line, and it was still keeping them awake at night. Moreover, the issue had to be a current issue that was on Lou Gerstner's plate. The people would present to me their strategic issue, and then I would run it up to the Corporate level where Lou Gerstner would say fine, this is an 'all right' project for this team to work on. That is the type of thing that we had.

Let me give you a really exciting example. Jim Vanderslice, at the time, was the head of the printer system division. Which, by the way, was literally a separate division. He was tapped by Lou Gerstner to go out to San José and take over the storage division. IBM had 75 per cent in that market, and proceeded to lose 50 per cent to EMC. You can imagine how much down in the dumps that division was. There had been several changes, different types of people had been tried to come in to run it, but it kept going down.

Interestingly enough, I had asked Jim Vanderslice to sponsor a strategic initiative when he was head of the printer division. So, when the announcement was made, it was three days away from the class, and I thought that I was going to lose him as a sponsor. So I called him up, and he said that this was great for him because he was ready to give them a project about his new division. The project was, 'what would you do if you were me'? The reason why I focus on this is I just wanted to show you how simple things can be effective.

The way that it worked was that the programme ran for two weeks, over a week-end. The Senior Executive would come in very early in the programme and would introduce the strategic initiative. He had to be there personally, and of course, he usually brought key members of his staff with him. He would introduce the strategic issue and would give the people as detailed a description of the issue as possible.

The one thing that we reviewed the strategic initiative for is that at the kick-off, we didn't want the executive to start hinting at paths that he wanted the students to go down. We just wanted the strategic initiative to be introduced with as much data that the executive had, to bring to bear on the issue that was made available to the people. But in no way did we want any hint of a path or a solution that his staff was wrestling with. We were really looking for kernels of new ideas. In no way did we want to influence them.

Indeed, no preliminary preparation took place. As a matter of fact, students didn't even find out what the strategic initiative was until this presentation. We didn't even advertise it to them beforehand because we didn't want their staffs back home working on it, so that they then came in with a prepared presentation. We wanted to tap their brain power in terms of coming up with kernels of new ideas.

We had a lot of confidence in our participants that they would come up with new ideas in such a short time, given the fact that I am sure that these problems have been worked on by teams of people over months and months. Of course, you would love to have things go on much longer, everyone would, but then of course, there is the timing pressure. It was quite a commitment on our part, I feel, to get this group of people out of their work place for two solid weeks. We were driven by the same factors that every corporation is driven by: how long can I take these people away from their workplace and of course, what is the cost of running a programme such as this? To be quite frank, I think that as we went on, we would probably have expanded the programme a bit. We would probably do some work at the work places, for example, but no, initially we wanted to get people in really quickly. We were trying to transform the company, and we wanted to get them in very quickly. We didn't want to tie the project up for months, or have it go over a year, or more, as some corporations do. Again, we were not looking for an implementable solution to the problem at the end of the two weeks. We were really looking for practical approaches to solutions, and hopefully getting some truly 'breakthrough' ideas to bring to bear on the project.

We would break these people up into three teams of eight, and they would work on the same project. Some people may feel that that is redundant. Why not, since you have three teams, solve three strategic business issues and multiply your success on that part of the equation by three?

I fought against that for a simple reason: if I know that I am the only one putting together a solution on a project, do I put as much into it as I would if I thought that I was in competition with someone else? If I am working on it by myself, I would say: 'fine, I shall do the best I possibly can, which of course all these people would do'. But in fact, I am the only one who is going to be covering it, I have no one to be matched against. So, we made a conscious decision to have all three teams working on the same project, and also hint at a level of competition.

Now, you must realize that at the end of the programme, as a matter of fact, the day before the last day of the programme, that senior executive came back for an entire half-day to listen to the presentations. So you can imagine the subtle pressure on these three teams, knowing that each one would be presenting separately to the Senior VP, and of course these people being the driven people that they are to achieve those ranks, were obviously driven to being better than the other teams. I think that we got a lot more out of it by having three teams working on the same project. As a matter of fact, I felt that that was a very successful design for IBM at the time. Sometimes we would change this approach to allow teams to integrate and combine their presentations. We would allow that. Not just one presentation, but at the end of the first week, we would have a checkpoint and if two teams were really down the same path, then we would allow them to combine. We didn't allow them to combine earlier on because we didn't want to end up with 'group think', 24 people working on the same thing. But it was very interesting, the combinations were very few and far between. They really wanted to compete against each other. Over the 24 or so programmes that I ran, I would say that there were partial combinations in no more than five or six. But one team would really strive to do something 'out of the box' because they were motivated to do something 'heroic', knowing what the normal paths would be. So, you usually got one presentation that clearly stood alone by itself, and interestingly enough, it was that presentation that had the most kernels of new ideas.

Week 1

	Monday	Tuesday	Wednesday	Thursday	Friday
a.m.			IBM learning maps Admn announcements Herman-Belbin ex.	Strategy discussion Network computing discussion	Leadership competencies General business discussion
p.m.			Herman-Belbin ex. Team competencies	Research and MFG discussion Executive assignment Software group discussion	PCCO discussion Team competencies Executive assignment work Software group discussion
			Course overview and objectives	Team competencies Executive assignments	Team competencies Executive assignments

Week 2

	Monday	Tuesday	Wednesday	Thursday	Friday
a.m.	Participant exchange	Global economic and political situation	Team and individual feedback		
p.m.	HR discussion Team competencies Chairman's perspective General finance and treasury	Research discussion Team competencies Executive assignment work			
	Team competencies Executive assignments	Team competencies Executive assignments			

Figure 7.1   Global Executive Development Programme schedule

The Use of External Coaches

External coaches were assigned to each team but they were not subject experts. Please note they were external coaches. I fought for this point a lot, because obviously, it was an expense to bring in external coaches. But I really felt that IBM, for the first 25 years of my career, was so insular that we really needed to bring into the corporation external views, and external people, to transform our culture of 'if it is not invented here, it cannot be good'. It is an arrogance level that you reach after achieving the success that IBM had up to that time!

So, we hired three external coaches. They were PhDs, basically trained in psychology; we looked for three coaches that had this type of profile, but at the same time worked extensively with the business, so that we wouldn't get the theoretical psychological view. These were people who did most of their consulting work with corporations in the private sector. Or, if they worked in the public sector, it was fine too. We were looking for coaches that were skilled in firstly, working with high-performance teams, which was part of the learning within working on the strategic issue. And secondly, these were coaches who were able to get people to think 'out of the box'. We were looking for breakthrough thinking. As I mentioned before, most of the classes, due to the fact that the transformation had just taken place, were really career 'IBMers'. They were really immersed in the old culture, so we really wanted these coaches to push them, and to get them to think 'out of the box'. And then, of course, during the teachable moments, to talk about their experiences with other companies. How other companies would handle the same type of problem which in most instances is very different from the way IBM would handle the problems.

Those were the type of coaches we used. They 'lived' with their teams day and night, and were not subject experts. We didn't want them to be experts on the subject. We wanted them to concentrate on focusing on how the team was working, and find teachable moments while the team was working to make corrections.

The typical example that I always use – not that I do not like marketing, but marketing people tend to be very outward and aggressive – is if there happened to be a marketing person on a team, that of course is the person who would usually jump up and want to take over. I observed the coach once, and he let that person take over for about an hour, and then he stopped it. He said to the marketing person: 'I want you to look around the room. As a result of your wanting to take this over, I have observed three people who have dropped off and are starting to star gaze'. It is a very simple example, but the point was driven home saying that with this type of behaviour, you have lost three pieces of brain power on this team of eight.

So teachable moments such as this will be found throughout so that people could improve their performance when they got back to the office and worked on teams, realizing that they could change their behaviours in order to keep a team intact and have it achieve its full potential.

These coaches also did individual coaching as well as teamwork facilitation. We left the last day totally to the coaches, and at the end of the programme, the coaches would pull together the entire team and give a general – with everyone present – team feedback. How the coach felt that they had performed as a team, and how that team could have been further improved. I should mention that this was a non-rated course, we wanted the people to feel comfortable. That they won't be looked at and rated by an HR department, so that they will feel free and open, and be acting in a risk-free environment. We encouraged them to take advantage of all of it. We said that we were not going to get back with the coaches and ask them to rate them, or make any comments about them. No senior executive would be able to tap into anything and I kept a very strict rule about that. You aren't trying to find out the successes of these people, or what they are strong in, you already know that, they have been appointed executives! You are really trying to get them to face up to their weaknesses and improve them. I really feel that the risk-free environment is the best approach.

After the team feedback, which would take half a day, the coaches would then book, on a voluntary basis, individual sessions with people, and give the individuals individual, private feedback. How did that work? It was absolutely incredible. I would say, without even trying to add the numbers up, 99.9 per cent of the number of people who went through the programme signed up for the individual sessions. I never knew what went on in those sessions, I was not part of them, again keeping it a risk-free environment. But the feedback that we got from the participants themselves in the individual sessions was outstanding. They would say that their one-on-one session with the coach was really one of the highlights of the programme So, that is the way we went about it – it was a total risk-free environment.

Programme Content and Design Issues

When you look at the typical IBM programmes of the past, if a programme lasted a week, we would probably hire ten or twelve world-class speakers. And, basically, I personally look at it as an entertainment show. These people were obviously very skilled in their subject matter, but since they made their living this way, they were very skilled speakers.

As I look back on these programmes, many of which I had attended, what value did I get? Was I entertained, or did I learn? I personally looked back on my prior experiences and thought that out of twelve or fourteen external speakers in a typical programme, I probably learned from two. That's a very low pay back, when you think about it.

So, we decided that in terms of the rest of the programme, we wanted as few external speakers as possible. And, by the way, and I'm not just saying this, we had come to this conclusion ourselves, but it was also the way Lou Gerstner felt.

He came to us and said: 'I understand that external speakers can be a value, but I do not want the programme loaded with external professors or consultants. I want the programmes loaded with my Senior Executives discussing their divisions, what they see as the qualities of leadership and how the new IBM should be, in addition to discussing projects that they are working on'.

What happened is that we ended up with two external speakers, and twelve Senior Executives, twelve people from the 42! A mixture, not the same ones every time, but we never had a speaker from outside those 42.

And they would faithfully come. Of course, it was probably because of the letter that Lou Gerstner sent them, that they would not only support a strategic issue, but they would also participate in every session. And that was it. Approximately twelve Senior Executives and two external speakers.

Let me go through the subject matters that we chose for the external speakers.

First, the things that really drove us were Global and Culture. We wanted these people to start getting a really global view of the world, and to understand what it is to work in a global culture. Hence, as you know, we worked with Dr. Yury Boshyk from IMD and then the Theseus International Management Institute. He would spend a day covering the geopolitical and economic situation of the world and opening peoples' eyes to the world, and it couldn't have been more timely. The Berlin wall had come down, billions of people, including China, were joining the 'free and open capitalistic society'; although no one wants to say that they are becoming capitalists, each one has his/her version of what capitalism means! The point is that billions of people around the world were joining our economic society in some way or another. This was a very timely subject.

The other external speaker that we had was Dr. Huib Wursten who works with ITM, a firm in Holland. They worked totally on studying cultures. They actually took the original work of Geert Hofstede who did a lot of his work with IBM in the 1940s, and expanded on it and kept the database alive. He would talk to the participants about the fact that, although we think that we are becoming a global culture, McDonald's everywhere or everyone wearing jeans, the statistics really show that a global culture is not forming.

These are superficial things that are happening around the world, but as a result of these things, according to their work, the core culture of the individual is actually getting stronger as a result of these superficial external influences starting to bombard the different cultures.

It was a very good session and the students were actually left with a categorization of the different cultures. So that they actually had a working tool, such that when they were working with a global team, they would know where these people were coming from.

For example, the American, individualist, 'go get him' type of thing, by contrast the Nordic countries, for instance, basically preferring to get things done through consensus. These are the proven facts of how these cultures work. Other cultures want to get things done through having a very active leader, and so on.

So they actually left with a tool and an understanding of the cultures in order to make them more effective in performing on a global team. And those were the only two external speakers that we had. All the rest were internal IBM Senior Vice Presidents discussing their business unit, its challenges, its competitive challenges as openly as possible. This was really phenomenal.

I had people standing in line here, and as the programme went on, it was never a problem to get either a sponsor for a strategic initiative or to get any of these 42 to speak at one of these programmes. Each one was booked for one and a half hours. It was also very interesting how many times they enjoyed this so much, that if they were there before lunch, they would stay for lunch, or if they were the speaker before dinner, they stayed for dinner. It was very encouraging.

Factors of Success and Results

As we have discussed before, if someone wants to ask about the critical success factors of a Global Executive, or any Executive programme in any organization, just as in real estate, it is location, location, location, in executive development the key success factors are CEO involvement, CEO involvement, CEO involvement. And I certainly had that, as I will describe to you later; as we chose the business action learning projects, it is the type of support that I got from the Chairman himself.

I would like to discuss a few other success factors and results. Because people are usually task-orientated, we were afraid that the task would just become the dominant thing and the learning would be in the background.

As a matter of fact, being the manager of the programme, of course I would introduce everybody in the morning and lay out the programme. And as a part of my introduction, I would stress that from my perspective, I was more interested in the learning that was going on, then the task solution. And I played that bit of the course because I was interested in achieving both! But I wanted to make sure that they stayed on the right track, in addition to just focusing on the task.

That is why I want to break the feedback down. I want to break the feedback down into two areas. I want to break it down into the participant feedback and the executive feedback.

In terms of the participant feedback, it was really amazing. When we asked participants to rate the course, and give comments, most of the comments would focus around the value of the course in terms of what they learned about working with cross-functional and international teams. I was so happy to see that come out number one. That was really what we wanted to achieve.

Obviously, the coaching, the teamwork, the decisions for every team – global, mixed functions, and so on – really worked and the people realized that all the brain power in the world doesn't reside in one geography! The brain power of the world resides around the world, as the brain power of an organization resides throughout the organization and not just in one spot.

Of course, the second thing that we were trying to accomplish was a buy-in of the new IBM strategy, and they all told us that they really had a better understanding and buy-in of the IBM strategy, the 'IBM of the future' strategy.

One of the questions that we specifically wanted to ask was: did the course result in changed behaviour? One hundred per cent of the people said: 'Yes, it really did result in my changing or I am going to change my behaviour in several areas when I get back, as a result of what I have learnt in this course'. For example, a lot of the comments were 'let the team do the work'. These are very driven individuals, very smart people. People like this tend to lean towards the 'know-it-all' category versus the 'ask-for-input' type of category.

Let's face it, they got to where they were by taking a stand and coming up with a novel idea, to get recognized in the first place. So, most of them said: 'I'm going to sit back and listen a lot more then I have done before. I'm going to communicate with the people a lot more then I have done in the past. I'm going to be more open and trustful with my knowledge, because otherwise the team will not understand the true inner workings of the strategic issue, if I am trying to keep some of it in my sleeve for my grandstand show at some point in time, as I am going to present this.

Those were the areas that they really stressed in which they would change their behaviour. We were really pleased with that.

The last point was the question: 'Would you recommend other executives like yourself in the programme?'. There was a one hundred per cent response, not one person ever said: 'I do not think that anyone should attend', it was 'everybody should attend'. As a matter of fact, it went to: 'why do you not get some of the older executives in here? Why are you concentrating on the new ones?'.

In terms of the successes, we also had a feedback questionnaire, mostly asking for comments, to the Executive who sponsored the project. This feedback was absolutely phenomenal. I could break it down into four areas, then I shall discuss another point which I left out until this stage.

The answers were that they all highly valued the output. As a matter of fact, I had one Executive who told me that he would have paid $750 000 for this type of consulting, and he actually sent that comment to Lou Gerstner. Of course, most sponsoring Executives did send their comments to Lou Gerstner.

We asked them if the output really influenced their decision making, and to a person, it did. There were new ideas that significantly influenced them.

They all volunteered to participate again, as a matter of fact! They would call me up if they had not heard from me for about six or eight months, and ask if they could do another one!

And, here is the thing that came about which was not in the design. As I mentioned before, the design was that we would just reach this point by the end of the programme, and we would take a look at some point in time later, in terms of if there should be some type of follow-up.

Well, it happened by itself! Several of the executive sponsors would call me up and say: 'there were some excellent points here made by team three, who could I get in touch with in that team to ask for a further expansion of the process on their side?'

I found two things happening: number one, they were working with individuals on the teams after the class, and number two, kicking off follow-up projects! Personally asking the teams to do some more work with them.

And, number three, on several occasions, I saw people from the teams being hired by these executives which, to me, was the bottom line of success. These executives were really impressed and they were looking at these people, and they would actually hire them away from another division.

We got a little concerned about that, but the decision was made not to stop it. Usually, it meant some motion of sorts, and that was a nice thing to advertize. 'This programme may also be good for your executive health!' We were very pleased with that.

We had gone to the stage of saying that maybe we should formalize an after-programme in terms of capturing the learning, and of getting the teams to stay in touch. But, as I said, that had already started happening, and then I decided to retire, and move on. So, I was not a part of that workload, but it was interesting that it happened by itself.

Getting back to a point that I missed, I said that the sponsor came in, and introduced the strategic issue. When Lou Gerstner came to these programmes, of course, it was a motivational type of leadership speech. But he would always make a comment. Like, 'I am anxious to see the results of your project. By the way, you do know that the second copy of your presentation goes to me on the same day?'!

After the fact I found out that there were follow-up meetings with the Senior Executives in the Chairman's office. How more successful can you get? After seeing all these events happening, not by design but by themselves.

CHAPTER 8

Johnson & Johnson: Executive Development and Strategic Business Solutions through Action Learning

Ronald Bossert

JOHNSON & JOHNSON is the world's largest and most comprehensive manufacturer of health care products serving the consumer, pharmaceutical, diagnostics and professional markets. It employs approximately 95 000 employees, and has more that 180 operating companies in 51 countries around the world, selling products in more than 175 countries. Sales for 1998 were $23.7 bn with consolidated net earnings at $3.7 bn, an increase of 11.1 per cent over 1997.

Effective leadership is required to continue the success and growth of the Corporation in a global competitive environment. A new style of leader is required, who can grow the various businesses by being able to work across boundaries with multiple working relationships, in teams, and can leverage multiple resources. Executives at Johnson & Johnson endorse education as a key lever to address the leadership needs of the company, however the traditional approaches to executive education were being evaluated regarding their impact on the business. Therefore, a new approach for executive education that focuses on real business problems is being incorporated into its programmes. This 'action learning' approach is a direct response to feedback by executives who want business-driven programmes which have immediate applicability and solve or address real problems.

Past Directions

In 1988, the Executive Committee of Johnson & Johnson approved a new Worldwide Employee Training Strategy, which had the following objectives:

- Focus on human resources as a competitive issue.
- Rapidly disseminate strategic knowledge on the Corporation's high priority business issues.

91

- Proactively understand changing business environments.
- Reinforce the Corporation's values and culture.

In addition to the various operating companies' role in this new strategy, Johnson & Johnson designed corporate core programmes for every management level. Each programme was designed to provide the fundamental knowledge and skills needed at each management level. In addition to the core programmes, other focused executive education programmes were established to address strategic agendas facing the Corporation. Table 8.1 provides a brief description of each of these programmes which were designed and delivered beginning in 1988.

Table 8.1   Corporate sponsored programmes

Programme	Theme
Executive Conference I	Setting the competitive standard
Executive Conference II	Creating our future
Advanced Management Programme	General management and business perspectives
Management Development Programme	Performance management
Superior New Product Development	New product development – a core competency
World Class Supplier Partnerships	Cultivating long term partnerships with key suppliers
World Class Manufacturing	Operations role in making J&J a world class competitor

New Directions

In 1994, Corporate Education conducted interviews with senior executives to define the current and future leadership needs of Johnson & Johnson. The interviews focused on business issues, opportunities, challenges, and the leadership skills required throughout the Corporation. Also, a series of benchmarking visits were conducted with some US companies, which have increased their investment in education and challenged their assumptions about development. The findings were documented in a summary report, which focused on three areas:

usiness issues.
ip development.
1al requirements and actions.

f this report, a new corporate education strategy was developed.

Key Findings

The executives interviewed strongly supported education as a key lever to address the leadership needs of the Corporation, and many expressed praise for programmes offered in the past. However, many mentioned that programmes need to be more business-focused, and the demands of the business make it difficult to free up time for broad education on general issues taught by outside faculty. They were looking for focused programmes which are business driven and have immediate applicability to real business issues.

In the past, education which focused on individuals becoming more knowledgeable or informed was thought to be useful. Today, executives are interested in programmes which provide a demonstrable, action-oriented link to current business issues. Many see the need for an approach commonly referred to as 'action learning' which refers to learning while working on real business issues facing an organization. This approach is viewed as a method to link education and personal development with addressing pressing business demands.

Response

In response to these key findings, Corporate Education developed a new strategic plan to address the overall needs of Johnson & Johnson. The new programmes are more action learning focused and address immediate business issues.

The Corporate Management Education and Development department was charged with the responsibility of designing new programmes which address the issues identified by the executives. The Department's focus is to create customized, high impact executive education strategies and programmes that:

- Help top management achieve their corporate strategic objectives;
- Provide a catalyst for change;
- Help shape top management's agenda.

To guide the development of the new programmes, the principle of development was that managers and executives learn best by doing. Based on the executive input, the priorities for Management Education and Development were established:

- Focus on leadership;
- Help leaders adapt to a global environment;
- Link management education more directly to Johnson & Johnson business issues.

Table 8.2 highlights the new programmes, some of which were rolled out in 1996. All address the common challenges of developing more effective leadership, teamwork and the ability to deal with a rapidly changing environment.

Table 8.2 Corporate sponsored programmes

Programme	Target Audience	Special Features
Executive Conference III	Senior executives and operating company Management boards	Natural work groups
		Executive committee involvement
		Delivered in regions
		Action plan outcome
Executive Development	Select operating company management boards and reports to board	Cross-boundary teams
		Nominated by senior executives
		Sponsored business issue
		Business recommendations
Leadership Challenge	New Executives New Board Members	Regional and company Executives/managing directors faculty
	New advanced managers New first-line managers	

An In-Depth Look at the Executive Development Programme

Getting Started

Corporate Management Education and Development conducted a number of briefings on the new strategy with the Operating Committees of the three business segments in 1995. The concept of action learning was new to most executives, so there were many questions, and in some cases, hesitancy in supporting such a new approach to executive education.

The interest and support for the first Executive Development Programme ~~_____~~ company group chairman in the Consumer Pharmaceuticals and _____ Operating Group. He had been on the advisory group for past _____ ation programmes, and was a believer in and advocate for the _____ s. He agreed to be the business sponsor for the first programme _____ d in March, 1996 and provided this challenge: 'How do we harness the strength and knowledge of our people to grow our businesses?' The programme was to be based on the following design principles:

- Action learning approach.
- Designed around an actual business issue.
- Focus on developing future leaders who can work effectively across boundaries.

Its focus was to be on the development of leadership skills and teamwork and the examination of a current strategic Johnson & Johnson business issue within the context of the external environment. The programme had three objectives based on the concept of action learning:

- To assist participants develop the leadership and team skills necessary to work across organizational boundaries.
- To generate ideas and recommendations on the Johnson & Johnson business issues.
- To assist participants in developing plans to apply the key learning to their own businesses.

Twenty-two participants were nominated by the six company group chairmen from the Consumer Pharmaceuticals and Professional Operating Group. The nominees were:

- High potentials.
- Key contributors to their businesses.
- From various functional areas.
- From various regions of the world.

It was agreed that each Executive Development Programme would be a highly customized intervention based on a specific business issue. For this first programme, the sponsor was interested in looking at a process to grow the various businesses in different types of markets such as mature, developing and emerging. After many discussions with other senior executives, the following business issue was developed which would drive the design and development of the programme:

- To develop plans to rapidly accelerate the market development and growth of a unique Johnson & Johnson product in markets at different stages of evolution;
- To identify the potential for synergy across other franchises and business units.

Three countries on which to focus were identified:

- Germany representing a 'mature' market;
- Sweden representing a 'developing' market;
- Poland representing an 'emerging' market.

Designing the Programme

For the design and delivery of the programme Johnson & Johnson selected Dr. Yury Boshyk, who became the Academic Faculty Director for the programme. Because of his move from IMD to the Theseus International Management Institute the location for the first programme was in the science and technology park of Sophia Antipolis, France, the Institute's location. Work on the design began in August. He and I met several times with our sponsor to further refine the business issue around which the programme would be designed. The basic thrust of action learning is to design a programme around a very strategic business issue facing the Corporation, and then drawing upon the talent in the organization to help address the issue, and generate ideas which can help move the business forward. We also met personally with the Johnson & Johnson managing directors and other executives in the three markets on which the programme would focus: Germany, Poland and Sweden. The purpose of these meetings was to understand in detail the local businesses and the environment in which they operate. Another important reason was to gain their support and involvement for the programme.

A team with representatives from the Theseus Institute, Johnson & Johnson, and other outside consultants , was put together to design and plan the logistics for the programme. Between August and February several meetings, videoconferences and telephone conference calls were conducted.

Delivering the Programme

In March of 1996, the programme was conducted at The Theseus Institute. Figure 8.1 provides a programme overview.

For the Corporation to try an executive education programme for close to three weeks in duration with twenty-two people from different businesses and orld was a risky approach. Senior management was used to more grammes, usually five days in length. The first week prepared the the business project. Faculty from Theseus facilitated sessions leadership and teamwork, Europe and the world economy, and isiness environment. Johnson & Johnson executives provided

Sun	Mon	Tue	Wed	Thur	Fri	Sat
	• Intro • J&J Leadership and Teamwork	• Business Environment • J&J Leadership and Teamwork	• Business Environment • J&J Leadership and Teamwork	Country Briefings	• Business Environment Analysis • Team preparation	Travel to in-Country briefings
• Team Planning • Cultural Event	PROJECT INTERVIEWS					Return travel
• Debrief • J&J Leadership and Teamwork	Analysis Report Presentation	Analysis Report Presentation	• Final Report Review • Debrief teams	Presentation to J&J Executives		

Figure 8.1 The programme overview

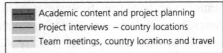

Academic content and project planning
Project interviews – country locations
Team meetings, country locations and travel

briefings on the Johnson & Johnson business. The sessions prepared background information on Europe and the context of the business issue.

Participants were divided into three teams, each with six or seven members representing various Johnson & Johnson companies, regions and functional areas. A separate team was assigned to Germany, Poland and Sweden. By the end of the week, the teams began preparing their protocol and questions for the interviews which were scheduled for the second week. Week two was spent in the three countries. The teams were thoroughly briefed on the local country by outside consultants who were local nationals. They also received additional information about the business from the local Johnson & Johnson Company. Each country team was further divided into sub-teams of two or three members, and travelled to various cities in each country which were identified by the local company. The sub-teams conducted interviews with government officials, health care officials and practitioners, current and potential customers, and best practice companies. Participants went into a real business situation; they got in the countries and talked to key decision-makers as well as others in best practice companies to help them benchmark their thoughts and perceptions as to how they could grow the business. The teams were encouraged to seek additional information which may not have been provided, and also request additional interviews if they so desired. The interviews were scheduled by the country consultants and the local Johnson & Johnson company.

A managing director of Johnson & Johnson commented 'Probably the best of it all was the feedback we have gotten from our customers and from our health care officials after their participation in it. Many of our customers felt flattered to be part of this Johnson & Johnson Executive Development Programme. They saw a new dimension of Johnson & Johnson, and that has deepened the relations we have with our people in our environment today'. Participants found the interview process to be exciting; they had a chance to get into the details of a market in a way one cannot in a classroom setting.

On the weekend of the second week, participants returned to the Theseus Institute with voluminous notes and findings. The final week was spent on debriefing the teams on the issues of leadership and teamwork, the analysis of their findings, and the preparation of a report and presentation. The analysis phase was where the country teams could look at the data which were collected, analyze it and then draw conclusions which they felt could be helpful in maximizing the business.

On Wednesday of week three, each team presented its recommendations to senior executives from the businesses involved and other executives. A detailed report for each team was distributed and a question and answer period scheduled after each presentation. The final session lasted about five hours. During the presentation process, the preparation challenged views and assumptions about the business; it helped the teams to discover how much they had learned and grown since coming together as a team seventeen days earlier. The presentations provided meaningful observations, good analysis and valuable recommendations for the Johnson & Johnson business.

Evaluating the Programme

Included in the design of the programme was an evaluation strategy. The programme had multiple customers including the six company group chairmen and the managing directors of the businesses in each of the three countries. These customers identified four major expectations for this programme. If the programme was to be successful, it should accomplish the following:

- This approach to executive development, where participants from diverse businesses focus on a business outside their own, should be able to generate useful, value-added ideas;
- Some of the ideas should be implemented in the business with a positive impact on the market;
- Participants should be able to apply some of what they learned regarding market assessment to businesses outside of the business issue and other regions of the world;

- The programme should stimulate collaboration, networking, and possible synergy among participants.

The following are some of the evaluation methods utilized:

- Application logs where participants were asked by their respective company group chairman to maintain a brief journal which addresses how they plan to apply the experiences from the programme to their own business.
- Each executive who attended the final presentations was issued with a summary sheet and asked to identify the most valuable ideas generated and the possible application to all Johnson & Johnson businesses.
- A follow-up telephone conference with all participants was conducted to assess the value of the programme and how they intend to apply the learning to their own businesses.
- An in-depth follow-up meeting was conducted with the sponsor to get feedback on the value of the Programme.
- Approximately nine months after the completion of the Programme, each managing director of the businesses in the countries included in the programme was asked to provide a summary of the recommendations they implemented, the results of the implementation, and an update on the business. The worldwide chairman for the business also provided similar information from a global perspective. The sponsor then prepared a letter and sent the information to all participants.

Feedback

The feedback received about the programme from the executives who attended the final presentations and the participants themselves was very positive. The executives praised the teams for generating meaningful ideas which can be used by the business. They also recognized the value of the action learning process, and how it could be used in other Johnson & Johnson businesses. The executive sponsor commented 'I just was flabbergasted at the enthusiasm the people had for this programme. I've been to many, many programmes and people say that's a great programme, that's a very good programme, but it was never enthusiasm about it that I saw in these people'.

The action learning process was believed to be a valuable and effective developmental approach for both teamwork and the personal growth of participants. It also can be transferred and used by participants in their own businesses. The interview process was viewed as having great value to the business by providing an outside objective approach, which resulted in a diverse set of recommendations. The methodology provided ideas on how information could be obtained in a systematic way to address key strategic business issues. It provided a fresh perspective.

Many specific, useful ideas were generated for the Johnson & Johnson business which can be used by the businesses in the three countries which were involved in the programme. The quality of the recommendations presented was believed to be equal to or better than those developed by outside consultants in other similar consulting projects. The advantage to this programme is that Johnson & Johnson retains the process and learning. Participants become in-company consultants. The Corporation has additional added value because the intellectual property is not leaving after the reports are presented. The process is something participants can transfer to their own market. One participant stated 'By using a case study like this, it does give you a different dimension and a very valuable dimension in utilizing your resources and challenging you...to see the learning as well as the application, and then hopefully the outcome of the information is applicable to your learning going back to where you came from, but also the leave-behind document and presentation and plan that you leave for the operating business and company'.

'One tends to get into a routine, and when I came back from Poland, I sat down and said, let's go back to basics, generate new creativity, and maybe give a new direction to the business' was reported by a participant. Another put it this way 'When I returned to my business ... we immediately formed two task teams in each country to study two businesses which were going to be critical for our long term growth ... and during the process, one of my managers said to me I've done a lot of analysis of my business, but my team members have totally turned my business upside down. She said I see things in a way in which I had never, ever thought I could look at from a new perspective and learn from'. The idea of putting an interdisciplinary team to work on a strategic issue was seen as a valuable approach which can contribute to strategic planning. Customers and other government and health care officials were very willing to talk and share ideas about critical issues facing Johnson & Johnson and health care.

Most participants reported that the team-building experience was the most valuable part of the programme. The opportunity to work on a heterogeneous team comprised of people from different businesses, functions, cultures, and management styles was viewed as a learning experience. Few participants knew each other prior to the programme and they quickly recognized the importance of effective teamwork which would be necessary to present some very specific recommendations for the business after seventeen days. There were many opportunities throughout the programme for participants to provide frank and open feedback to each other and improve their team effectiveness; this was viewed as a very important part of personal development.

Continuing the Process

Based on the positive feedback provided after the first programme, we proceeded to plan the second Executive Development Programme which was conducted in November, 1996. Teams looked at a number of external barriers which exist and have impacted the adoption rate of various surgical procedures. These vary by country and involved increased contact with the government and regulatory agencies, major employers, unions, and insurance payers. Each market requires a different mix and different solutions to accommodate these differences. Four countries were selected to focus on these barriers: France, Germany, Italy and the United Kingdom.

The process used to design and deliver this programme was similar to the first, although there was more emphasis on teamwork. There also was a 360 degree feedback instrument integrated into the programme including one on one feedback sessions with a faculty member.

We again received excellent feedback from the participants and the executives who attended the final presentations. By March of 1999, there had been a total of six programmes delivered and several are planned for 2000.

Lessons Learned

With six Executive Development Programme offerings completed, there are some key lessons learned.

The selection of an appropriate executive sponsor is critical. We were very fortunate to have two executives who believe in executive development involved as the sponsors for the first two programmes. It is critical to have senior management understand the process and have them play an active role in the programme planning and implementation. A sponsor must be willing to communicate the purpose and process to the organizations involved.

Action learning teams are not task forces. The Executive Development Programme is about personal development with a business focus. Individual development must be balanced with a focus on the business issue. It is not an either/or situation, and it is important for an executive sponsor to understand and support these dual purposes. Teamwork and individual executive development are fundamental to programme design. It also is important to explain this balance to participants. Successful business people want to 'get on with it' meaning they are interested in getting to the project work right away. However, it is important to prepare participants with the necessary background information and team building which are critical to the outcome of a programme. It is critical not to focus on the problem-solving too soon.

Attendees were high potential executives and managers who were carefully selected. The high quality of the participants is very important to programme success. They were bright, enthusiastic, and very interested in generating valuable ideas and recommendations which could help our businesses grow.

The business issues which serve as a starting point in designing a programme must be strategic, meaningful and viewed by participants as being important to Johnson & Johnson. Make-work projects would not be effective.

Action learning programmes are very complex and challenging to manage. There are numerous key players who must be involved at every stage of development. A true collaborative partnership was established with the Theseus Institute to design and deliver these programmes. Such a partnership in the design and delivery is very important. Intensive administrative and logistical support is paramount to the success of a programme. There are so many details which can impact a programme that a team approach is absolutely critical.

An evaluation strategy should be designed before the programme begins. This will increase the probability of a success because expectations and deliverables are explained up-front.

Participants need time for reflection and relaxation. This is a continuing challenge because of the extensive time away from the job for participants. Most participants question the value of such an intensive programme when they are going through it; however, just about everyone who attended these programmes reflected on how the intensity was worth it.

There also needs to be a more effective way to provide participants with feedback regarding their recommendations. We are currently exploring strategies to address this, one being a yearly reunion conducted on a regional basis.

Leveraging the Learning

One of the key issues in executive development and action learning is how best to retain and use the information and knowledge generated during and after action learning programmes. Johnson & Johnson has begun to assess how better to utilize this information and knowledge and leverage them better within the company in the spirit of continuous improvement.

In March through to June of 1998, four MBA students from the Theseus Institute, under the direction of their faculty advisor, Yury Boshyk, completed a consulting project for Johnson & Johnson. The project was completed through an examination and analysis which:

• Detailed the component elements and processes involved in the Johnson & Johnson Executive Development Programmes, and analysed the views and experiences of programme participants, country consultants, and administrators who have been involved in the programmes. The process looked at evaluating the impact of these programmes both developmentally and on the businesses;

• Benchmarked global best practices in the field of knowledge management (not restricted to action learning executive programmes) including how other organizations and executives develop continuous organizational and individual executive learning, improve business results, and evaluate their action learning programmes;

• Assessed computer software and other knowledge management tools, as well as videoconferencing that can be utilized in action learning programmes, including leveraging the learning beyond the direct experience of participants.

The project involved extensive literature searches of both electronic and published sources and telephone conferences with participants, other Johnson & Johnson executives and the country consultants. A detailed report with specific recommendations was presented to Johnson & Johnson in June, 1998. The recommendations are currently being reviewed and many have already been implemented.

The Future

The six Executive Development Programmes have provided a solid foundation for the action learning approach to executive education at Johnson & Johnson, and there are several other action learning models being used throughout the Corporation. The approach is a direct response to feedback from our senior executives who were interested in action-oriented initiatives which were directly linked to current business issues. I believe that the action learning approach is here to stay at Johnson and Johnson.

CHAPTER 9

Motorola: Combining Business Projects with Learning Projects

Kenneth H. Hansen

IN many aspects Motorola is unique among the Fortune 500 companies. From a modest beginning in the heartland of the United States the corporation has grown to produce approximately $30bn in annual revenue with 130 000 employees located in 45 countries around the world. It has accomplished this growth by focusing the corporation's energies on one primary business, the enhancement and development of the electronics communications industry. Because Motorola is engaged in the leading edge of communications technology, it has built close working relationships with governments, universities and regulatory institutions around the world. These relationships help Motorola both influence and work within the communities and environments that regulate the communications industry. Motorola prides itself in working in countries in a partnering relationship of free trade, where Motorola assists the country in developing their communications capabilities and in turn benefits from the evolution of the markets for communications products. There are many instances in Motorola's history where the corporation has invested in a country for ten years or more without seeing significant profitable return. Motorola believes this level of commitment is required to develop the communication industry, and in turn, the market opportunities for the corporation. Several examples of this philosophy of long term commitment include the Republic of China, India and South Africa. Motorola senior leaders often commit to the leaders of emerging market countries that 'we are here to invest in your society for the long term and you can count on us as a partner in improving your communications infrastructure and the standard of living of your people'. More importantly they have examples in the history of the company to justify these commitments. The corporation considers these long-standing relationships, build on high integrity and ethical standards, and respect for the individual, as part of the intellectual property of the company.

One might argue that these concepts are not unique, but are the goals of all major companies that function in the global environment. However, when integrated with other facets of Motorola's culture and history, one begins to understand the uniqueness of the corporation and the role that continual education and action learning plays within it.

Leadership

While Motorola has grown to produce approximately $30bn dollars in revenue annually, it is one of the few Fortune 500 companies that can easily identify its history through three generations of management. Each of these leadership teams has been directed by a succeeding generation of the Galvin family. Paul Galvin founded and led the corporation from its origin in 1928 through the mid 1950s. In 1956 the power of leadership was transferred to his son Robert (Bob) Galvin to provide leadership through the decades of the 60s, 70s and 80s. And, in the 90s the seat of power has transferred to the grandson of the founder, Christopher (Chris) Galvin who is currently the Chairman and Chief Executive Officer of the corporation. This transition of leadership within one family has resulted in a consistent long term commitment to the growth of the electronics industry, a focus on enhancing the technologies of communication as a contribution to the betterment of the global society and a family-type commitment to the companies' employees. Often referred to as Motorolans, the employees of the company are viewed as a primary competitive advantage of the corporation and investment in maintaining the knowledge and skills of this asset is considered an investment in the future.

Focus on the Electronic Industry

Throughout its history Motorola has focused its energies on the emergence and development of the electronics industry. That history is evident in the Museum of Electronics at Motorola's headquarters in Schaumburg, Illinois in the United States. Here you will find a timeline indicating the development of the corporation from its first inventions, a battery charger and the automobile radio, through its latest contributions to communications, the first operational low orbit satellite communications system known as Iridium. During its 70 year history, operating at the leading edge of the electronics industry, Motorola has continually had to reinvent itself to develop and promote leading technology. During each decade the company has been required to abandon markets and products that had previously been very lucrative. As the value proposition in the communications industry has shifted the company has been required to push on to new frontiers in electronics, pioneering activities in radio and television, semiconductor manufacturing, mobile communication, paging, cellular and satellite communications. All of these innovations resulted in periods of heavy investment, repaid change and renewal, rewarded by high levels of profitability and rapid growth. This continual renewal and reinventing of the company within a value system of high levels of ethics and individual integrity often places Motorola managers in the position of maintaining the cultural values of the organization while achieving very aggressive performance and growth goals.

Commitment to Continual Learning

In this environment of the extended Motorola family, dealing with continual renewal and rapid change, the training and reskilling of the workforce has become a natural setting for the development and practice of industrial training methods and concepts. Motorola University (MU) operates as the corporation's internal training organization, serving all Motorola businesses and the corporate office. In addition MU provides training consulting and services to external distributor, partners and customers. The university currently employs 650 full-time associates and approximately 400 contract associates located in 22 countries. MU maintains 12 learning centres around the world and in recent years has developed on-line training capability that can reach approximately 80 per cent of the Motorola global employee population. Training is focused on preparing Motorola employees to adapt and develop their knowledge and skills to meet the business goals of the future. To carry out its charter MU develops/sources all levels and types of training (*management*, *engineering*, *quality*, and so on) required by the Motorola business units. All activities of the University are directly linked to the business initiatives of the corporation and the support of the business units.

Action Learning

In this setting of continual renewal, the concepts of 'action learning' have become an effective means of generating consensus and focusing the work of the organization. In the late 1980s Motorola had invested heavily in technologies in paging and cellular telephonics. The cost of entry into these markets was substantial, both in the development of the technologies and the development of the infrastructures within each country to enable the distribution of pagers and cellular products and services.

A very successful education programme titled 'Rise To The Challenge' had increased the awareness of the corporation's leaders to the fact that heavy penetration of the global markets would be required to meet the goal of becoming the leader in both the paging and cellular markets. A small taskforce of Senior Executives had also recognized the opportunity for growing these markets in the Asia/Pacific rim.

Throughout its history Motorola has operated as a decentralized company with each sector developing its own technology and marketing strategies. This decentralized structure has enabled the corporation to quickly react to changes in technology and markets. However, the structure also has a downside, it makes it very difficult for the various sectors to develop and implement coordinated plans to address the market with effective solutions. To resolve this difficulty, commonality of purpose is driven through the various businesses' focused initiatives that address the common needs of all the sectors. The penetration of the Asia/Pacific markets became one of these initiatives.

Deborah (Debby) King-Rowley, MU's Director of Executive Development, was given the challenge of developing an education intervention to focus leadership of all Motorola sectors and functions in a joint effort to plan and implement Motorola's strategy in Asia/PAC. Her proposal centered around an action learning initiative titled 'Senior Executive Programme (SEP)'. The concepts Debby proposed were adopted by the senior leadership of the corporation and implemented over the next several years.

Since that time the processes of SEP (*Action Learning*) have been used to provide the framework for numerous Motorola corporate initiatives. These initiatives include:

- Doing business in Asia/PAC.
- Motorola's role in the communications industry.
- Entrance into emerging markets.
- Management of regulatory standards.
- Becoming a premier software company.
- Brand management.

The processes of the Motorola SEP can be outlined starting with the selection of the project and the SEP team.

Project Definition

The project addressed by an SEP is selected and defined by the President and CEO in collaboration with the Motorola Management Board. Each project represents a major corporate issue that crosses all Motorola businesses and functions and lends itself to a cross-organization plan and collaborative solution. The issue is defined at a high level, with limited direction that might inhibit the creativity of the SEP team.

A member of the Office of the CEO and/or the Motorola Management Board is identified as the champion for each SEP team, sets the expectations for the team and provides the interface with the Motorola Management Board.

Selection of the SEP Team

The selection of the SEP team is one of the most critical steps in the action learning process. Team members are selected from candidates nominated by their business units and reviewed by the Corporate Management Board. The selection criteria includes the proper mix of experiences, responsibilities, organizations and functional representation.

While several team members are selected for their knowledge of the issue that will be addressed, the majority have limited expertise in the topic. One of the goals of the SEP is to educate an ever increasing number of the corporation's executives on the issue.

The team includes both line and functional executives (finance, human resources, and so on) selected from those businesses that will be impacted by the project. Most importantly the team members are selected form those executives that are positioned and capable of influencing their business units/functions to implement the outcomes of the SEP. In some cases participation as a member of an SEP is assigned as a development activity for the executive.

Membership in an SEP is an addition to the normal job activities of the executive and will consist of no more then 25 per cent of an executive's assignment. Participation in an SEP has become a valued opportunity for executives since it recognizes the individual's ability to participate in the planning and implementation of the corporation business strategies. The executive's participation will also provide exposure to top management and the opportunity to develop new networks with corporate leaders.

The team normally consists of 20 to 25 executives representing a wide cross-section of the businesses and functions of the corporation. Both Motorola University and the Organization Development organization assigns a representative to support the work of the SEP. Generally one executive is given the responsibility for coordinating the initial meetings and logistics of the team.

SEP Operation and Logistics

The SEP team is given a broad charter by the champion. An example might be to: *define and implement the strategy and processes Motorola will use to manage the brand image of the corporation.* The Champion takes care not to recommend solutions so the creativity of the team is not limited.

The SEP team manages itself in addressing their task. They determine their own work schedule, goals and timelines. The team also determines how they will measure and report their progress and how they will facilitate and manage their work. Through their connections to the businesses they have the ability to draw on resources beyond the team members themselves.

The SEP will continue to function until the assigned goal has been achieved. In actuality teams have remained functional from four months to more than five years.

SEP Education and Learning

Learning interventions are scheduled for the SEP team as their needs dictate. The team members must become the most knowledgeable people in the corporation on the topic they are addressing. This learning is provided in the form of external speakers, team training, research, reading, benchmarking, etc., at the time that it is needed to support the work of the SEP.

The primary education takes place during the initial phases of the team's work. This learning addresses both developing the abilities of the team to work together to achieve a common goal and increasing the team's knowledge of the issues they have been asked to resolve. Learning of course takes place throughout the entire project and takes many forms.

Institutionalization of SEP Work

As the work of the SEP progresses the changes they recommend must be implemented and institutionalized to achieve their goal. Many actions can be implemented to institutionalize the results of the SEP's finding. In general these actions can be described in two categories. First are those actions that the SEP members are empowered to implement by influencing their management, peers and associates in their own business unit or function. This normally accounts for approximately 80 per cent of all required actions. Second are those actions that require approval and action by the Corporate Management Board. These actions normally relate to policy changes, corporate level structural changes, and so on.

What Have We Learned?

The concepts of the SEP/action learning to resolve corporate-level issues, develop corporate-wide strategies, and drive change are effective when the appropriate team members are assigned, their goals are clearly defined and adequate support is provided. To institutionalize change and implement the work of high level action learning teams we have found that new ways of thinking about change are required if we are to gain the return on the investments in the SEP. At best we may have 1500 people at the top of the organization that truly understand the changes that are proposed and the actions that must be implemented. A systematic approach is required to mobilize the entire organization and gain the momentum that will make the proposed changes a reality. The experience in Motorola indicates that the following activities have a major impact on implementing and maintaining the changes required.

Align management

Additional learning has to take place throughout the organization for the changes to become embedded as the culture of the corporation. To accomplish this a number of the SEP teams have sponsored training and action learning programmes throughout the various levels of the organization. In its most effective form this training is cascaded down through the various levels of the organization. At each new level the training is supported and facilitated by the higher levels of management. In this concept of cascading the learning, managers at each level first learn, secondly they implement, thirdly they teach others and fourth they support the implementation initiatives of others. This cascade of learning can be diagrammed as follows:

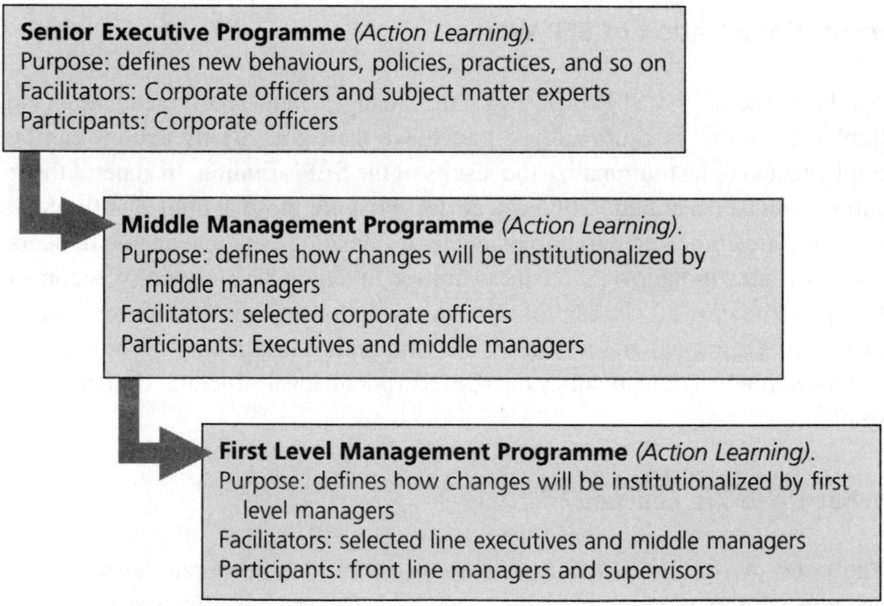

Senior Executive Programme *(Action Learning)*.
Purpose: defines new behaviours, policies, practices, and so on
Facilitators: Corporate officers and subject matter experts
Participants: Corporate officers

Middle Management Programme *(Action Learning)*.
Purpose: defines how changes will be institutionalized by
    middle managers
Facilitators: selected corporate officers
Participants: Executives and middle managers

First Level Management Programme *(Action Learning)*.
Purpose: defines how changes will be institutionalized by first
    level managers
Facilitators: selected line executives and middle managers
Participants: front line managers and supervisors

Figure 9.1 Cascade learning

Action Learning becomes an effective method of cascading the learning and ownership of the changes required throughout the organization. In Motorola the SEP teams often establish the policies, practices and behaviours that must be changed to achieve the goals. At the next levels of the cascade, action learning is used to help employees impacted by the transition to take ownership of the processes and methods that will be required to implement the changes at their levels of the organization.

Align gatekeepers

There are many processes and systems that must be revised and adapted to provide the structure for implementing behavioural changes and new practices. If these processes and systems are not adapted and continue to support the past behaviours the organization will revert back to the behaviours and practices of the past.

These processes and systems are often defined by the functional organizations such as finance and human resources. These functional organizations influence and often control the accounting, staffing, performance management, and so on, processes and systems that must be adapted to provide the risks and rewards that encourage individuals throughout the organization to support the changes. It is critical that these 'gatekeepers' understand, take ownership and support the changes. They will have a tendency to protect the old systems and ways of doing business since they have often built their personal success by being among the best at implementing the past processes and systems. It is part of the work of the transition team to give these 'gatekeepers' a compelling vision of the future that encourages them to make the changes required.

Mobilize movers and shakers

In every organization there are individuals that are viewed by their peers and associates as the 'Movers and Shakers' within the organization. These people may not appear on the organization chart as the leader but they are people who, for various reasons, influence others. It may be that they are recognized as moving up in leadership, it may be that they have unique technical abilities. Whatever the reason, they have the ability to influence others. This influence can be either positive or negative in implementing change. It is important that these people understand the recommended changes, why they are being implemented, and become a positive influence on others. One means of accomplishing this is to involve these 'movers and shakers' as champions for the changes being implemented. If involved appropriately these people will become a major asset in institutionalizing the proposed changes.

Hire and promote people with new behaviours

One means of insuring the transition of the organization in adopting the new behaviours is to make these behaviours a prerequisite for the people hired into the organization and for people that are given higher levels of responsibility through promotion. The organization will watch closely to see if the people that are supporting the change will receive additional authority and responsibility. Conversely, if those people that oppose the transition continue to receive recognition and promotion it will send a strong message that the leadership of the company is not serious about making the transition. Who is given positions of authority and responsibility will be the clearest message to the people throughout the organization of the true intention of management.

Recognize and reward role models

It is important, especially in the early stages of the transition, to make visible the early adopters of the new behaviours and practices by recognizing and rewarding them for their active support. It is also critical that the processes, systems, recognition and rewards that encourage and support the old behaviours and practices are stopped. To accomplish this the reward and recognition strategy you will implement as part of the transition must be proactively planned and effectively implemented. The momentum of the past will continue the recognition and reward behaviours of the past if there is no planned intervention to change them.

Align new employee orientation

The orientation a new employee received during the first days of their employment often sets their behaviour and attitude patterns for future years with the company. During a time of significant change it is very possible that the new employee will receive mixed messages concerning the intent of the organization. It is important that the employee's formal orientation reflects the future intent of the organization and outlines the behaviours and practices expected of the employee in support of the new ways of doing business. When we think of new employee orientation we normally refer to entry into the company at the lower levels of the organization. However, even more critical is the effective orientation of new employees entering the organization at the senior management and officer levels. These individuals will impact the behaviours of hundreds and even thousands of people throughout the corporation.

Capture communications channels

The planning and implementation of consistent and widespread communication that reinforces the changes being implemented is also critical to the transition. In most situations a small number of people have spent time studying the issues under consideration in great depth. These studies have allowed them to make proposals and gain top leadership approval for the changes being implemented. In doing so they have developed high levels of understanding allowing them to gain ownership in the transactions taking place. However, in most situations this group will consist of less then five per cent of the total population. The other 95 per cent have no idea of the new directions and expectations. All means of communication should be used to convey the message. This will include; company newsletter, web sites, letters from the president and senior leaders, union leadership if applicable, etc. If the web sites are not maintained or the newsletters convey the old expectations they will be confusing to those people throughout the organization that are trying to interpret the new directions.

It is also important that the communication of the transition occupies a major 'share of voice' to the organization. If other information of great importance occupy the same channels, the impact of the messages concerning the changes taking place will be greatly reduced or lost.

Audit for performance

The final step in institutionalizing the new behaviours and practices that will drive the transition is to conduct audits to determine if the changes are actually being implemented and embraced throughout the organization. These audits also provide an opportunity to gather feedback and adjust the strategies as required to carry out the transition.

The audits should be well designed and those individuals doing the audits well trained. Designing the audit, training of the auditors, conducting audits and gathering feedback, are all in themselves opportunities to involve additional people, provide recognition and showcase leaders as a means of institutionalizing the changes. Using well-positioned line managers as the auditors significantly strengthens the impact of the audit process.

Summary

Action learning in Motorola has proven to be an effective means of defining and resolving very high level corporate strategic issues.

The results of action learning are greatly enhanced when the issue that the team is asked to address is clearly defined and a senior executive as the champion supports the work of the team.

Action learning embedded in a larger process of strategic problem solving can be a powerful tool for renewing and establishing new direction for the organization.

Action learning projects in themselves do not result in major change in the organization. Those changes must be reinforced through a well-orchestrated change process, which includes adjusting all the levers that support the behaviours and practices of the people involved in the change.

CHAPTER 10

Action Learning at Philips Electronics: from Training to Transformation

Nigel J. Freedman

Introduction

FOR MORE than 20 years action learning has been at the heart of Philips' management education activities, and this chapter will deal with three very different approaches. Firstly the 'European Octagon', which has also been adopted by several other companies, is based on an assignment from the Board for high potential middle managers. It has been updated recently to become a truly global programme.

Secondly, at the business unit level, powerful project approaches for strategy development with a strong action learning focus for management teams have been used since the mid-1970s.

Thirdly, in the first half of the 1990s 'Operation Centurion', a unique major turnaround process, involved tens of thousands of managers at all levels in a cascaded series of action learning workshops, which helped substantially to bring the company back from a situation of crisis.

The following section places these various approaches in a simple framework for action learning that helps to highlight the underlying characteristics, after which each is described in some detail. Experiences and issues are discussed in the final section.

A Framework for Action Learning

Action Learning covers a wide range of approaches that aim to link learning and 'doing'. In the context of business-driven action learning, the following framework (Figure 10.1) shows a range of possibilities for '*content*', i.e. the nature of the topics on which attention is focused, and '*context*', which is the setting in which people are brought together to work and to learn. Together the two dimensions determine the extent to which real change can be achieved through the learning process.

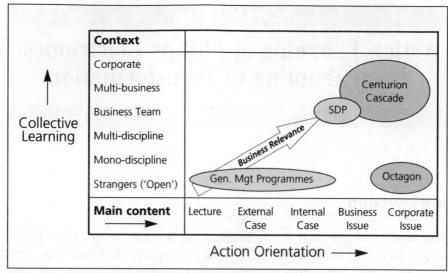

Figure 10.1 A framework for Business Driven Action Learning

It is likely that the most effective learning occurs when action learning is strongly coupled to *collective learning*, which can be achieved in various groupings of people in an organization. There is a range from pairs, clusters of individuals, through small family groups, complete management teams, to total corporate management. Frequently a large number of people know what should be done, and yet nothing happens. Actions leading to real change happen when a *critical mass of critical people* have learned enough to be dissatisfied with the current situation *and are aware of each other's readiness to act*.

The shared drive to acquire relevant learning and to act on it jointly can make all the difference between passive listening and the active implementation of action projects.

The Octagon Programme: A Corporate Project Assignment for High Potentials

Background and Objectives

For more than 20 years the Octagon programme has been seen as a valuable training for high-potential middle to senior managers. After frequent updating it has maintained a high degree of top-level support despite many changes in the composition and structure of the Board of Management, which now has few members who have a long history with the company.

The Octagon is an action learning programme for managers in their thirties from all parts of the world, and consists of three residential modules which are held in the key regions USA, Asia and Europe. An assignment sponsored by a Board member is undertaken, requiring about one day per week between the modules during a three-month period. The objectives of the Octagon in its most recent form are for the participants to gain:

- Greater insight into the business environments, practices and cultures of world regions.
- Knowledge and skills through analyzing and preparing strategies and solutions for a major company issue.
- Experience in managing a complex project under time pressure, and in the use of modern IT facilities in managing distributed teams.
- Insight and skills from working with peers from other businesses, functions and cultures.

Participants and Structure

Twice a year approximately 24 middle to senior high potential managers who are on the 'Corporate Interest Group' list are invited to participate in an Octagon, all costs being covered by a corporate management development budget. The target population is regionally representative of the firm's structure, namely: Europe 60 per cent, North and South America 20 per cent, Asia/Pacific 20 per cent.

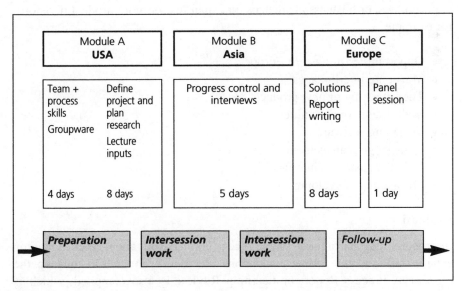

Figure 10.2 Octagon structure

The key features are:

- A single corporate assignment, BoM member as sponsor.
- Modular, three months duration, 20 per cent of working time.
- Three 'triad' locations: modules in USA; Asia; Europe.
- Work mainly in three sub-teams of eight ('Octagons'), making one consolidated report.
- Local contacts, field trips, interviews, presentations per region.
- Facilitation, programme management and administration by internal HR staff.
- Consulting skills tuition and process guidance are given by external faculty.
- Topic-specific inputs are provided by internal and external specialists.
- Intensive use of modern IT facilities: e-mail, Internet, Lotus Notes Groupware, video conferencing.
- Reporting to a panel consisting of BoM sponsor and top management.
- Optional follow-up meeting after six months to review implementation, both by sponsor and by participants.

Experiences and Issues

Topics

Typical assignment topics have been corporate-level issues, regional opportunities, or business challenges that span two or more product divisions, for example:

- Opportunities in Eastern Europe
- Managing interlinkages
- The launching of new products
- Multi-media opportunities
- Managing software
- Knowledge management
- IT in the customer interface
- Management development

Evaluations

In general the participants have been enthusiastic about their Octagon experiences, and the formal evaluations are used each time to tune up the process. A Process Report or Learning Review is also compiled, which is discussed with the top management Panel at the final reporting session.

The objectives are usually met to a good extent by a majority of participants, but obviously not everyone is equally satisfied. Individuals put in different amounts of time, energy and ideas, while some have more affinity with the overall approach or with the assignment topic.

The main reason for the high profile of the Octagon is probably the satisfaction among top management over many years, with the usually high quality of the information and the recommendations generated, and with the broad learning that they or their subordinates have apparently gained. In most cases the reports received very wide circulation, and triggered further presentations and action projects. There are many cases where specific major changes can be directly attributed to good Octagon studies, however it has not been the custom to try to assess the 'ROI' of the approach.

Implementation

An unsatisfactory aspect for some participants has been the feeling afterwards that their hard work has led to a report that has ended up in the cupboard. In some cases this has been true, for a variety of well-known reasons, but in general top management has been satisfied with the outcomes and has done a lot to push the implementation when they have been given good recommendations from the Octagons.

A growing issue results from the flattening of hierarchies and the changing responsibilities of top managers. It is often less appropriate for a Board member who sponsors a corporate-level assignment to wield influence in an area over which he does not exert formal authority, and yet many corporate strategic issues span several sectors, regions and functions. The sponsor may not always be the same person as the 'client' who eventually becomes responsible for the key steps in implementation. The alternative of only having assignments in one specific business area would defeat one of the main goals of the Octagon, which is to train managers to understand the realities of operating in the complex environment of a diversified multinational.

Care is therefore needed from the very beginning to maximise the chances of effective implementation, by thoroughly preparing the assignment with the (right) sponsor, by involving key people at various levels throughout the project, and by stimulating the participants themselves to cover implementation and change issues during their work.

Managerial relevance

During the first module several days are invested in learning a particular consulting methodology that provides a powerful conceptual framework. This guides the participants via a clear definition of the assignment that they will cover, the generation of creative hypotheses to be tested, the identification of data sources, and the formulation of key issues, leading to sound fact-based recommendations. Many people have found this methodology, which is used by a major consulting firm, to be very valuable afterwards in their approach to solving business problems. It also helps to provide a common 'hymn-sheet' to keep 24 potential leaders singing in tune for three months.

Facts vs. opinions

It is a long tradition that Octagon participants are allowed to interview anybody in the company, including the Board of Management, and in general this right is respected and broad cooperation is given. A tendency often noted is for participants to take the opportunity they have been given, and to spend too much time in interviews with Senior Management within the company. Finding their way in the 'corridors of power', while in itself even being a sub-objective of the programme, can cause the data-gathering to become more opinion-based than fact-based, more internal than external. The planning and conducting of interviews may take precedence over the less exciting work of searching the Internet and reading analytical reports.

Announcing the assignment

The assignment is devised in close consultation with one or more members of the Board of Management, the initial idea having come from sources such as Corporate Strategy, Division Managers, Corporate HR or Board Members. Normally the assignment is announced to the participants only after they have been together for a few days, and have worked on team and process skills. This ensures that all begin with more or less the same level of preparation on the assignment itself; this may not be optimal regarding the 'business result' objective alone, but has been found to be a good solution on balance when considering also the learning objective.

The role of the Chairman

At the end of the first week the Octagon Chairman is selected by the group itself, to manage the process and to coordinate the sub-groups for the duration of the project. The participants are invited to draw up their own criteria for the role of Chairman and to manage the election as they wish.

The demands on the Chairman are high, the visibility in the company is high, and the potential both for learning and for making a mess are also high. The choice is important, and it is not unknown for a change of Chairman to be forced by the turn of events, as the group comes under pressure and the stress level builds up. A deputy-chairman is usually appointed as a back-up.

Other roles per sub-group are for example: chairman, secretary, information manager, IT coordinator, report writer. The groups (normally three, but this may change during the assignment) are usually formed based on the profiles that emerge from the team-skills sessions in the first few days, after which some re-allocation will occur according to capabilities and interests, and to deal with cultural, regional or functional aspects.

The pain and pleasures of IT

Having taken the decision to use the new Global Octagon as a vehicle for understanding how to manage distributed teams, and the value of modern IT in doing so, considerable top-down pressure was necessary to bring participants up to speed with Groupware technology. Following an edict from the Board all were required to acquire a laptop with agreed specifications, but at the beginning the increasingly decentralised organisation caused a number of problems. Even when laptops were made available centrally it was difficult to get local support for everyone to become comfortable in using Lotus Notes Groupware to allow simultaneous access to shared files.

There was talk of people 'being dragged kicking and screaming up the learning curve' during the first two runs of the new global programme. Nevertheless most people were grateful for the experience, and many went on to implement Groupware in their own organisations.

Pro's and Con's of the Octagon

In the foregoing section many positive and some less positive aspects of the Octagon have been mentioned, and indeed the programme is viewed in Philips as a valuable educational experience for 40 to 50 high potential managers a year. Nevertheless it is positioned in the Framework for Action Learning (Figure 10.1 above) at the lower right of the chart, indicating that the 'Business Relevance' is still relatively low. This is because although the issue dealt with by the assignment is always a live company challenge, few participants are working on their own business areas, most are 'strangers' when they come together and they go their separate ways after about three months. The *collective learning* cannot easily be translated into *collective action*. Their roles are closer to consultants than to managers as far as the implementation of real change is concerned. Others, who have not themselves been through the data gathering and the discovery process, must pick up the baton and run with it.

A positive feature of The Octagon is that it can be valuable to have creative people who are not directly involved in an issue to take a completely fresh look from their unique perspectives. Many very good, practical, ideas have indeed come from Octagon programmes.

In the following Sections two other Action Learning approaches will be described that come closer to the ideal of both Collective Learning and Action Learning.

The Strategy Development Programme: Action Learning at the Business Unit Level

Background

During the mid-seventies an approach to strategy development for management teams was developed in Philips with the help of Igor Ansoff and the French consulting firm Société Euréquip. The method became widely known as the SOR, the Strategic Orientation Round. It combined basic strategic planning techniques with group dynamics in a manner that led not only to concrete business plans, but also helped the team members to adopt Strategic Management as a way of managing for the longer term. The essence of this approach lay in the coupling of action learning and collective learning in a business team, while systematically involving several supporting groups in a planned series of meetings to get the organization actively participating at several levels.

Various derivatives of the SOR have been applied successfully in Philips and in other firms, while the approaches have also been adapted to provide frameworks for teaching strategy and strategy process, for example in case workshops in the company and in a number of business schools.

As strategic planning techniques evolved, for example from simple SWOT Analysis to Industry Analysis, Business and Technology Portfolios, Scenario Planning, and Hyper-competition Arenas, the *collective learning* approaches for business team projects have been steadily adapted to embrace these techniques.

One version, the Strategy Development Programme (SDP), was created to assist business teams to re-think their business strategy and to involve managers and specialists also from other related units, while developing their communication, teamwork and analytical skills for strategic management.

Figure 10.3 depicts the particular framework for strategic management that lies behind the SDP approach.

The accent is placed in these action learning programmes as much on the *process* of strategy as on the *Information and Analysis* aspects, which are the

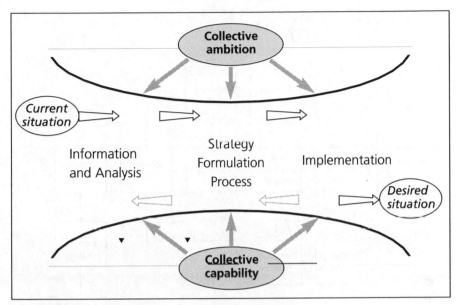

Figure 10.3 The ingredients of strategic management

tools and techniques of strategic planning. Strategy is handled more as a social, dynamic, team process; in Mintzberg's terms, '*formation*' rather than '*formulation*'.

Design of the Strategy Development Programme

Main design features

- The sequence of activities to cover the chosen strategic planning logic.
- The structure of the team and supporting resources.
- The management of communication and exchange of knowledge among the participants, and with other relevant units and levels of the organization.

The analytical steps may include some (only *very* occasionally all) of the items shown in Figure 10.4, according to the business situation.

A frequently used design comprises a series of core-team meetings of one to one and a half days each, with intervals of two to three weeks between them for inter-session work by the core team and its supporting groups. Some of the work may be carried out in parallel, for example a Business Portfolio Analysis and a Technology Portfolio Analysis. The overall duration can be typically two to three months, however 'pressure cooker' versions have often been used, consisting of two or three intensive two-day workshop sessions, a few weeks apart.

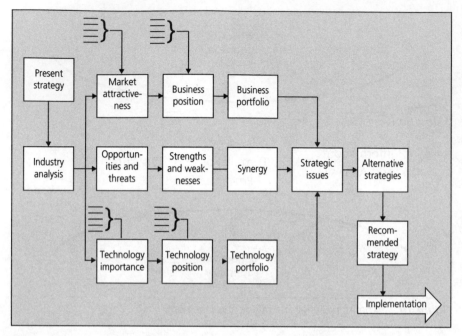

Figure 10.4   Strategic planning logic of the SDP (some options)

SDP organization structure

A key feature is the allocation of tasks between a 'Core Team', usually consisting of six to ten members of the management team plus one or two specialists, and supporting 'Aspect Groups' representing for example the key functional areas for the particular business. A typical structure is shown in Figure 10.5.

The Aspect Groups are usually members of the departments run by the management team members, supplemented by selected specialists from other units or for example suppliers or customers. 'Aspect Leaders' coordinate the work of these sub-groups, whose meetings are scheduled to ensure that their ideas and their output are fed in to the Core Team at appropriate times.

A small Support Group coordinates the programme, comprising typically the Business Unit manager as chairman, a secretary, and a facilitator/consultant. The latter has been most frequently an internal person belonging to HR, Strategy, or Organisational staff, or occasionally from outside the firm.

Communication in the organization

The development of collective learning and the effectiveness of implementation can be greatly enhanced by proper communication between the Core Team, the

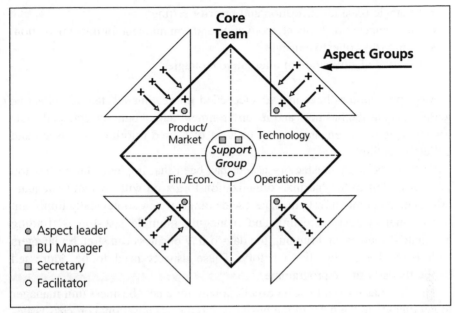

Figure 10.5 SDP team structure

Aspect Groups, and members of the organisation who are not officially part of the SDP programme.

Both upper-level management and lower-level employees need to be involved in regular communication about the process and about issues as they emerge, with due regard for confidentiality and diplomacy. A considerable amount of time is spent on planning and carrying out this communication, which is critical in creating the conditions for effective implementation of recommendations.

Related to this is the choice of core team members and of those who could better remain outside it. For example a dominant high-level manager may be encouraged to stay in a 'to-be-reported-to' position, and invited to meet regularly with representatives of the participants or the Support Group.

The learning dimension

Participants have the opportunity to gain knowledge, skills and insights matching the main objectives of the programme, namely:

- A structured, project approach to strategy formulation in a management team.
- Analysis of markets, companies and internal capabilities via a range of modern concepts for strategic management.

- Strategic issue identification and priority-setting.
- Management involvement, motivation and commitment for implementation.
- Consensus/collective insight.
- Creative identification of alternative strategies.

Most programmes have indeed succeeded in creating substantial *collective* learning about the business and its environment and about concepts and tools for strategic management, leading to a set of shared priorities for issues and collective action.

Perhaps the least satisfactory aspect has been that implementation has too often been left to the 'normal' organization to get on with, without adequate effort being put into how to manage a wide range of new strategically important tasks simultaneously. Creating and managing multiple task-forces, finding adequate resources, and running the day-to-day business can stretch managers well beyond their familiar territory. These aspects need to be addressed explicitly early in the programme.

The SDP has proved to be an excellent way for a new business unit manager to get quickly to the heart of the business and the organisational process issues involved. As a developmental vehicle for high potential managers who are included in the core team it has also proved very valuable.

Action Learning for Major Transformation: Operation Centurion

The Crisis of 1990

For nearly 100 years Philips had been one of the world's largest electronics companies, with a high reputation for innovation via activities such as Lighting, the Rotary Shaver, the Audio Cassette and Compact Disc. In early 1990 the situation became desperate as financial institutions lost confidence and the share price dropped to an all-time low. Disillusionment due to poor and inconsistent performance quickly led to the appointment of Jan Timmer as the new President in mid-year.

It was already clear that with years of declining profits in the face of murderous competition, responses were needed that went to the very roots of the company's way of operating.

The challenge of revitalizing a company of over 250 000 employees and worldwide sales of more than $25bn had begun.[1]

The Change Process

A decision was quickly taken by Timmer to embark on an ambitious programme known as Operation Centurion, the architecture of which was strongly influenced by Professor C.K. Prahalad who became the leading faculty supporting the operation. The key feature of the approach was to avoid the frequently seen 'slash and burn' of pure downsizing, by taking a longer-term view of what it takes to 'create a winning company'. *Action Learning* became a critical theme from the start.

The Centurion design provided a phased sequence for the attention given to improving operational performance, relative to the attention to innovation and growth.

Phases	Activities
I Restructuring (Performance gap)	1 Sealing the leaks 2 Efficiency drives (personnel, stocks, fixed assets, debtors/creditors, purchasing)
II Revitalisation (Opportunity gap)	3 Daily sales go on customer and quality campaigns 4. Strategic direction and growth 5. Workforce revitalisation

Figure 10.6 Operation Centurion design model

While all five of the above items were dealt with to some degree from the start, the priorities for attention shifted over time. In the first instance a small number of severely loss-making activities were sold or terminated. Then the start was made with the long-term process of 'Creating a Winning Company'.

In practice work on Phase II, for example via Task Forces on a new Strategic Direction or on fundamentally new ways of organizing work and involving people, needed to be established early on in the change process.

It was considered very important that as many people as possible had the overall model in mind, because to anticipate the hoped-for 'light at the end of the tunnel' was crucial for its motivational effect at all levels. 'Restructuring' is hardly a motivating theme if sustained for long, but the pain can be justified if more exciting innovation possibilities are seen to be ahead.

The key features of Operation Centurion were as follows.

Cascade

Top-down cascaded 'Centurion Sessions' formed the heart of Operation Centurion, and became an intensive company-wide Action Learning process. Over 500 three-day workshops were held from 1991 to 1993, each one creating new change projects or furthering the implementation of existing ones. Bottom-up 'Town Meetings' throughout the company provided a complementary action-oriented two-way communication path.

Centurion Sessions consisted of workshops lasting three days, with between 20 and 70 participants representing three or four hierarchical levels, usually within one business except at Corporate or Country level. An external consultant provided process facilitation, giving specific cognitive inputs as required, with the manager responsible for the business as 'owner' or chairman. The design of the initial Corporate-level session used to kick off the overall cascade, and mostly adopted per Division, was as follows:

Day I	Day II	Day III
A Crisis Scenario, Magnitude of the Task	*Examples of Change in Other Firms*	*Priorities, Commitments, Projects & Action Planning*
Coming to terms with reality – performance, choices and managerial orientation	Fighting back – a methodology for revitalization	Identifying and accepting goals for performance improvement – role of top management in revitalization

Figure 10.7   Centurion I session sesign   C. K. Prahalad

The agenda on the first day confronted participants with the state of the business, benchmarked against the best in class, followed by group work on formulation of the key issues facing the business. In businesses where a major turnaround was necessary this was the point at which the whole group was quite intentionally confronted with harsh reality by being pulled into the so-called 'Valley-of-Death'. The establishment of a sense of urgency was a critical *emotional* part of the change cycle, in order to prepare for the personal commitment to stretch targets in the following steps.

Day two was used to present modern concepts and illustrations on 'Building a Winning Organization', including Strategic Intent, Core Competences and approaches to major transformation in other large companies. This built the knowledge and the faith needed for the following phase, in which participants worked in groups on the formulation of, and commitment to, stretch targets to take the business to new levels of performance.

The third day was devoted to project formulation, action planning, and to making firm commitments.

This process was cascaded downwards in similar sessions with large groups to lower levels, where specific targets were put up for 'buy-in' discussions and translation to the next operating levels.

The whole cascade process was started with the top 120 managers including the Board of Management (labelled the 'Centurion I' Group), and continued for each Product Division normally to 'Centurion III or IV' level, and for most National Organisations or Regions.

Most groups continued to hold follow-up sessions at intervals of 4 to 6 months to review the implementation of the change projects, and to plan the next stages.

Some 30 000 people were involved in Centurion Sessions and over 600 change projects launched in the first two years of the operation.

The Centurion I Group established 22 *Corporate Task Forces* to tackle major issues such as customer orientation, control of inventory and receivables, purchasing, accounting systems, R&D effectiveness, management skills, values and behaviours, and strategic direction.

External consultants helped substantially with the cascade process on a worldwide scale, bringing the advantages of objectivity and the ability to confront; also external information, examples and best practices, plus meetings facilitation and advisory capabilities.

Urgency

Critical to the whole process was the instilling among senior management of a shared sense of urgency for major change, for example by well-prepared competitive benchmarking comparisons, presented in a manner to shake managers quickly out of any complacency.

An important factor here was the application of much more stringent criteria for profitability, cash flow and investment compared to the past.

Stretch

A key theme in the Centurion Process design was the notion of Strategic Intent,[2] a concept that has been at the heart of achieving commitment or 'buy-in' to reaching new levels of performance among large groups of employees at all levels. Prahalad & Hamel's idea of 'the impossible, achievable target' was made operational by using outside examples of how 'stretch' can lead to creativity and supreme performance when properly managed.

Emotion, consensus and commitment

A basic assumption underlying the Centurion model was that people would not be committed to new challenging goals unless they felt an emotional identification with them. This they will have only if they have either personally been involved in setting these goals, or are provided with sufficiently appealing incentives to adopt them.

Centurion meetings gave an opportunity for free expression of personal feelings with no 'sacred cows' permitted. Often a great deal of emotion was shown in putting away the past and adopting new stretch targets in a mutually supportive atmosphere. The 'Valley of Death' phenomenon mentioned above was recognised as a key factor leading to emotional commitment to change.

The first decision in the Centurion I meeting in October 1990, which was to cut the headcount by some 45 000 people, was reached by 120 people collectively and not by a top-down instruction from the Board. In a highly emotional process, managers found that they could do collectively what was previously impossible individually.

Projects, action learning and building competences

Centurion meetings gave an excellent platform for *collective learning and action learning*. The concrete output from each session was a set of stretch targets and *projects* that were selected to achieve new levels of performance. The intention was to change the way of managing, by forcing people to find new ways of doing things. Projects proved to be a very effective way of learning, and of building new capabilities.

Similarly the 22 Corporate Task Forces provided a vehicle for involving hundreds of people in searching for new approaches. Most of them undertook extensive external benchmarking to establish targets for best practice. External faculty and consultants provided valuable inputs that enhanced the learning of all involved.

Changing behaviour and style

A great deal of emphasis was placed on the 'soft' aspects of management as conditions for reaching 'hard' results. A new *mindset* was the goal.

The *Centurion spirit* was about raising ambition, about business not as usual, challenging established beliefs and norms, and listening to others. Trust, openness and honesty became key words in the Centurion approach.

Centurion progress 1990–95

From 1990 to mid-1995 the Centurion process led to a substantial improvement in almost every operating ratio, despite the recession and particularly unfavourable market conditions for companies in the Consumer Electronics business.

	End 1990	End 1994	Change
Sales	55.8	61.0	+9%
– Volume		+11%	+22%
– Price		–3%	–11%
Net Debt	14.8	6.4	–8.4
Group Equity	11.6	14.9	+3.3
RONA excl. restructuring	8.5%	20%	+135%
Profitability (% Sales)	4.2%	6%	+59%
Net Inventories (% Sales)	20.7	17.1	–17%
Receivables (months)	1.9	1.5	–21%
Personnel (comparable)	304 600	253 000	–51 600
Share Price (guilders)	20.30	51.40	+153%

Figure 10.8 Centurion progress 1990–95

In 1995 Philips saw further improvement in sales and profits and the share price rose to over 80 guilders, a factor of four times the figure during the crisis of 1990. Nevertheless analysts reacted negatively to third quarter results, which hinted that asset management was not improving as fast as expected, and that the Centurion process was running out of steam. The competitors were not standing still, and complacency was being allowed to creep in. This led to increased attention to 'unfinished business', that is to more and continuous efficiency improvement.

The Second Wave: 1995–98 Onwards

In October 1996 Cor Boonstra succeeded Jan Timmer as President. Some of the challenges at that time are described in *Business Week*.[3] Shortly afterwards he launched a new 'Governance Model' designed to inject a more performance-oriented culture and to shake the firm again to new levels of performance. The approach in this second wave of the change process was substantially different from the first, the main themes being structural decentralisation into 100 'businesses', dissolving the Division/Country matrix organisation, and the termination or sale of many operations that were not meeting shareholder value criteria. In particular the diversification into software and services initiated by Timmer was strictly cut back, with a firm focus on core businesses.

During the stock market 'high' of mid-1998, the Philips share price temporarily passed 200 guilders, a factor of ten times the figure at the low point of 1990. The market was reacting very favourably to the new attention being given to shareholder value. In early 1999 the markets appeared to be awaiting clear signals of sustainable growth in the company.

The two phases under Timmer and Boonstra need to be seen as 'waves in a continuous change process', and not as specific projects. The one is not necessarily more effective than the other, rather they were probably the appropriate approaches for the firm at the time, the second building on the successes and correcting the weaknesses of the first.

What we have learned about business driven action learning

Five years of Operation Centurion have given a number of insights that may well be of value to other organizations, particularly to large complex firms. A significant feature was that this approach began in a time of crisis. The following points stand out.

The design of the change process

Creating a sense of *urgency*, by using carefully presented facts or scenarios, has been a difficult and yet critical factor in focusing attention on the need for deep change. Sustaining that urgency has proved to be even more difficult.

Emotion is a critical component of the change process, and needs to be used wisely. An emotional cycle was a key design feature of at least the earlier Centurion sessions.

Resistance to change can be greatly reduced by '*peer pressure*' in large groups. Less familiar perhaps is '*peer support*', whereby difficult decisions become easier when all face them equally. The initial headcount reduction by 45 000 people proved to be surprisingly less impossible than most people thought, since all colleagues were faced with the same challenge and pain. Exchange of experience was also very helpful here. This is the essence of *collective action learning*.

Speed is essential. Despite the rapid response to the crisis in 1990, with hindsight some have said that they would have preferred to move much faster. The lesson here is, as one top manager said, "*change at least twice as fast as you can, and start long before it is possible*"!

A *Cascade Process* involving well-facilitated multilevel meetings, repeated every few months, can give a status-free forum for stimulating collective action learning and achieving real change. For top-down sessions there is a natural minimum duration of two to three days for the dynamics to work effectively. Consensus takes time: compliance can be deceptive: achieving real commitment requires real effort.

Units that held Centurion sessions at top level but did not cascade the process to lower levels usually found that implementation of stretch goals did not work well. The critical 'buy-in' process was missing. There is a (subtle) major difference between a traditional hierarchical deployment of targets, and a translation by lower levels of proposed stretch goals into accepted and owned commitments.

Learning

Perhaps one of the major positive 'soft' changes that were seen was the increased readiness to learn. Exchange of best practice across divisions, benchmarking against competitors and firms in other industries, a willingness to listen to lower-level and younger people, and a marked increase in the demand for management and technical training programmes, were signs of a healthier respect for learning. The earlier arrogance was departing.

The cascade process was co-ordinated by the Corporate Management Training and Development function, and for two years all normal management training programmes were suspended. Instead, Centurion became a new way of combining management meetings with education. Many corporate-level taskforces recommended new or revised training programmes, which gave the impetus for rethinking and expanding internal management training. *Action learning* through work on live issues or projects, and *collective learning* in intact business or 'family' teams became a high priority in the company.

Change agents and consultants

Hundreds of three-day Centurion Sessions were held, and hundreds of Town Meetings, in the early 1990s. Nearly all of these were facilitated by an outside consultant or by an internal staff or line manager. A small 'Core Faculty' from prominent European and US Business Schools provided a strong intellectual input, experience of other companies' change processes, and the facilitation of top-level meetings. One of the main reasons for choosing people from business schools was the accent to be placed on *learning*, though in a *doing* mode.

Change Agents Training workshops lasting two to three days were given to over 400 line and staff people in several countries, with the intention of creating an army of internal resources to continue the change process. The content was primarily focused on the design and facilitation of Centurion Sessions and Town Meetings. A survey showed that the success rate was disappointing, and that only a modest number were being really influential. There were simply too few people available with the right combination of skills that senior managers could rely on.

The massive mobilization of people in the Centurion cascade has been a valuable, business driven, action learning experience.

CHAPTER 11

Scancem: 'What Did We Earn and Learn'? Emerging Markets and Business Driven Action Learning

Miko Weidemanis and Yury Boshyk

SCANCEM is one of the leading cement and building materials companies in the world with over 10 000 employees, active in 35 countries, and with its headquarters in Malmo, Sweden. Scancem has major operations in many parts of the world but in 1997 the board was considering and interested in expanding its activities in a new emerging market region. Before doing so in a significant way, it was decided to utilize its annual action learning programme for high potentials and then its Senior Management Seminars to access the past experiences that Scancem had in emerging markets. At the same time they were to address the issue as to whether or not the company had developed the right competencies to work well in new emerging markets, especially in South East Asia.

Scancem's Business Driven Action Learning Programme

Business driven action learning has always been used used in Scancem's high potential programmes. What follows is a brief description of one of these programmes and the interconnectedness with Scancem's senior management, the general learning process from 1997 to 1998, and business issues relating to the company's efforts in working in emerging markets.

Programme Structure

Every year Scancem holds what is called a Programme for Management Candidates (PMC). About 25 to 40 people every year are selected by their managers into the Scancem Group pool of young potentials. The candidates for this PMC must have the following profile: be an employee at one of the Group's (more than 50 per cent owned) companies for at least the past three years; be considered to have potential for more demanding assignments; be in age about thirty-three (plus or minus three years); have linguistic proficiency (good knowledge of two foreign languages, of which one must be English); and, possess a higher educational degree (post-gymnasium). Of this number, about 18 to 22 are then chosen to attend the PMC after consultations with business area human resource heads and the Senior Vice President for human resources. The selected candidates are, therefore, sponsored by their business area and the leaders of these businesses also sponsor the business driven action learning projects. Like many other companies' experiences, not many executives in the beginning understood the benefits of sponsoring a business project but after the first programme volunteers became more forthcoming. Their 'mentors' are the Human Resource (HR) heads of the respective business areas. The PMC enjoys great prestige and is very highly considered in the company. Needless to say, the competition to be nominated and accepted is stiff.

A typical programme would have seven phases and would run for nine months from March through to September, with participants still working on their regular 'day' job. It starts a few weeks before the programme launch with an individual review with the 'mentor' on needs and skills for personal development. The second part – the formal launch of the programme – takes place over five days and is focused on teambuilding and leadership, using outdoor exercises and other well known methods. This usually takes place outside the Nordic region. At this stage, the 'project work' is introduced.

Each Business Area with participants in the programme has the 'opportunity and the obligation to propose a project'.

In 1997 the project work was on the topic of 'how we in the Scancem Group up till now have succeeded in penetrating new markets' or as it was later coined: 'What Did We Learn and Earn in Emerging Markets?' Five countries and regions where Scancem had experience were selected: Angola, the Baltic Republics (Estonia, Latvia and Lithuania), Ghana, Poland and Russia. The high potentials were divided into teams with no one being allowed to work on a project from their own business area or geographical responsibility. Each team was also assigned a Project Leader – a senior executive appointed by the Business Area – in charge of important businesses in Scancem. These Leaders helped the teams to 'open doors' in the company and helped the teams clarify their thoughts and analyses. Already at this stage it was planned to have these high potential project team reports integrated into the Senior Management Seminars later in the year and into 1998.

Work on the projects continued for the next few months. The 1997 programme teams also visited the countries and the Scancem businesses in those emerging markets and interviewed all the people who played a role in creating the Scancem presence in those markets. In June, or about half way through the PMC, the participants were brought together for a few days of intensive briefings on the company: its structure, strategy, business areas, processes and culture. This helped them better appreciate the context of their project work.

By the beginning of August most reports had been completed and the next stage was the preparation of the presentations to the CEO and the executive committee. A few days before that, the participants were brought together to spend some time preparing these presentations and learning about managing and understanding cultural diversity. About one half day was allotted to a discussion and presentations on the history and future of the Scancem Group. These discussions were led by the CEO and the most 'senior' of the Scancem executives who passed on to the younger generation, in today's terms, the embedded knowledge and experiences of the Group. This was followed by presentations of the report findings and recommendations to the CEO and the executive committee, Project Leaders, and the Business Area leaders who sponsored the projects. These presentations inevitably lead to very lively discussions among all the stakeholders and clearly demonstrated the value of having real business issues as a foundation for business driven action learning.

The business benefits are clear to everyone. First, there was general consensus on the value for the company of having documented past experience – from who was involved, to the actual processes used and lessons learned on how these markets were developed by Scancem. Second, the high potential participants got a deep insight into the company's practices and competencies. But the greatest benefit was the personal learning and teamwork that took place during this challenging action learning programme. At the same time, the role they played in the programme led to promotions for nearly half the participants very soon after the programme.

The concluding part of the PMC takes place the same way the programme started – with an individual review with the Human Resource head of the Business Area from which the participant works. They discuss the experience of the PMC and further developmental needs and other issues related to career planning.

Next Steps: Senior Management Seminars

A month after the presentations to the executive committee the Scancem Group Senior VP for Human Resources launched the follow up to the PMC projects through the Senior Management Seminars. These were planned a year in advance and dealt with a wide variety of topics for the top 200 or so managers in the company. These came together in separate groups of 25 at a time for eight meetings throughout 1997 and 1998 over a period of five days. Each time they met, one day of the five-day seminar was devoted to emerging economies. Half of the day was spent looking at the experience of a major multinational in one emerging market (a 'best practice') and the experiences of many multinationals in many emerging markets. Both subjects were presented by outside speakers. The rest of the day was spent working in teams analysing the reports from the PMC particpants. Each of the senior management teams was assigned a country report to consider and then they were asked to make a presentation of their findings to the whole seminar. They were asked to consider the following questions in their presentation to the group and in their analysis of the PMC reports:

1. What did the Scancem Group do right in its emerging markets businesses? What could have been done better?
2. What is needed to grow a profitable Scancem business in new emerging markets?
3. How should we make what we have earned and learned better known in the Group?

As one can imagine, the presentations and discussions generated a great deal of valuable insights on both the shortcomings and strengths of the Group and helped to develop a consensus at the highest levels on ways to improve performance and ways forward for new market opportunities. While the company discovered that there were some areas for improvement, it was encouraging for everyone to see that these were also common to many companies struggling to improve results, especially in emerging markets.

Some of the ingredients for success were identified as being the following: early market entry; the right local partners with the respect and authority needed to open doors and make things happen; a relationship of trust and respect for the local partners and the local community; a long view on investment; support and understanding by senior management, including the ability to make quick decisions, and an appreciation of the cultural and political background of the country; cooperation and sometimes, coordination among different Business Areas; and tying human resources management to the strategic goals, including selection of the right expatriates, and the wise use of internal company experts – and finally, a good dose of luck and right timing!

What the discussion also revealed was that, like many other companies, the talent, competencies and experiences from previous ventures into emerging markets were not well leveraged for future growth opportunities, and that some very practical, and relatively easy things could be put in place to improve the situation. These included the use of the company intranet, the creation of a special team involved in emerging markets and a Business Intelligence unit, and a built-in process of 'knowledge capture' on any new projects of this kind. For example, several groups mentioned that internal expertise on such matters as managing under superinflationary economic situations existed in the company and could be used more extensively in emerging markets where inflation is a major consideration for management. In fact, one of the first things to be implemented was the development of a manual on guidelines for a business area heavily involved in emerging markets.

The board is also presently considering other initiatives based on the feedback from the Senior Management Seminar presentations and discussions. In 1998 Scancem ran another PMC with a business project that once again utilised the learning on emerging markets from previous programmes and Senior Seminars. The PMC particpants were asked to recommend how the company could establish a major presence in the second largest city of a newly emerging country and market.

Conclusion

Scancem is committed to continuing this action learning approach to high potential and executive development. The success of the programmes speaks for itself both in terms of business results and the personal development of partcipants. The integration of many different elements was also another factor in their success because we integrated and combined the specific and the general (emerging markets and the Scancem experience); the historic and the futuristic (what did we do at Scancem in the past and what do we need to do in the future); the perspectives of the younger and older generations (the high potentials and the senior executives); and, finally, the business issue, individual and team development were all tied together: earning and learning came naturally and constructively to all.

Scancem programme for management candidates

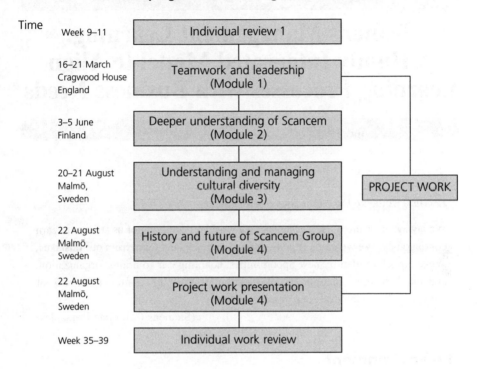

Time

Week 9–11	Individual review 1
16–21 March Cragwood House England	Teamwork and leadership (Module 1)
3–5 June Finland	Deeper understanding of Scancem (Module 2)
20–21 August Malmö, Sweden	Understanding and managing cultural diversity (Module 3)
22 August Malmö, Sweden	History and future of Scancem Group (Module 4)
22 August Malmö, Sweden	Project work presentation (Module 4)
Week 35–39	Individual work review

PROJECT WORK

Siemens Management Learning: A Highly Integrated Model to Align Learning Processes with Business Needs

Matthias Bellmann

Learning is the key to continuous improvement.

We always measure ourselves against the world's best. Each of us strives to learn continuously. We welcome and offer open feedback, and learn from our mistakes. We are quick to identify new opportunities, adapting our solutions, organization, and our behaviour accordingly. We are building an international network of knowledge in which everyone gives and takes.

(Siemens Corporate Principles)

The Environment

THE FOLLOWING trends have been recognised in the field of management training for some 15 years, irrespective of the type of business:

- The time companies spend on learning in formal processes is being reduced per training unit (seminar, workshop), even though the perceived need for learning is rising.
- Traditional learning processes are being increasingly separated from work processes. This is evident if one considers the choice of locations where training is held (company in-house training centres, business schools, seminar locations). The learner consequently has the feeling that the greater the distance from the actual workplace. the less the relevance of what is being learned.
- The 'seminar' method of training (classroom instructions as a combination of lectures and exercises over a couple of days) is becoming more popular, which may explain why efforts are being made to standardise and commercialise the subjects and processes to be learned. At the same time, there is growing criticism of the efficiency and the effectiveness of this learning method for practical work.[1]

The underlying reason for the growing polarity between the reality of training and what really needs to be learned is the rarely recognised and even more rarely applied recognition of a far-reaching paradigm of change that is best described as the trend towards the 'learning organization'.[2,3] While the human capabilities required for the development, manufacturing and distribution of goods in the industrial phase are mainly acquired through the public education system (schools, vocational schools, universities) and then – apart from a few modifications to ensure practical application – used for the whole of a person's working life, knowledge itself is becoming the dominant factor of production as we migrate from the post-industrial to a knowledge-based society.[4] This is a knowledge that becomes quickly redundant and must be renewed in ever shorter cycles. The public education system can no longer – or only inadequately – meet this challenge. In the past it may have made sense to keep the organization and content of work separate from continuous learning. Today, however, learning new and additional skills has become a permanent, highly integrated part of the process of realizing added value, and this will become even more important in the future. The learning organization is therefore a producer of new marketable knowledge and management may transform this knowledge into saleable performance on the market.[5]

Changes in Management Training – The Siemens Way

For these reasons many companies have made efforts over the past years to fundamentally rethink and revise their training systems for management development. Siemens, one of the world's market leaders, with 150 years of experience in the field of electrical engineering and electronics and with 15 business groups maintaining a global presence in virtually all countries of the world, found itself faced with the challenge of redefining its management training in view of a business environment that was undergoing change at a rapidly increasing pace, mainly caused by the globalisation of activities and by inter-group and inter-regional businesses.

In the course of this redefinition, Siemens – with enormous support from top-level management who was convinced about the need for an efficient and transparent management development system – seized the opportunity to risk a radical new beginning instead of merely continuing to develop the existing sequence of long-standing training systems.

The starting point for reform was the result of a demand analysis of current and future business operations (and qualities required from managerial-level staff). Four main demands were found:

- Identify, specify, develop, and measure behaviour patterns which are essential for business success.
- Promote and support the 'learning organization'.
- Reinforce the Siemens principles of personnel development (individual initiative, transparency, and competition).
- Less system, clearer values.

Four main demands were also ascertained for the content and structure of management training:

- Reduce the complexity of the learning systems and introduce a clear programme structure tailored to future needs such as knowledge management and virtual team processes.
- Demonstrate and measure the business contribution of learning by working on concrete business tasks in a clearly structured project-oriented learning environment.
- Promote knowledge management across functions, groups, and country borders and establish permanent networks among managerial-level staff.
- Achieve progressive internationalization through uniform world-wide programmes that can be adapted to local and regional requirements.

From Management Training to Management Learning

The change of name – from training to learning – reflects a radical change in philosophy. 'Management Learning' was (and is) a conscious departure from 'management training'. While training is event-oriented (mainly seminars), the highly integrated methods of learning are business and results-oriented. While training is usually short-term and separated from one's daily work, Management Learning is an ongoing process aimed at integration into daily work. The training approach focuses on individuals, and the trainers (faculty) are held responsible. Management Learning focuses on teams and processes, and the participants – who prefer to call themselves 'contributors' – bear the main share of responsibility. Training courses usually aim at presenting subjects within a set curriculum. Learning strives towards full utilization and expansion of potential. While training generally provides a person with tools and a store of knowledge, learning fosters the establishment and growth of the mental concepts required for gaining and applying knowledge and for exchanging experience and expert knowledge with others. Training attempts to structure learning processes, while 'learning' tries to stimulate these processes and ensure their continuance. Learning leads participants towards empowerment instead of channelling individuals towards a constrained path. Last but not least, it is a process owned by the participants, instead of by an organiser who assumes the role of owner, thus creating a customer-supplier relationship that is detrimental to learning.

That is why Siemens Management Learning is based on three basic principles:

- It is oriented towards performance and results. Learning is part of project work in a real business environment, where knowledge applied is, wherever possible, self-taught.
- Siemens Management Learning is the co-operative attainment of personal qualifications. Prior to project work, individuals are responsible for acquiring knowledge on their own initiative. They then apply this knowledge in a network of competencies to an actual project.
- Siemens Management Learning fosters the world-wide exchange and transfer of knowledge by documenting learning processes and results (including project results) in its company-owned intranet. It should take place, first and foremost, as intranet-based cooperative learning.

These principles of Management Learning support the following corporate objectives:

- To strengthen business and customer orientation.
- To encourage people to take responsibility for their own learning in a decentralized organization.
- To create a worldwide pool of business-relevant knowledge as the foundation for a learning organization.

To meet these objectives, all management training events (about 30 seminars) scheduled as part of the company's management development programme were replaced in 1997 and mandatory 'Siemens Management Learning' was introduced world-wide. This was preceded by six months of preparation that entailed intensive benchmarking and selection of future external partners. 'Regional learning councils' – which were established in all large-scale regions (Europe, Asia Pacific, North America and South America) – took part in this process. These councils included representatives from the corporate groups as well as from International Siemens Companies. At the same time, 'regional learning managers' were appointed and made responsible for the implementation and coordination of all regional and local Management Learning activities, thus decentralizing the entire operation.

The Management Learning system now consists simply of five programmes worldwide: a Management Introduction Programme, a Basic Management Programme, an Advanced Management Programme, a General Management Programme, and a Siemens Executive Programme, abbreviated as S5 to S1. These programmes have different target groups, goals, and scopes, but their structures and principles are identical (see Figure 1).

S5 is aimed at employees who clearly have above-average potential for future managerial tasks. The aim of the programme is to reinforce self-management capability in the company's various fields of endeavour.

S4 prepares employees for their first managerial task and is therefore aimed at the acquisition of management skills. As a rule, participants are estimated to have managerial potential that goes beyond the first level of management.

Both programmes are carried out locally, with the International Siemens Companies responsible for their implementation and further development. Organizations in smaller countries cooperate with neighbouring countries in order to guarantee economies of scale. They are assisted in this task by the regional learning councils and the regional learning managers.

S3 is targeted at managerial staff with several years of management experience and with extensive functional responsibilities in a core process, for example, as head of a profit centre with responsibility for revenues and results. Consequently, this programme focuses on promoting entrepreneurial potential. S3 is a regional programme that is carried out for the International Siemens Companies and is held in English only. The regional learning councils are responsible for organising S3 within the scope of the specified uniform structures, and the regional learning managers are responsible for delivering the programme.

S2 is for managers responsible for the operation of businesses with a global scope, such as a Subdivision or a Division. It is carried out centrally in a uniform manner for the entire world and is supervised by a programme manager. The aim of S2 is to develop entrepreneurial capabilities into leadership abilities.

S1, the Siemens Executive Programme, is aimed at the holders of, and the successors for, the approximately 250 key positions in the company. It deals with central corporate issues as stipulated by the CEO and their implementation. As in the case of S2 and S3, the language of the programme is English.

All the programmes have a uniform structure (see Figure 2). They consist of a combination of workshops, distributed (distance) learning, and 'business impact projects'. As a rule they take one year. This length of time was chosen because:

- The programmes accompany or are integrated into activities.
- Time is needed to develop lasting learning attitudes and to establish a stable network.
- An individual's acquisition of knowledge must fit that individual's schedule.

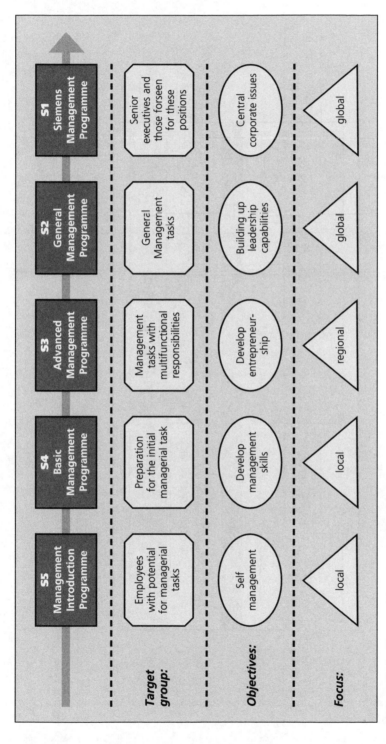

Figure 12.1 Siemens Management Learning

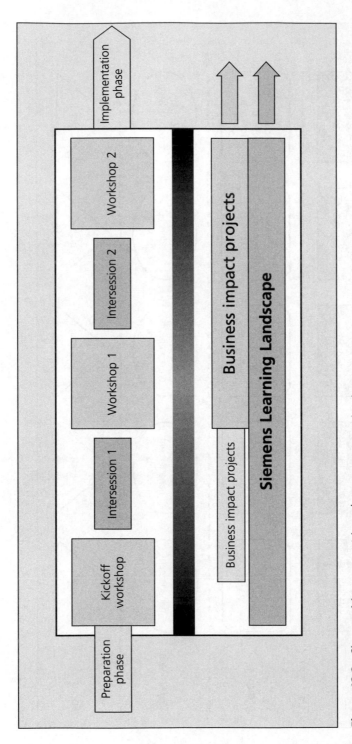

Figure 12.2 Siemens Management Learning programme structure

The main aim of the workshops, which last about one week, is to focus on the learning and management attitudes of the participants and to initiate personal change. At the same time, core skills – for example, financial, strategic and change management – that would be needed at the targeted managerial level are introduced. Contents of the workshops can always be applied immediately to one's own work and/or during the course of self-learning phases or team learning phases following the workshops. These 'intersessions' utilise the networking of the participants on the company's own intranet and continue group learning by means of a virtual workshop via the network. This is the Siemens distance learning structure. For example, one workshop element in S2, 'Strategic Management', is continued and completed in teams connected via the intranet for several weeks directly after the respective workshop, as an integrated business simulation.

Apart from receiving the best external knowledge available, 'distance learning' also provides learners with Siemens-specific knowledge via the intranet. Great effort is taken to adapt the experience and best practices gained in the Siemens department units and operating units for the intranet and to make these available via various means of access (e.g. the current curricular structuring of MBA programmes). It is already possible to retrieve a great many Siemens-specific subjects under the title 'Siemens Learning Landscape", for example, on subjects such as 'accounting and finance' or 'strategy', outlining best company know-how on that particular subject (see Figure 3). This enables managers to access best or, at least, good practices independently from a formal learning situation exactly when this knowledge is required, e.g. to optimize purchasing processes or to redefine customer relationships. The goal is to set up an integrated 'knowledge landscape' with many other company initiatives and to continue to develop this on a permanent basis, something which goes far beyond the actual demand of Siemens Management Learning.

All further information on Siemens Management Learning, including programme brochures, application procedures, etc., can be found in the company's own intranet.

The focus of Siemens Management Learning is on developing an effective, feasible 'action learning' component, transferable to all other actual business requirements. Because of Action Learning, cross-functional, cross-group and cross-country learning can be practiced on actual business opportunities, thus realising the actual, measurable benefit for Siemens' businesses. Detailed analyses of the experience that other companies (e.g. General Electric, Allied Signal and Bell Canada) had gained through this method of learning helped to implement the version of 'action learning' designed especially for Siemens.

The Siemens version of Action Learning – a process and its associated

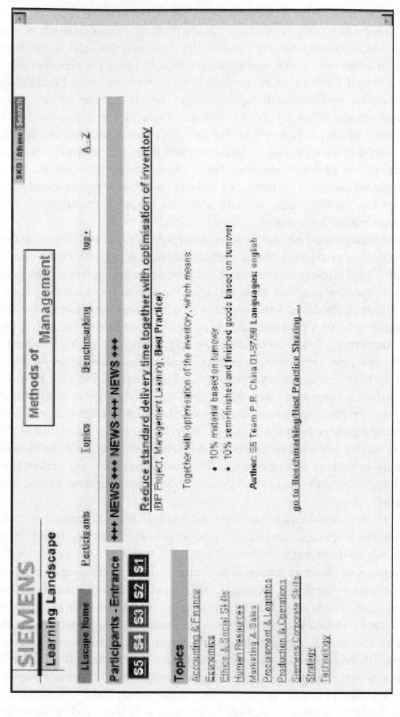

Figure 12.3 Siemens Learning Landscape

instruments were developed under the title 'Business Impact Projects' (BIP). BIP is characterised by the following principles.

The subjects (known as business opportunities) for this learning phase are generally identified by the participants themselves in one of the Siemens Divisions, and a 'coach' is selected to lead the project. This coach has business responsibility for the process targeted by the project, permitting him to decide whether the project results will be implemented. The business opportunity must be according to the respective level of management – S5 to S1-- and be solution driven. A 'BIP marketplace' has been set up on the Siemens intranet to enable a potential coach to advertise business opportunities without being directly addressed by participants. As a basic principle, BIPs are processed in teams of four–six participants, none of whom belong to the field of work which originated the business opportunity. In a systematic process the goal of the BIP as defined by the respective team is narrowed down in collaboration with the coach so that the project can be completed within a period of approximately four months (out of the 12 months allocated to a programme) and can lead to a measurable contribution to the business of the respective part of the company. A specially developed procedure based on 'best practice' experience, [6, 7] ensures that this is done. It systematically narrows the project ideas, which are usually too extensive at the outset, and reduces them to create an effective lever that can be used to make a concrete and measurable contribution to basic business tasks. The implementation of the project results in concrete business processes is an indispensable and critical part of the BIP methodology. The projects are finally documented on the intranet and made available to other corporate groups.

Some examples of current BIPs are: reduction of redundancies between sales and service in one business area, improvement of material stock system for one material category, reduction of scrap rate in manufacturing in one production line, implementation of a self measurement process for delivery performance, making a pilot for electronic commerce in a business group, operator support via remote access in one business unit, world-wide sales strategy for one product in electronic business, cost rationalization for one product group in tele-communication business, optimization of a sales channel for one product group and increase of market access, via multimedia, for a few businesses in one region.

BIPs are monitored by a standard process and their financial impact is confirmed by accounting methods. The completed BIPs have fulfilled initial expectations. They not only offered participants a unique, challenging and exciting learning opportunity, but also contributed to bottomline results. So far, business impacts valued from $10000 to $1.5m have been realised. The Siemens Management Learning concept was able to refinance itself within the first 18 months, recovering development costs and the costs of operation. This is perhaps not the most advanced argument for a combination of work and learning but it is certainly a very convincing one.

Initial Experience

There is no doubt that risks were entailed in developing the new Siemens Management Learning concept, implementing it worldwide for all programme stages in less than one year, building up the required resources, informing the entire organization of the goals, contents, and procedures of the new programmes, and almost completely replacing all former training elements. But the experience gained, to date, has shown that the new model meets the requirements of the organization exactly and provides good support to further worldwide company initiatives. Moreover, it has been received very positively by participants.

The highly integrated programme elements (workshops, action learning, and distance learning), the empowerment to make local and regional modifications according to local culture, the immediate applicability of what has been learned to one's own work as well as the support and active participation of the top management, were all criteria that guaranteed success. Last but not least, it was right to create a model from the outset that was in itself a learning system, one that not only permitted constant improvement but actually made such improvement a mandatory part of the system. For example, partners, persons responsible for the programmes, participants, and external service providers all check to see if modifications need to be made after every programme sequence and – if deemed necessary – these are implemented immediately, affecting programmes at appropriate levels.

A number of new cultural elements of management development and learning were consciously introduced into the company through Siemens Management Learning. These included the orientation of learning processes towards performance and results, making use of virtual learning environments, the worldwide exchange of knowledge gained from learning processes using the latest technologies, and the integration of learning and work. The persons responsible knew from the beginning that turning these requirements into lasting changes in the behaviour of management personnel would take time. Making success visible for all people involved within a short time is perhaps one of the most basic ways of motivating people to invest their time.

Up until now, Siemens Management Learning has focused on the vertical development of elite personnel with clearly above-average performance and potential for advancement. In a forthcoming second phase, the knowledge and techniques already acquired will be transferred to forms of horizontal development. Which means that now:

- Special target groups, for example, in the area of human resources or project management, will experience learning development adapted to their specialised interests and requirements (which nevertheless also includes cross-departmental managerial development), and
- Executive staff at and for a particular managerial level (for example profit centre managers) will undergo supplementary learning processes which support and encourage the development of the initiative that is demanded of them.

The first such programmes had started when this contribution was submitted.

CHAPTER 13

Volkswagen: Action Learning and the Development of High Potentials

Guy Mollet

Introduction

WHEN I met Richard Davis, he was an investment banker and he had been working with Morgan Stanley for the best part of the last two years. He was a little over 24 years old and he looked exactly that age. It was in one of the overcrowded Northwest lounges of the Davis terminal in Detroit. We were both waiting for a Dallas connection and we started chatting. I was in the middle of a benchmarking study focused on the development of high potential managers for the Volkswagen Group and he was flying to some remote place in Texas where he would meet with the CEO and with the CFO of a health food processing company. 'To analyze their assets' he told me, 'in order to see whether we would consider buying them.'

He specified that the buying decision would be his.

I was amazed and I asked him about his Morgan Stanley career.

This company picks the best graduates freshly from campus, gives them a two-week training and then they're off in the real business life. In Richard's case, selling and buying companies. Long working hours, 8:30 am to midnight or more and hardly any weekends free. Very regularly they were trained and briefed and they were requested to study new material. He had demanding schedules, always ready and expecting to be called back at the office. But the pay was very good, he said. And on the top of that he was entitled to 'the limo treatment,' free restaurants and to first class flights. I inquired about his family life? Not yet he said, no time for it. He told me that he was gathering experience as much as he could, having a lot of fun doing it and that later, in a year or two, he intended to look for a 'better job'. Some companies had already called him, with the promise of doubling his salary. Nowadays, on a yearly basis, he was making close to $100 000.

Here I was, working for a traditional European corporation where we also recruited the best college graduates; we also had programmes to develop them with the hope that they would become the executives of the future. The difference was that our college graduates were 29 when they started working for us, that we expected them to 'dirty their hands' before we would consider giving them any responsibility. On the top of that, they would be paid according to our 'honest to all' pay scale and they would certainly never receive a 'limo treatment'. 'This would spoil them and we don't need spoiled brats in our organization,' was the standard line of thinking.

Suddenly I knew what to do, in order to maximize the development of our best people.

1. Attract and recruit the best-trained brains.
2. Give them assignments that stretch them beyond their capabilities.
3. Give them immediately real responsibilities, no case studies, and expect them to deliver excellent results.
4. Follow them up and give them according to their needs, as much training as they (and you) can afford.
5. Reward them well for their achievements and celebrate their successes.
6. Expect them to be very flexible.
7. Do this on a continuous basis.

The Context at Volkswagen

The Volkswagen Group is a complex, diversified and decentralized organization.

It encompasses four distinct brands, Volkswagen, Audi, Seat and Skoda. Outside Europe the activities are coordinated through regional structures: the North American Region (Canada, the USA and Mexico), the South American-South African Region and Asia Pacific.

Most of the HR activities are kept totally decentralized. The Brands as well as the Regions are responsible for the planning, the recruitment and the development of their employees and their managers. We believe that the cultural and the social diversity of our employees is an enrichment for our organization.

In the early nineties, the Group Management Board (subsequently referred to as 'the Vorstand') felt that there was not enough synergy between the management teams worldwide. They also believed that the transfer of know how as well as the networking between the international managers needed to be improved.

Thirdly and maybe most importantly, they wanted to prepare the future. The goal was to ensure the availability of highly motivated, skilled and experienced multilingual management personnel for staffing key positions and to run the worldwide VW businesses.

The Actions

Decision

In December 1991, the Vorstand decided to set up a task force with the specific goal of developing international management processes. The two target groups were the 300 Group Senior Executives and the worldwide 'high potentials.'

In the spring of 1992 I was appointed as team leader of this task force. The team was called 'Group Management Development' (later to be referred as GMD).

In this article I shall only focus on the programme that we specifically designed for the benefit of our high potential managers. It is an outstanding example of action learning.

Design Team

The GMD team members were chosen for their competence and their willingness to do something new. I attracted people from all over the world belonging to very different business fields. I wanted the team to be a picture of the cultural diversity of the VW Group. Purposely, only four out of ten were HR managers.

Research

We started with a self-assessment and with an internal benchmarking study. We visited our four Brands as well as the Volkswagen companies in the North American region, South Africa and South America as well as in Asia Pacific. The idea was to get a good feeling of how our different companies were selecting and developing their best people.

We also initiated an international benchmarking study. After a preliminary survey we eventually visited Bechtel, Ford and General Electric in the USA, ABB, British Petroleum, Continental and Nestlé in Europe. During the same period we conducted several in-depth discussions with eight European Business Schools. We knew that this programme needed the support of an outside academy and because we are a European based corporation, we wanted to work with a European School.

This pre-work took place in the second half of 1992 and in the first quarter of 1993.

Ideas and Concept

This whole research convinced us quite rapidly that we needed to develop a programme that was totally different from everything that had been done in past in the Volkswagen Group.

Traditionally our programmes were either internal training modules or we sent, somewhat randomly, our best people to attend specific seminars in some of the good international business schools.

The first important decision that we took was to work with Ashridge College in the UK. This academy had appealed to us for the quality and the international expertise of their faculty. It was also the only school that was ready to develop with us, from scratch, a programme tailored to our specific needs at Volkswagen.

The concept that we imagined and that we developed with Ashridge College was a mix of academic input and real life project work. The whole programme takes one year, it encompasses up to 40 days of project work and it has three distinct training modules (see Figure 13.1).

In order to verify our concept we invited in March 1993 a focus group to help us fine-tune this programme. Around 30 participants joined us for two days to discuss both the content and schedule of our proposal. We put together an international group of people that included high potential managers, some of their bosses, project owners and also some faculty members from Ashridge.

The selection process for the candidates of the first round followed and the first cycle of the programme was launched in August 1993.

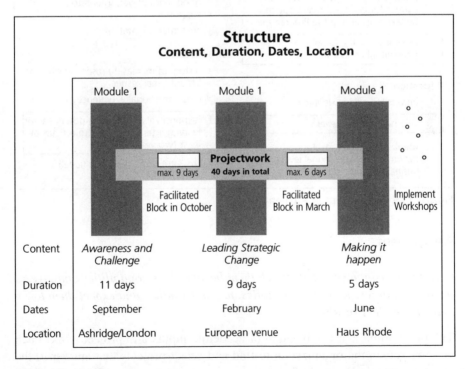

Figure 13.1 Programme structure

Description of the Programme

Selection of the Candidates

Attract and recruit the best-trained brains

The goal is to identify high potential managers with at least five years of experience in the VW Group. We are looking for people with a solid academic background and with an outstanding professional track record. They should be fluent in German and English and they should be willing to be geographically mobile. Each Volkswagen company is given a *numerous clausus* of participants that they are allowed to present every year. Figure 13.2 gives more details.

Target Group – Criteria

Potential development

- ☐ could be on the succession list, for a SE candidate position, within five years
- ☐ at a good learning point and/or career stage
  ideal: two years success within the current function, no new position to be taken up during the Programme.

- ☑ openness for the benefit of intercultual cooperation

Education

- ☐ university, college degree

- ☑ very high English level

  ideal: negotiating level
  minimum: conversational level plus business terminology

Performance/behaviour

- ☐ continuous outstanding performance
- ☐ two-three outstanding successes, where he or she had an important specific influence
- ☐ good team player, integrator, supporter
- ☐ customer orientation

Job history

- ☐ history of increasing responsibility; has brought real results
- ☐ cross-functional experience
- ☑ responsibility for leading others and/or leading interfunctional projects for at least two years
- ☐ cross-cultural experience (ideal)

Figure 13.2 Target group – criteria

Assignment

Give them assignments that stretch them beyond their capabilities and give them immediately real responsibilities, no case studies, and expect them to deliver excellent results.

The programme is a combination of academic inputs and project work. Each year we screen the organization to find and select projects that answer to the criteria shown in Figure 13.3.

Project Orientation
☐ a real project, not invented, with substantial impact beyond the programme
☐ learning experience
☐ networks with front line experts
☐ includes implementation phase, where possible
☐ focus on the future and not just reviewing the past
☐ should generate genuinely innovative approaches
☐ either new project or supports existing project
☐ measurable results
☐ benefits from multifunctional and international input

Project Content
☐ link to Group strategic goals of service, quality and/or profit
☐ challenging, but can be done
☐ quantifiable results within a ten-month period
☐ achievable part-time, approx. 40 days within ten months, by teams of four people
  (to ensure reserve; project teams will decide how they allocate/manage their time
☐ encourages 'learning by doing'

Figure 13.3   Project criteria

The idea is to find projects where the owners have a lack of resources. We try to convince the owners to use and work with a team of high potential Volkswagen managers instead of hiring outside consultants.

As an illustration, here below is the list of the projects that were selected for the programme that ran in 1996 and 1997.

1. Change connections between suppliers and automotive manufacturers.
2. System for video conference within VW Group and main suppliers.
3. Worldwide distribution strategy for spare parts.
4. CKD interlinking brands and overseas.
5. Local content India.
6. Future concept for GEF, integration GTMC and major international events.

In a first selection phase, the project owners are requested to present their project to the group of 30 participants of the programme. Each project gets bought in by a team of five to six high potential managers. We always make sure that the project team is a mixture of different nationalities and functions. The estimated workload to realize such a project is 40 working days. The project team gets a theoretical sabbatical time of 40 days to attend the academic modules and to work at the project. They are requested to keep their current jobs and the reality shows that this assignment purposely stretches them far beyond the standard working times. Because they are outstanding performers, their supervisors remain usually very demanding and they are compelled to deliver their normal share of daily activities. Because of the high pressure, every year the programme counts one or two dropouts.

The project owners are always senior executives. They act as customers and as coaches for the project team.

GMD coordinates the project activities and coaches the team members. Ashridge College gives the team the academic support and the individual supervisors try to keep a healthy balance between the daily activities and the project related workload of the participants. There is a very close working relationship between the GMD and Ashridge, in respect to the definition of the content of the programme as well as in the supervision of the project.

Academic Input

Follow them up and give them according to their needs, as much training as they (and you) can afford.

The role of Ashridge College is threefold. First, in a joint effort, we have developed with the faculty a series of tailored programmes targeted to the needs of the participants.

Secondly, the College is in charge of the continuous feedback of the participants for the whole duration of the programme. In module one, when the teams meet for the first time, a basic evaluation is conducted, using Meyer-Briggs. Later on the performance of the participants is measured in relation to the success of their project work.

Thirdly, together with GMD, Ashridge coaches and guides the participants in the realization of their projects.

Three formal meetings are organized during the duration of the programme.

During the *first module* the participants learn to know each other. There are teambuilding exercises, they are assessed and they get a feedback of their profiles. It is also then that the project owners present their projects and that the sub-teams are created. Finally and very importantly, the intercultural awareness is highlighted. We believe that one of the critical success factors of a global company is the ability of its managers and leaders to understand, accept and build on the richness of their cultural differences.

The *second module* takes place after six months. The projects are reviewed and the academic focus is leadership. Finally, at the end of the year, in *module 3*, the projects are consolidated and presented to the CEO and to the other members of the Vorstand of the Volkswagen Group.

Every participant also receives an individual coaching that encompasses the evaluation of his performance during the project as well as his personal development plan for the future.

One of the main features of this programme is the continuous feedback offered to the participants during the whole process. As mentioned before, Ashridge uses standard assessment tools during the modules and also in the follow up of the projects.

The participants are also requested to evaluate their peers. We pair them and request them to cross-assess one other team member. At the end of the programme, a closed and confidential feedback is given by each pair of participants to their chosen colleague.

It is however entirely up to the participants to decide upon the level of assessment and feedback that they think they need. The project owners and the supervisors of the participants are also contributing to the overall evaluation of the programme and its participants. GMD coordinates this whole assessment process and consolidates the results in a join effort with Ashridge.

Rewards and Benefits

Reward them well for their achievements and celebrate their successes.

Once again, the overall goals of this Junior Executive programme are to prepare our best managers to be the leaders of the future. In a global company it is vital that these individuals get an excellent understanding of how the company works. They have to become familiar with the complexities, the cultural differences,

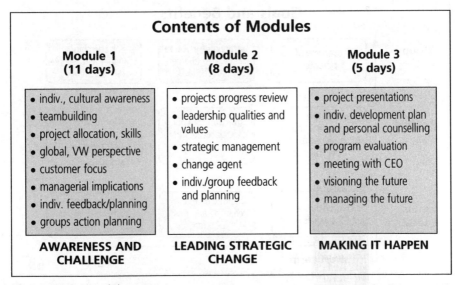

Contents of Modules		
Module 1 **(11 days)**	**Module 2** **(8 days)**	**Module 3** **(5 days)**
• indiv., cultural awareness • teambuilding • project allocation, skills • global, VW perspective • customer focus • managerial implications • indiv. feedback/planning • groups action planning	• projects progress review • leadership qualities and values • strategic management • change agent • indiv./group feedback and planning	• project presentations • indiv. development plan and personal counselling • program evaluation • meeting with CEO • visioning the future • managing the future
AWARENESS AND CHALLENGE	**LEADING STRATEGIC CHANGE**	**MAKING IT HAPPEN**

Figure 13.4 Module content

the ambiguities and the major strategic challenges which the automotive industry faces today and in the future.

The participants of this programme are challenged to work at a real international project, in a multicultural team, with colleagues from other functions. They rapidly develop project management skills, teamwork skills and a sound knowledge of the way our corporation operates. They grow a self-awareness, they learn to handle power and they develop a worldwide international network of colleagues and partners within and outside the Volkswagen Group.

On top of that, they are given, on a regular basis, academic inputs that are targeted to their individual needs and to the needs of the projects that they are working on.

Figure 13.5 gives a summary of the specific goals and benefits of this programme, long term and short term.

The project owners have followed their teams throughout the development of the studies and they demand solid results for their project. If the project owners wish it, the project teams participate in the implementation of their recommendations.

Finally, at the end of the year, each team has to present the results of its project to the members of the Vorstand. This places them in the floodlights at the highest level of the company structure.

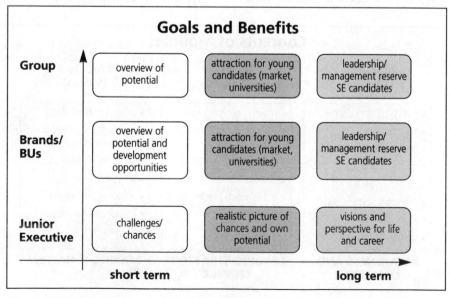

Figure 13.5   Programme goals and benefits

Conclusion

This programme is one of the building blocks of Volkswagen Coaching GmbH that was created in 1995 at the initiative of Dr. Hartz. It is now in its fifth cycle and over 150 high potential managers have had the opportunity to participate. The reality is that subsequently most of them have either been promoted or have at least been offered a better job.

Future Development

Do this on a continous basis.

The challenge facing us is not the structure nor the content of the programme but the selection of the right participants and the follow up of the alumni.

As we learned from our benchmarking study, one of the critical success factors of any developmental programme is continuity. Another success factor is the holistic approach of management development. Any investment in people development should be aligned with the strategy of the company and it should be integrated in a global management development process. Figure 13.6 shows a simplified picture of such a process.

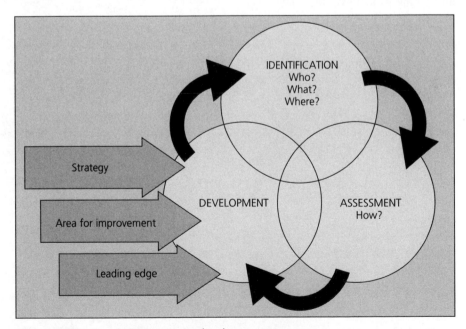

Figure 13.6 Group management development processes

The first circle is the identification of the individuals. Who are they, what is their background, their education, what job are they in right now, what is their job history and so on. Secondly one has to assess how the individuals are performing in their current job, what lies ahead of them in the future and what are their developmental needs. Thirdly, how can they be developed in order for them to perform better and to get prepared for their future jobs and for the future challenges that will face them.

Developing such a process and running it for many years optimizes the quality of management and allows an organization to prepare its future.

The example that I gave at the beginning of this chapter shows that Morgan Stanley has a 'throw in the water and swim approach' towards management development. At Volkswagen we have a slightly more conservative attitude in at least one respect. We select our target group among high potential managers who have already proven that they are the best compared to their peers. Our basic criteria are very severe and there is no guarantee for anyone who has attended this programme, that it will open all the doors to top positions in the Volkswagen Group. We still firmly believe that it is up to everyone to make his or her own career. We are willing however to spend a lot of money and effort in order to try and prepare our best potential leaders for the future success of our organization.

The Group Junior Executive programme is one of our most powerful tools in helping us achieve this goal.

Notes to Chapters in Part I

1   DaimlerChrysler: Global Leadership Development

1. See their *Strategic Organization Design: Concepts, Tools and Processes*; and the more recent, *Competing by Design: The Power of Organizational Architecture* (New York: Oxford University Press, 1997).

3   DuPont: Business-Driven Action Learning to Shift Company Direction

1. The original programme covered eight weeks: two weeks in-session; four weeks back on the job; and two weeks in-session. Participants complained that this was too long a time to be away from their jobs and we had a hard time getting people to commit to attending. We redesigned the programme to three consecutive weeks, taking out what previous participants said was least valuable.

   In some respects, we think a three week programme better mirrors what is happening in business today. The pace of work life (and life in general) is so fast that we often do not have as much time as we may want to accomplish what needs to be done.

2. We are not always aware of all the interactions between sponsors and teams. Typically the on-going relationships involve team participation in strategy meetings with business leadership. We believe the most important thing a sponsor can do is to communicate back to the team what follow-up has been accomplished based upon their recommendations. The team acts as consultants in that they have learned a great deal about the business issue. The business may continue to reassess the recommendations long after they have been made and, perhaps, as business conditions change. In this capacity, the team may be consulted for future changes in strategy.

3. The business units have varied as to whom gets invited to participate. For example, some include new supervisors only, others include seasoned supervisors (both first and second line), and still others have included potential candidates for supervision.

4. We find that the process of self-selection depends on the culture within a business. Some businesses have made participation in the Core Modules mandatory, others mandatory at some levels. Since the Leader Labs are only in the beginning phases, the businesses we are working with are requiring that the 'graduates' of the Core Modules participate in the Labs.

5. Business Leadership have total responsibility for an entire product line/enterprise. Site leadership refers to primarily manufacturing sites. We have many 'sites' that are multibusinesses, i.e. several product lines are manufactured at the same facility.

6. Those who deliver the core modules we refer to as facilitators. Coaches are those who counsel participants in the Leader Labs.

    Groups are trying to link the projects with other corporate initiatives such as outcomes of the corporate employee satisfaction survey and manufacturing initiatives that include uptime (increasing the time that equipment and employees are functioning) and producing products and asset productivity processes. In general, we let the groups define what they expect to determine as 'success' (as long as they identify both individual and organizational learning as one of the expectations).

    In the early phases, participants are asked to work on aspects of a problem that is within their control. They are then expected to network with other groups within the business. At multibusiness sites, they can then work with other business units. Our goal is to have a few move on to working across countries on some problems. In this way, they can become better self-directed and collaborative learners and we can use even more complex issues for the development of middle management and executives.

7. We get a sense that most of what we have learned in other action learning experiences still holds true. This is that management must show a commitment to the effort. Their participation in the selection of the experiences, review of the proposals and outcomes, communication of the results, and so on is critical. We are also learning that the collection of data is important. The project summary sheets ask the participants to identify their 'investment' and to estimate the organizational impact in financial terms. We are hoping that by accumulating the data, we will be able at the end of the year to demonstrate the return on the Leader Lab investment.

10 Philips and Action Learning: from Training to Transformation

1. Freedman, N. J., 'Operation Centurion: Managing Transformation at Philips', Long Range Planning **29** (5), pp. 607–615, 1996.
2. Hamel, G. and Prahalad, C.K., 'Strategy as Stretch and Leverage', *Harvard Business Review* (March-April 1993).
3. 'Ultimatum at Philips', *Business Week*, 17 November, 1997, pp. 30–31.

12 Siemens Management Learning: a Highly Integrated Model to Align Learning Processes with Business Needs

1. The Price Waterhouse Change Integration Team. *The Paradox Principles. How High-Performance Companies Manage Chaos, Complexity, and Contradiction to Achieve Superior Results*. Chicago, London, Singapore: Irwin, 1996, pp 223ff.
2. Charles Handy, *The Age of Unreason*. Boston: Harvard Business School Press, 1989.
3. Peter M. Senge, *The Fifth Discipline. The Art and Practice of the Learning Organization*. New York: Doubleday/Currency, 1990.
4. Ikujiro Nonaka and Hirotaka Takeuchi, *The Knowledge-Creating Company: How Japanese Companies Create the Dynamics of Innovation*. New York: Oxford University Press, 1995.
5. Karl Erik Sveiby, *The New Organizational Wealth. Managing and Measuring Knowledge-Based Assets*. San Francisco: Berett-Koehler, 1997.
6. Robert H. Schaffer, *The Breakthrough Strategy: Using Short-Term Successes to Build the High Performance Organization*. New York: Harper Business, 1988.
7. Robert H. Schaffer, *High Impact Consulting. How Clients and Consultants Can Leverage Rapid Results Into Long-Term Gains*. San Francisco: Jossey-Bass, 1997.

PART

II

Facilitating and Enhancing Business Driven Action Learning

Guidelines on Coordination and Teamwork

CHAPTER 14

Strategic Management by Project Group: Lessons Learned

Colin Hastings

Strategy: Problems We Hear

A NUMBER of years ago I asked a group of senior managers to outline the problems that they experienced with the strategy process in their organizations. There was a wide range of responses, but essentially they clustered into four main groupings.

1. We have no strategy, we need one but we don't know how to go about developing one

I call this the *strategy development problem*. It still seems extraordinary in this age of sophisticated management development, that senior managers are saying this. But it is still the reality, particularly where, as a result of delayering, we have a younger generation of senior managers suddenly finding themselves rapidly promoted up into board management strategic positions. These people have survived the rat-race by being doers and suddenly find themselves having to think strategically, having to think in the abstract, having to think long term. They are struggling with the very idea of strategy itself, and finding that they alone as a top team cannot comprehend all the complexity involved.

2. We have a strategy, but not everyone at the top agrees with it

This is the *buy-in problem*. It reveals the conflicts that often take place at senior team or board levels where either a strong autocratic CEO or a strong visionary may dominate the top team and bulldoze a strategy through. Another version of this is the visionary who has all the strategy worked out in his or her head but finds it very difficult to communicate it to the rest of the board. This kind of person is always six steps ahead of those surrounding them. This is also a problem where there are the vestiges of central corporate planning departments who develop very clear and admirable strategies but often do it in isolation from the rest of the organization.

3. The Board has an agreed strategy, but no one else understands it

This is the *communication problem*. It raises the whole issue of how you get the wider organization on board with understanding strategy and understanding their role and contribution to implementing it. It begs the questions of what processes are required to achieve that. In my judgement, whatever the type of strategy implementation that is required, whether it is a crisis driven one where somebody comes in to force the organization in a new direction, or whether it is a more participative one, at some point in time you are going to need a process where you engage the wider organization with the nature of the strategy and its implementation.

4. Everyone understands the new strategy, but nothing is happening

This is the *implementation problem*. Too often the top team is very clear about what needs doing and they assume simply by communicating this that it will happen. Not so. A visionary client of mine, ruefully reflecting o the lack of progress in implementing his strategy, showed a remarkable degree of insight when he said of himself 'I think, therefore it is'. There is a large amount that needs to be done to help the implementers turn the concepts into reality.

New Challenges – the Goals of the Strategic Management Process

The nature of the environment in which modern organizations are working was graphically summarized for me on a wall poster in an office in a major international organization. It read *'this is to notify you that the light at the end of the tunnel has been permanently switched off!'* Most people in most organizations feel at times that they are handling huge amounts of complexity, ambiguity and uncertainty. And yet at the same time, they are expected constantly to sustain competitive advantage, to build increasingly rapid speed of response, to innovate continuously, to attract, develop and retain talented people and to win their commitment. These are huge challenges indeed and a strategy process has to be able to cope with them. In my experience a clearly defined strategy process, based on the use of carefully constructed and guided project teams, involving significant numbers of people across the organization, can go a considerable way towards creating such a process. What has emerged over recent years is a new mindset. It is the idea that we have to create some different mindsets for the process of developing and implementing strategy. It is a shift away from a bureaucratic procedure which is what we had in the days of corporate planning, towards another model where the top team as the brain of the firm is seen not to be all seeing and all knowing, but to require considerable input and help in the continuous process of devising and implementing strategy. That has now come to be called strategic management. Projects that involve talent across the organization are a key mechanism to do this. Putting these together we have the idea of strategic management by projects. It is a process of shaping the future of the organization. I use the word shaping because I think of it almost as a sculpture, like working a piece of clay that is gradually being moulded and shaped into a form as new ideas and directions emerge. Henry Mintzberg called this emergent strategy.

Strategic management by projects is also a process through which we create a sense of mission and direction amongst people within the organization. We talk a lot about mission statements but often these are empty pieces of paper. What senior managers are usually trying to achieve is to create a sense of mission within their organization. Mission statements don't create that. The process of strategic management by projects however can. It can also act as a vehicle through which ideas, innovation and change are explored, assessed and implemented. In doing so, it helps people in the organization to get to understand the uncertainties and the complexities and to work their way through them by analysis, identification of best practice elsewhere and the invention of solutions that uniquely fit their own situation.

The Key Players in the Process

Strategic management by projects is a systemic process: that is to say it is highly interactive and it requires the activities of a large number of people and a large number of elements of activity and information, all interdependent on each other. In understanding how to manage the process it helps to think of the key groupings which will contribute to its success. Each has particular problems to face and contributions to make.

The Top Team

Strategic management by projects can be quite threatening to the top team. Underlying this is perhaps the fear of losing control. As one senior manager said to me, 'because I am not in control it must be out of control'. That mindset will present problems in managing modern organizations. But we must recognise that, particularly for organizations that have been relatively bureaucratic in their approach, this represents a quantum leap in ways of working. If the top team members behave in a way which doesn't give space to those involved, they can often act quite unconsciously to douse the energy of the whole process. Even for those whose management style is naturally more participative, there are also very real problems of how to absorb and understand all the information that is coming from the project groups and how to work efficiently as a top team to make decisions based on this input.

The Project Leaders

For many who find themselves in the project leader role it is a daunting experience. If they are people perhaps who are technical specialists, they have a relatively limited exposure to the wider organization and a relatively limited network across the organization. This may disadvantage them because the role requires credibility and contacts right across the organization. For many of them even leading a team, and in particular a multi-disciplinary team that cuts right across the organization, may be a new experience. Couple this with the fact that projects of this nature are usually highly visible in the organization and it is no surprise that project leaders feel ill prepared for the task.

Project Leaders' Bosses

This group of people often are in danger of being left out in such a process. Their young high flyers are involved in the project groups, the top team is involved in the process and they somehow get by-passed. As a result of this, and partly because they have the most vested interests to protect, they can become points of resistance and blockages to change. They can do this in particular by influencing the people who report to them who are involved in the projects and placing demands on them which mean that they cannot meet their line role requirements and their project requirements. Ensuring that this group is well briefed and well involved provides a significant payback.

The Project Teams

Even now in organizations project teams are formed with gay abandon. The evidence however suggests that the results overall are disappointing. Making multi-disciplinary project teams work effectively is not easy. Quality does not happen spontaneously, particularly where the projects to be done are by their very nature complex and frequently ambiguous at the start. In addition, project team members often have very mixed feelings about being involved in these teams as they try to balance the pressures of the strategy process and their line management roles.

Process Coordination

It is vital to have a small group responsible for overviewing the process and continuously for energizing and coordinating it. It requires at least one person full time with considerable assistance from others to take the overview of what is happening to ensure that it is staying on track.

How to Make the Process Work – What are the Rules of the Game?

Most organizations who try to create a process of this nature have no clear picture of how it should work, who the key players are that need managing, what the key success factors are and what the key stages or elements of the process are. Being able to explain to the organization clearly what will be happening, how it will be happening and when it will be happening is a vital first step in ensuring the success of the process. Figure 14.1 outlines the major elements of a strategic management process.

Stage	*Goals*	*Way of Working*
Launch	Broad direction Excitement	Come together
Explore	Finding alternatives Defining problems/issues	Work apart
Exchange	The big picture Reducing the options	Come together
Test	Testing feasibility Testing commitment	Work apart
Focus	Commit to specific actions Re-launch	Come together
Implement	Make it happen	Work apart

Figure 14.1 The strategic management process

The *launch* is vital in communicating to a wide number of people the nature of the overall process. This is done by bringing people together. Groups then split apart to work their projects and go through the *exploration* phase as they seek to understand the nature of their projects, to define the problems and issues, and to suggest alternative ways forward. These outputs are then shared in another phase of *exchange* where the project groups, the top team and other senior managers come together, in conference format, to get a broader appreciation of what has been found out so far, to see the overall picture, to begin to see interdependencies between different strategic issues, and perhaps at this stage to begin to reduce some of the options that will be taken forward. The board has a key role at this stage. There then follows another phase of working apart in project groups where there is more *testing* of both the feasibility and the approach to be taken and the testing and building of commitment across the organization to that particular approach being taken. Once again, after that there needs to be a coming together, a *focusing* of all the action that will be finally implemented. This is the point at which the top team and the key implementers commit themselves to particular actions. Subsequently these actions become the core of the *implementation* phase where responsibility and accountability for making things happen is allocated. This is done usually through a combination of the line structure and project groups.

In reality, these steps or phases are not discreet, they overlap. Different projects also go through them at different speeds. I like to think more of the process as a kind of a Catherine Wheel which is continuously spinning. Strategic Management by Projects is not a one off – it is a continuous process. This is represented in Figure 14.2.

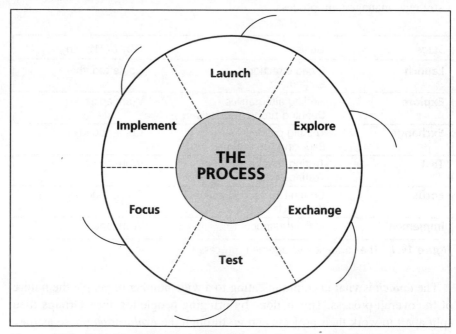

Figure 14.2 Strategic management by projects – the Catherine Wheel

Lessons Learned

There are so many factors involved in creating a successful strategic management process and in particular creating one that gets the best out of a changing portfolio of project groups. However, the key learnings that I have taken out of my experience of facilitating these processes can be summarized under six major headings.

1. The Involvement of the Top Team

Clearly their impact on the success of the process is fundamental. If they are not seen to be supporting it actively and constantly others involved will begin to conclude that it is not a priority and day-to-day work will come first. We should not assume that the board have all the skills necessary, all the awareness necessary to conduct such a process. They will need preparing and developing just like any other of the key players.

Activities	Do's and Don'ts
• Commission design of process/launch • Agreeing success criteria for process • Viable role in launch • Digestion of emerging issues • Task definition for Strategy Groups • Regular review of overall process • Informal interaction with Project Group leader • Identify appropriate Project leaders • Ensure 'spare' resource for quick response when needed • Shaping inputs from below to achieve concensus • Use of crises or discontinuities to move forward • Keep Divisional Management positive	• Give the groups short time deadlines to report back (max. two months) • Don't get into too much detail at Board level before involving the Project Groups • Don't just 'play the game' – you'll be found out • Be very open in interactions with Project Groups • If you're not prepared to invest substantial time, effort and money into the process, don't start it • Teambuild with the Board and Divisional Management first to create the right climate • If you're not prepared for some discomfort, don't start the process • Be patient – it takes time

Figure 14.3   The involvement of the Top Team

2. The Vital Sponsor Role

The sponsor is the godfather of each individual project, the vital link between the project, the top team and the wider strategy process. The sponsor is not there to do the work but to provide guidance to remove particularly political obstacles.

Activities	Do's and Don'ts
• Sponsors work together on the nature and key result areas of the role • Bring key stakeholders together • Provide resources • Regular review meetings with Project Team • Involving in scoping and clarifying the project • Fighting 'political' battles for the Project at senior level	• Be clear how Sponsoring is different from line management relationships • All groups must have a sponsor • Ensure frequent reviews out with the sponsor • Negotiate time for group members • Demonstrate commitment tangibly by removing obstacles to the Project Group's work • Ensure cross-pollination and exchange between different projects • Be open to challenge by the Project Team • Listen, support and challenge • Be clear whether the Project is an open or closed one

Figure 14.4 The vital sponsor role

Many sponsors fail to realise the importance of this role. They see it as a kind of sinecure or formality. It is not. They have a vital role at key points, particularly in the initial scoping of the project and subsequently at key decision points in deciding which way it should move forward.

3. The Process for Project Scoping

More projects fail because of lack of clarity about the impact they are supposed to be producing than for any other reason. The approach to project scoping

Activities	Do's and Don'ts
• Project team discuss outline brief with sponsor • Write up their understanding of desired outputs and impacts • Circulate/discuss with key stakeholders • Articulate areas of disagreement • Define broad options and practical implications • Get eventual agreement on scoping	• Be clear about whether the Project is an open one or a clsed one • Scoping of open strategic management projects has to be an interactive process • Beware the dangers of 'dumping' additional elements into a Project brief • Don't pretend there is agreement on Project scope when there isn't • Often the Project scope (initially) is simply to get clarity about what the issue/problem is • Ensure all the key stakeholders are consulted on the Project brief

Figure 14.5 Project scoping

usually consists of a sponsor hurriedly writing down some terms of reference, the project team accepting those as gospel, going away and doing the work and coming back three months later to find that that was not what the sponsor or other key stakeholders expected. Effective projects may spend as much as 50 per cent of their elapsed time simply getting agreement amongst key players about what the project is designed to achieve.

4. Creating Effective Project Teams

I have already alluded to this. It is not easy. Teams need help and development to understand how to perform effectively, particularly given the nature of the problems they are likely to be involved in. Some kind of facilitation help, especially at the beginning, is almost essential.

Activities	Do's and Don'ts
• Link with other groups/people outside • Bring key stakeholders on board • Build coalitions • Do Project start-up teambuilding • Appoint the right sort of leader for the Project type (open or closed project) + necessary credibility/network • Meetings regularly with Sponsor • Internal marketing of the Project in the Organization • Define the problem *then* plan activities/tasks	• Members should ideally volunteer. There needs to be a good mix of backgrounds and some 'sceptics' included • All groups should have some training or consultancy help on hand – many find it a difficult process, especially initially • Identify sources of know-how inside and outside the organization • Ensure thought be given to the presentation and synthesis of information at an early stage • Don't become inward looking

Figure 14.6 Effective project teams

5. Energising and Coordinating the Overall Process

Once again, I have referred to this and in particular the importance of the special group to do this. This is one of the acid tests of the top team's seriousness and resolve. Are they prepared to commit some people (and money) on a full time basis to make the process work? It cannot be done and won"t be done if everyone is expected to fit it in around and on top of their day-to-day jobs.

6. Communicating the Process

It is vital that the wider organization understands what is happening even if they are not fully involved in the detail of it. A strategic management by projects

Activities	Do's and Don'ts
• Appoint clear process coordinator and strategy steering group • Programme extra Board meetings to deal regularly with emerging issues • Ensure adequate budget and resource provision • Project Groups report back publicly to Board • Project Group leaders' meetings/Sponsors' meetings • Provide regular support to Project leaders • Map resistance • Build spare resource for quick response when needed	• Ensure frequent review/checking out with the sponsor • Encourage Strategy Group leades to get together regularly • Strategic management process by Projects may not be suitable in all corporate or national cultures • 'Keeping it all together' requires sophisticated information exchange and mutual learning • Different ways of working required for strategy formulation and implementation • Don't let Sponsors neglect their role • Think hard before appointing Project leaders

Figure 14.7   Energising and coordinating the overall process

process reaches every corner of the organization. No one can hide and no one will be unaffected by it. It is only good management process therefore that people are aware that this may happen and are also helped to see how they may even contribute indirectly both to the projects and to strategy development, and of course in particular to strategy implementation.

Activities	Do's and Don'ts
• Create many opportunities for people to understand the process and its implications • The Strategy Room – a showcase for what's happening • Stering group develop overall internal and external communications strategy • Set up some formal exchange mechanisms (workshops, presentations, meetings etc) • Encourage Strategy Group leaders to get together regularly • Encourage direct linkages and support between teams	• 'Remember where you came from' – i.e.. what is clear to you (because you've been through a thinking process) is not to others. Explain and explain again. Stay tolerant • Communication and the desire to explain, try to understand and make sense should know no boundaries. The Board has to model this from the start • Overcommunicate – redundancy is OK • Clear, simple themes to focus detailed implementation • Ensure Divisional Management are carefully briefed about the process and their role in it, otherwise they become 'blockers'

Figure 14.8   Communicating the process

CHAPTER 15

GE Executive Programmes: Checklist and Tools for Action Learning Teams

Stephen Mercer

A Typical Project Approach

Introduce project issue to the teams

Overview of briefing material

Meet team coach

Individual preparation of briefing material

Briefing by business contact

Team project planning

Team selection of 'Project Week'

Team sets up data gathering and interviews

Project Week

Analysis/report writing

Presentation to business sponsor

Methodology to attack a project

Preparation

Implementation

Team process issues

Closure: recommendations and presentation

Reflection/feedback

Preparation by Project Team Members

Review issue statement

Consider 'going in' assumptions/biases

Reading briefing material

Preparing for the briefing

Constructively handling the briefing

Digesting the briefing book/briefing

Understanding the problem, the 'unstated problem' and the 'deliverables'

Implementation

Planning the project approach

- Data needed
- Interviews (who)
- Interview guides

Team process approach/ground rules/leadership/roles

Scheduling team meetings

Field work

- Gathering preparatory data
- Setting up interviews
- Conducting interviews (pairs)

Communication and field data processing

Hypothesizing the presentation

Support structure

The project 'business contact'

- Clarification
- Facilitate contacts
- Sounding board
- NOT a GOFER

The project 'coach'

- Observer/mentor
- Team process
- Individual leadership style
- Individual team contribution
- Sounding board
- Feedback

Team Process Issues

Objectives
Setting up the team
Preparing the team for action
Information Gathering

Objectives

To test your leadership and team skills
To learn how to make the group effective in a short period of time
To expand the group's capacity
To deal with ups and downs in the group's emotional energy
To discover areas for personal improvement
To get real time peer feedback AND
To Deliver A Quality Product

Setting up the team

Groundrules
Leadership
Goals
Roles
Resources
Tools/Techniques
Dealing with Conflict
Making Decisions
Communicating
Participation

Preparing the team for action

Division of tasks
Communicating
- Parallel processing of information
- Single focal point
- Daily faxing/phoning/e-mail

Listening
- Asking the right questions
- Extracting information
- Cross referencing

Capturing information in standard form

Method of integrating information

Information gathering – Interviews

Map of:
  Who needs to be interviewed

  What you expect from interview

Possible candidates:
- Decision makers
- Key influencers
- 'Knowledge repositories'
- Those impacted by outcome
- Ultimate implementers
- Colleagues in other companies
- Key faculty
- …

Prepare interview guide

- Open ended questions
- No leading questions
- Probe questions

Listening with an open mind

- Get at right issue
- Frame of reference of individual
  (Background/function/knowledge/style)
- Emotional content of answers
- What is NOT said as well as what IS said
- Playback – 'here's what I heard'

Suggestions to ensure the proper execution of the interview

'What To Do'

1. Plan the aspects that will form part of the interview

2. Memorize the objectives and make them your own

3. Explain the interview procedure

4. Put yourself in the 'listening position' in a neutral manner

5. Propose the topics and re-introduce in a neutral manner any topic not dealt with exhaustively

6. Be flexible

7. Follow the logical sequence of the person talking

8. Keep any straying off the point 'under control'

9. Start from a general analysis to then relate the topic in concrete terms with your project

10. Be relaxed and reassuring

'What Not to Do'

1. Do not allow any type of personal reaction to 'show through'

2. Do not be too detached

3. Do not guide and do not express personal opinions

4. Do not slavishly follow the guidelines, but leave room for improvisation

5. Do not 'telegraph' the answer you hope to hear

6. Do not interrupt the respondent

7. Do ask questions which can be answered simply by Yes or No

8. Do not use slang, acronyms, or unclear, idiomatic expressions

9. Do not create defensive barriers

10. Do not make commitments youcan't personally assure will be kept.

Information gathering – sanity check

- Test hypotheses with client mid-course – you don't want to be faced with: 'Didn't you talk to ...'
- Your goal is to develop solid recommendations and have them seriously considered, not to get the glory. If you've 'greased the skids' in advance and client says 'I know that' or 'I'm doing that' in the final report it is no big deal.

Closure

Reconvening – initial data dump

Making sense of things – analyzing the data

Developing recommendations
- Alternatives
- Assumptions

Writing the report
- The bottom line
- Appendix/backup

Presentation/dialogue

Preparing for recommendation

Establish time limits

Data dump

Organize the data into information (recommendations and solutions are not part of this)

Duo's: each duo shapes one central idea underlying the recommendation

Debate: each idea (gaps, deductions, inconsistencies, insights)

Redo the exercise: Trio's – Different members (just get the ideas out – non judgmental)

Is the idea: clear, specific, attention-getting, innovative, practical, quantum

Establish assumptions and decision criteria

Make selection – key conclusions/ideas

Identify options considered

Anticipate clients' questions

Key questions

What are the key factors affecting project issues? What are your assumptions?

Identify the key criteria used to decide

Identify key short term 'impactors' upon which success depends

What are the two or three things the business leader should know that were not known before?

Shape several clear options
- pros/cons
- why chosen/rejected

Focus
  Not a laundry list of recommendations
  What should be done Monday morning?

What is the risk of NOT implementing vs risk of implementing?
Would YOU take the job.?

Developing recommendations

Shape the ideas of team members

Build – don't destroy

Recognize personal biases/blind spots

Honest respect for differences

Get things done without vertical power

Don't be 'nice' to each other (The Road to Abilene)

Finalizing Recommendations

Shape mutually exclusive options

Evaluate options – develop solid arguments

If disagreement exists:

- Break into two parallel groups
- Each write a pitch (will crystallize your thinking and clarify the effectiveness of your position)
  Present to each other
- Defend – then blend

Preparation of the presentation

The team as a whole develops supporting ideas in bullet form (no wordsmithing)

Divide the tasks to write the first draft of the pitch

Assign two people to write the whole pitch

Include:

- Useful quotes in the pitch
- Options in the Appendix

Rehearse

Making the Presentation

Know your audience

Golden minute

What is the key point?

Anecdotes

Team effort – NOT individual presenter

Dialogue

Integrate into making the presentation

Know your audience

First minute is 'golden moment'

Go on the attack right away (tell them what you're going to tell them ...)

What is the key takeaway – the point you're trying to make (brevity, few bullets)

Eliminate (ruthlessly) things that don't add to your point ('kill your children')

Use anecdotes/examples/non-numerical statistics (look right, look left – one of you will be gone)

Don't assume your point is clear (everyone has a different perspective/ interpretation) (think as if you're communicating in a foreign language)

Personalize 'I believe...', show commitment

This is a team effort – all involved, everyone backs you up 'Don't hang presenter out to dry'

Appoint 'specialist'. Everyone has a particular expertise area. They answer questions – not presenter

Team watches audience – not presenter

Take hold of the session – control the time/appoint a timekeeper

If discussion goes off track, call time out

Make sure there is a dialogue – the presentation is a vehicle to take hold and guide the discussion

Content NOT appearance

Clear takeaways / Clarity and specificity / Don't tone down or sugarcoat / One central idea / 2–3 supporting points

Clear recommendations, unequivocal, actionable

You have to take a stand

Show options you considered, why recommended course was selected

Options should be fresh, original, NOT same old bathwater

Why were rejected options discarded? Support with appendix material as needed

Put some emotion/passion into pitch

Don't be timid / Courage of your convictions / You did analysis, talked to people not them.

If you believe it, don't back down

Be willing to take a risk – dare to be different

Be clear about what you want 'What do I do Monday morning ...'

Leave time to sum up/get closure

Don't ever 'wing it'

Rehearse questions in advance

Don't beat a dead horse

Engage the entire client team

Don't get derailed by peripheral questions. Come back to your theme.

'Ask for the order'

What was accepted?

What was rejected? Why?

What was unresolved? Why? What needs to be done to resolve?

Someone should summarize

Don't be defensive

Bottom line:

- Strong opening
- Personal/team commitment
- Anecdotes/statistics
- Powerful closing
- Ask for order

Reflection

Team process feedback

Individual contribution

Peer feedback

Lessons learned

Reflection/Feedback

Constant observation/awareness

How do we:

- Make decisions
- Build relationships
- Resolve conflicts

- Repair relationships
- Maintain energy level

Assign a buddy to give you personal feedback

Use your coach

Team Process Questions

How did team leadership evolve?

How did you select your presenter?

How clear were your goals? (Did you have a common purpose and direction?)

How did you plan your action?

Were individual roles clear?

What were the roles played by various individuals?

How were these roles chosen or assigned?

How well were group resources identified?

How well were group resources used?

What tools/techniques did you use to make your team more effective – a high performing team?

What could you have done to make the team more effective?

How did your team maintain its energy level? What were the sources of energy drain/ energy gain?

What mechanism did you use the deal with problems? How were conflicts surfaced and what was the routine for solving them?

How were decisions made? Did the process promote the best ideas and foster commitment?

Did you go down the 'Road to Abilene'?

What were your communications processes/patterns and how were they established?

Did people LISTEN?

How did you develop participation by all team members?

Did some people withdraw from participation? Did others withdraw if they didn't get their way? The extent to which everyone is part of the group.

How was disagreement handled?

Did anyone display defensive behaviour? What was it? How was it handled?

What was the level of trust and openness on the team? Were you honest about conflict?

How did the team work together when it was split up? When it reassembled?

Were group members supportive of each to other?

How was individual performance recognized?

How much attention was paid to process? (How the group is working?)

What behaviours helped the team?

What behaviours hindered the team?

What would you keep the same if you did this again?

What would you do differently?

Team Feedback Session

Sample group process questions

1. If actual group performance is equal to the group's potential performance minus its process losses, what prevented this group from achieving its potential?
2. What leadership skills did the project require?
3. Who emerged as the leader(s) during this project? Why?
4. Who has most strongly influenced your team's focus and direction?
5. How much influence have you had on the team?
   - too little
   - about right
   - more than you'd like
6. How extensively was your expertise utilized?
   - too little
   - about right

   more than you'd like
7. What team leadership lessons can we draw from this experience?
8. What can we say about the team's development? What enhanced, what inhibited its development?
9. What can we say about the quality of communications during this project?
10. What's enhanced/inhibited innovative or creative problem-solving in this team?
11. How were decisions made on this team? Why?
12. What generalizations can we make about the impact of stress on individual behaviour? Risk-taking?

13. For each team member, including yourself, list two behaviours which contributed to the successful accomplishment of your team's objective.

14. For each team member, including yourself, list two behaviours which hindered the team in accomplishing its objective.

After you have answered each of the above questions, please share with each team member the answers to questions 13 and 14. Each member should accept this feedback as constructive suggestions for their consideration.

Comments should not be 'explained away', however, clarification can be requested.

If there is sufficient time, you should discuss your answers to the other questions.

Feedback/after action review

Individual reflection

- What behaviours (you and others) helped the team
- What behaviours (you and others) hindered the team
- What would you keep the same
- What would you do differently
- One area for personal improvement

Team discussion of team process

Team feedback from coach

Feedback from team to 'buddy'; feedback to you from 'buddy';

Feedback to you from coach.

CHAPTER 16

Facilitating Leadership Through High Performance Teamwork Leadership

Mary Rose Greville

IN this article I will describe the process by which one global corporation builds its leadership capability for the 21st century, through a particular form of the action learning process – business driven action learning. The goal of the programme is to build multicultural leadership and teamworking capability, while examining a critical business issue.

The business findings are presented to the top management of the organization by the multicultural teams established at the beginning of the programme. When the teams succeed in working well, the presentations are excellent. Naturally not all teams succeed in working well together. When this is the case, the participants' individual leadership, team and multicultural learning can be even more transformational. But not always.

In describing how I do this in action learning, I thought that the best way was to actually tell the story of the programme, by building the picture from the first session. While it is probably impossible to distil the quality of the experience, from the point of view of the participants, it would be a pleasure to describe, from the point of view of the facilitator, the energy, insight and personal learning of the participants as they go through the process. It is so satisfying when things work, and so interesting when they meet resistance! Happily, the programmes are enormously successful, by a range of criteria which I will outline as we follow the storyline.

The Opening Event

Among the 32 participants participating in the last programme, we had 25 nationalities from all over the world. One of the key issues in the programme, and in delivering the results at the end of the programme to top management, is how these participants, all senior managers, are going to work together in multicultural teams, and also how they are going to learn about multiculturalism.

So the goal of the first session is to create a multicultural learning community, to which everybody feels they can belong.

We do the usual introductory session, introducing the concept of action-learning, the key business issue, the deliverables to the top management representatives, and the key individual goal of developing each participant's leadership and teamwork capacity in a multicultural setting. This is quite formal and meets their need for clarity about the general objectives and goals. We then have the challenge of focusing on the process issues, a challenge which persists throughout the programme – they want to start on the task immediately.

However, they have the usual uncertainties about their presence in the group, and the issues of acceptability, which need to be addressed immediately. So we undertake a community-building activity. I have chosen to follow the 'formal' programme introduction with a fun activity which has a serious purpose. Many of these activities are available and serve the same purpose. I have chosen the autograph session as a way of immediately building bridges and valuing differences.

The participants are given a sheet of paper listing 17 questions. They have to get a different 'autograph' to each of the questions, from a person who has participated – they have to identify someone who does an extreme sport or who has travelled to a very unusual place, and so on; it's simply an ice-breaker. I originally found an autograph list in a Pfeiffer and Jones training and development manual, and thought that it was a great idea.[1] But I built my own because I wanted to look at events that they would have experienced as managers, so I asked who had been down-sized, and who had been in a joint-venture, who has been in a closure, who had led a major change, as well as other questions such as who is born under my astrological sign? Who likes to go skiing, who likes to write? Amazingly enough, in every programme, you find people who write for journals or magazines, who write poetry, it's quite extraordinary! Who has done extreme sports, who plays a musical instrument? You usually have an entire orchestra in the room! I then ask who had signed in answer to which question, so that everyone identifies the golfers, the sailors, the bungie-jumpers, the rock-climbers, the writers and the volunteer workers. All of this creates a sense of common humanity, a lot of laughter, tension release, and a lot of fun. Then we do the usual 'introduce the person beside you', so that everyone knows who is in the room. Having broken the ice, we then go into the multicultural activity.

Multicultures

We do an exercise in which I ask each group of people to introduce their own culture. This is very simple, however it is also very effective because they describe their own culture. I then build in some of the research findings from Geert Hofstede, Fons Trompenaars, Kurt Lewin, and some of my own research into their answers.[2] The participants self-select into a group representing their own culture. Each group answers a set of questions about what it's like to be a manager in their culture, what it's like to be a direct report in their culture, or a team member in their culture. The questions are directly related to the key concerns of the programme. The participants are also asked to prepare a short charade or role play illustrating a key aspect of their culture. I first ask them to identify what they are proud of in their culture, and secondly what they are not proud of. The second of these questions is more important than the first. This gets all the negative stereotypes out in the open immediately, put there by the people themselves. I usually model this at the beginning. I'm Irish, so I talk about what I'm proud of – the Nobel prizes for literature, the music, the friendliness of the people. I then say what I'm not proud of in Ireland, such as the drink culture and the Northern Ireland situation. This models openness. The responses of participants vary, but are usually very open and rich, and elicit understanding rather than criticism. For example, South Americans will say they are proud of family life and their sense of fun and enjoyment of life, and not proud of political corruption and ecological pollution. The Germans will say that they are proud of their philosophers, poets and composers, and not proud of the war.

All of this is funny, rich and deep, and it also helps people to recognise and respect differences. The answers to these questions and to others such as 'what not to do as a manager in my culture' and 'what not to do as a direct report in my culture' provides accurate data to illustrate Hofstede's work. I introduce the concept after it has been introduced in the role-play, and then the participants confirm the data,which grounds the process in their actual experience, rather than just introducing them to a set of theories, however valuable. In addition, however, the participants will be working in teams together over the next three weeks, where the multicultural issues may be very significant. This session is, as a result, seen to be of immediate value. It is also very illuminating because there are very different answers in different cultures. For example, in the United States, when you think that a manager is wrong, you tell him, even in a meeting, whereas Japanese participants will say that under no circumstances should you do that. This also tells the participants what they can and cannot say to each other in the course of the three-week programme. It also tells the participants, depending on the culture which they are going to, what they can and cannot do in their contact with the members of that culture.

The charades or role plays are a lot of fun, but also illuminating. The British often do queuing, or the class factor in British culture.The Italians like to illustrate their preference for the dramatic, or the verbal, the Japanese frequently illustrate respect for age, and ways of showing respect to others, things that must be understood in the culture. One good example of a charade was provided by three Dutch participants, illustrating what it is like being Dutch. They found a small basin, put water in it, and stood in it, supporting each other: they said that in the Netherlands there is a lot of water, not a lot of land, and they have to support each other in order to survive.

At the end of this session, naturally, the participants are all talking to each other, frequently about their culture differences and the deeper meaning of some of the behaviours, the values and assumptions on which the explicit culture is based. I encourage them to ask such questions over dinner. As a result of this, there is no cultural masking, no pretence that we are all the same. It becomes very explicit that we are different, and that we must value the difference, rather than trying to blend into a corporate similarity. All of this also has the intention of making sure that nobody gets inadvertently offended. It's so easy to give offence across different cultures. You don't want a participant to be profoundly offended by something that someone else said, when the person never intended offence, and is unaware of their input.

There is an additional dimension. In this session, when focusing on the theories, I highlight the countries to which the participants will be travelling in their multicultural teams. This helps them to be particularly aware of some of the dimensions when they are in interviews with customers, competitors, regulators and suppliers in their 'host' country. In one programme which took place in Asia, based in Singapore, the participants travelled within the region. These themes were important, and essential to the behavioural learning of the United States, South American, and European participants in the interviews they conducted. They also provided a powerful theme for the whole programme.

The session is not particularly innovative, but it works very particularly in this programme because of the programme goal. The participants are not there to learn about culture for the sake of learning about culture. They are there to learn about culture for the sake of working together in order to deliver a very high quality product to their own top management at the end of the three weeks. It has a very immediate relevance for them. All of this is done in about three and a half hours of the opening session. It is fast and furious, and a lot of fun, but also very serious in its intent and its consequences.

Day Two

The goals of day two address both the business issue and the leadership and teamwork issue. The business issue is addressed in the morning, the leadership and multicultural teamwork issues in the afternoon.

In the morning they work on the geopolitics of the world. They get a radically different view of the world! The countries they will be investigating as part of their business issue get special attention. Then I have the challenge, familiar to many facilitators, of coming in to the group in the afternoon and focusing them down from this exciting, new global perspective back into 'internal space' i.e. this team, this programme, their personal leadership challenges.

In the most recent programme, I used the Birkman Relational Method, an exceptionally powerful and detailed instrument.[3] It has the value of providing team feedback in the form of a relatively simple four-quadrant grid. In the Leadership Grid they are provided with insight into their interests (what motivates them), their usual behaviour (what they do well naturally) and their stress behaviour, all in the context of the team setting. It also provided amazingly valuable data about 'components' of their behavioural repertoire, such as their authority style, their preferred ways of giving and receiving feedback, their preferred ways of working in teams, their specific ways of responding to change, the amount of time they need before reaching decisions, the pace at which they prefer to act. In these areas, eleven in all, participants identify their usual behaviour, when their needs are met, their needs, and their stress behaviour profile when their needs are not met.

I chose this instrument to replace two others – a 360 degree feedback instrument, replaced when we discovered that most of the participants had already done their 360 degrees. I had combined these with the Belbin team roles profiles – which very nicely complemented the 360 degree feedback, but was no longer necessary given the comprehensive nature of the Birkman.[4] However, we asked every participant who had done a 360 degree to bring it to the programme, so that they could refer to it and check it against their Birkman results. On the afternoon of the second day, I introduce the instrument. They are placed in groups with the same Birkman profiles and asked for the answers to certain simple questions about their interests, usual behaviours and stress behaviours. Working in like 'type' groups gives them comfort with their own profiles, and powerfully validates the instrument's value to them. It is also lots of fun. I then give them their individual feedback on the Birkman Leadership Grid, which is the team role feedback instrument, and send them to their team rooms for the first time. When they go to their group rooms, they are also asked to identify a team 'Vision Statement', to include their task, as specified by their business issue, complete with a values statement about the quality of the work they intend to produce.I also ask them to produce a list of 'Ground rules' for monitoring their own behaviour in the course of the three weeks. They then compare their vision statement and ground rules with their personal resources as a group, as identified by the Birkman Leadership Grid. They quickly identify their strengths and potential weaknesses as a team, based on the Birkman data. The high 'face validity' of the instrument is a great help at this stage. The team profile shows them, as a team, what their interests are, what motivates people as being very different from their usual behaviour, which is their usual productive behaviour when they are working well. It also identifies their stress behaviour, which becomes critical, particularly for the third week of the programme because they are frequently under considerable stress at that stage. I go from team room to team room, coaching where needed, just observing when coaching is not needed, or clarifying a point of interpretation of the Birkman, the Vision Statement or the Ground rules.

On the first day, we create an openness to learning about others, and in particular about different cultures. On the second day, there is already an openness to learning about themselves and their teams.

Day Three

This is taken further on the third day. Once again the design involves working on the task issues in the morning, and on the leadership and teamwork issues in the afternoon.

By the afternoon of the third day the participants are really enjoying the programme, the energy is high, the sense of commitment palpable. At this point I introduce the Birkman components, working with the teams, as teams, seated at separate tables in the main room. The components are introduced, and I ask the teams for examples of usual and stress behaviours in each of the eleven components in turn.

The Birkman components identify some of the participants' behavioural modes such as their authority style, their preferred ways of giving and receiving feedback, their preferred ways of working in teams, their specific ways of responding to change, the amount of time they need before reaching decisions, the pace at which they prefer to act. In these areas, eleven in all, participants identify usual behaviour, when needs are met, and their stress behaviour profile when their needs are not met, for example for someone with high usual behaviour and high stress in authority, and/or low usual behaviour and low stress in authority.

Once again the instrument is validated by the ease with which a group of participants from 25 national groupings can describe behaviours and incidents so readily, based on the simple definitions provided by myself, based on the Birkman literature. The examples of behaviours, especially stress behaviours, range from the hilarious to the near-tragic, always accompanied by 'if I had known at the time, I could have behaved differently'. This process, in class, also has the value of making stress behaviour in a team a 'normal' occurrence, and something that can be effectively or ineffectively managed. It presents them with the tools to identify stress behaviours, and the tools to manage them in the interests of the person experiencing the stress, and in the interests of the whole team. This becomes extraordinarily valuable in week three of the programme. Its 'take-home' value to the participants is also incalculable.

Reticence tends to be a personal issue for some people who move more slowly into a process like this than others. One of the things that has to be respected in this is that people do move into things at a different pace. However, at this stage, the participants, while involved in an intellectual game of 'spot the appropriate behaviour', are also identifying patterns in their own behaviour, across a range of such behaviours, and with relative degrees of comfort and, naturally, some discomfort at times. At the end of this session, I give them their personal feedback on the components, which they compare with their guesses about themselves. We then work with the components in the teams. In addition to their Leadership Grid, the teams can now put on the walls, the behaviour of each, related to, for example, a preference for teamwork, or a preference for working alone ... very valuable information in this context.

The key learning for the team members here, which they will have to put into practice in the next three weeks, is that individuals differ in many respects, including their capacity to sustain long periods of teamwork, and that this must be factored into the allocation of tasks over the coming weeks. This also sharpens the insight into what they themselves as leaders need, back at work, and what their direct reports, and bosses, may also need. At the end of this day the participants are very absorbed by what they are learning about themselves and others. They are also a bit overwhelmed, and need reassurance that there will be ample time to absorb this data over the coming two days, and over the coming two weeks. What is clear to all participants at this stage is that good teamwork is based on respect for individual differences. Differences can be respected more easily and more fully when they are named and recognised. Any good instrument can contribute to this goal in a team setting.

When using Belbin combined with the 360 degree feedback the participants felt a little less overwhelmed at this stage. However, all of the participants on this programme said that they found the information provided by this instrument 'deeper' than the 360 degree, and many claimed to have found it more insightful and revealing than anything they had done before. This naturally depended on what they had been exposed to in the past. Prior to using the Belbin team roles combined with the 360 degree feedback, I have used The Myers-Briggs Type Indicator for the same purpose.[5] However, it has been my experience that North American and Anglophone participants in general have had previous exposure to the MBTI, and want something 'new'. I weave their MBTI into their Birkman feedback in week three.

Day Four

On day four they focus on briefings provided by experts in their business issue area, and their host country. They also prepare their first presentation as a team, based on their knowledge to date, derived from the inputs, the library, the internet, and any other sources of data, deriving testable hypotheses about the state of the market globally, its impact on this particular local system, its economic, social, demographic and technological status. The presentation preparations, in teams, is video-recorded, so that the teams can look at it on day five, when they do their team process review. The day largely concentrates on 'task', while I hover in team rooms, providing observations and coaching as required. I usually gain some insight into potential problems in the team dynamics at this stage, and from time to time intervene to 'hold a mirror up' to the group process.

Day Five

On day five each of the teams makes its first presentation, accomplishing its first major task as a team, and in the afternoon, prior to departing for their host country, each team does a process review. For this purpose I provide them with a video-recording of their teamwork process, some checklists from Katzenbach and Smith's 'The Wisdom of Teams',[6] some input on 'High-Performing Teams', and references to the Birkman's explanatory power in identifying the key behaviours which the team will have to monitor carefully on their return. They are encouraged to look carefully, celebrating the positive, but not slipping into 'Groupthink', as described by Irving Janis.[7] They are asked to revise their groundrules in preparation for the next week in their teams. Then they break up into sub-groups, and depart for their host countries. I carefully collect all the team documentation from the walls of their group rooms, and keep them carefully for their return.

Week Three – Day One to Day Three

When the participants return to the classroom on the beginning of week three, the challenge is to make sure that they return to their group process issues while the task of assimilating all of their interview data and the stress of making decisions about recommendations to top management looms in five days' time. Yet, if they fail to address the group issues, when issues need addressing, they can, and have, run into major problems of content and quality of presentation. Conflict resolution styles are important here, and clearly and helpfully identified in the Birkman instrument, so I do a quick revision of the Birkman, with particular reference to the 'Stress Pages' of their feedback, which they read individually, and then share with their teams. This is quite a strong 'bonding' process, and causes the group to re-visit their groundrules and to revise their vision statement. Once again the energy for both the task and the process is high, as every facilitator will know, given the task of making a formidable feedback, and the rest of the team, one by one, giving the person their feedback. The recipient comments on the feedback at the end, and may ask questions of clarification during the process. Those giving feedback are specifically asked to be careful about words such as 'aggressive' or 'dominating', or for that matter 'withdrawn', which, as every facilitator knows, are judgments, not behavioural observations. During the process I move from team to team, picking up 'trigger' words, or obscurities. The activity can be particularly difficult for Asian participants, as it is counter to their cultural norms. They often choose to receive full feedback, but only to give positive feedback in return. This is usually accepted and understood by other team members.

The process is a very rich one, again. The 'feel-good' factor is, as every facilitator knows, very high in a process like this. The content of the feedback is usually quite similar for each participant, despite the cultural diversity in the groups. Most participants experience this as an affirmation. In groups which may have had some difficulties, particularly if these are unresolved, it is necessary, as facilitator, to monitor the process more carefully. Paradoxically, the individual and team learning may be even greater, in particular about 'jeopardy factors' or stress behaviours, than in the groups who succeeded in managing differences more effectively. However, the immediate acceptability of some of the feedback may be discounted in such groups. The feedback process, at this stage in the programme, removes the uncertainty about how one has been perceived by one's colleagues. More importantly, it also provides some sense of both celebration and closure to what many participants have, in follow-up interviews, described as a 'life-transforming experience', or more modestly 'the best programme I have ever attended in my life'.

CHAPTER 17

Executive Team Facilitation: Some Observations

Thomas E. Ollerman

WHY am I here? This is one of the most critical questions asked by team members and must be addressed by an executive wishing to facilitate an executive leadership team. An executive must resolve the fears that are associated with unresolved issues often experienced by team members not familiar with team dynamics or working in a team environment. The resolution of these issues during this initial stage of team development often provides team members with a sense of purpose, a sense of assessing how they fit into the team and the expectations of the executive, and it allows them to test their sense of membership with other colleagues on the team.

The Mission Statement

Their agreement on a clearly defined mission statement is critical during this orientation phase. A mission statement is a brief, concise statement which leads to a sense of focus and direction for team efforts. The mission statement should be specific enough to serve as a benchmark for setting priorities and evaluating the strategic value of the team's performance, but not so specific as to state goals and objectives.

Some qualities to consider in developing a mission statement include:

- Its purpose is to liberate energy, mobilize, federate, enthuse and make people think.
- It should be satisfying, reasonable, equitable, ambitious, possible, and consistent with the corporate culture.
- It should look beyond the foreseeable future.
- It must be clearly expressed.
- It must NOT be an economic goal only.
- It must NOT be parachuted in from above.

One must always remember that the process of formulating the mission statement is more important than the resulting mission statement.

Consensus Decision-Making

An executive's ability to demonstrate listening skills is crucial for facilitating consensus decision-making. Consensus is a decision or result that reflects the views of all the team members who can publicly support the team's decisions to the rest of the organization. This skill requires that each member feels they have had a full hearing chance to convince the team of their opinions.

Some guidelines to keep in mind are:

1. Avoid voting, averaging, and trading positions to get agreement on other issues.
2. Involve all members' viewpoints on the issues being discussed.
3. Explore the reason behind each member's view.

Some key facilitating behaviours oriented towards consensus decision-making involve the executive's ability to ask opinions and opposing viewpoints, ask or summarize discussion key points, get agreement from the entire team, summarize the team's progress on the assigned task and most importantly, ask for clarification of each team member's opinion in order to eliminate any misunderstandings by other team members.

Consensus decision making does not equate to 100 per cent agreement. As nearly everyone knows, 100 per cent agreement is next to impossible. Consensus does equate to 100 per cent commitment to decisions. Commitment to decisions is achieved through a thorough discussion and participation among team members. Consensus occurs when each person on the team can say that he or she has had a chance to speak, has spoken, and has been sincerely heard. Consequently, each person has either persuaded the team to his or her way of thinking or has not persuaded the team. Either way, the team's decision is accepted, possibly with reservation, but always with a commitment to the decision and to the implementation of that decision. Obviously this approach to decisions takes time and trust, so don't expect excellence right away. Eventually, however, this process yields team synergy with accompanying bottom line results.

One of the best ways to assess an executive facilitator's intervention skill and impact upon a team is to use a Team Process Check at the conclusion of each meeting . This is a rating scale of one to ten completed by each member of the team at the conclusion of a team meeting on six dimensions. These dimensions include: Remaining on track with the team's stated agenda; total team participation in the process; the team's overall listening behaviours; to what extent there was shared leadership by all of the team members; the quality of the decisions made by the team; and ratings on each member's perception on the usefulness of their time spent during this team meeting. These ratings are made public and open to team discussion at the end of each team meeting in order to establish criteria for improving their team interaction process. Any recommendations or changes are recorded by the team recorder to be used at the next team meeting as focus points for continuous improvement.

In order to provide feedback to a team, an executive must have some criteria for observing team members and their process working together. Behavioural feedback that lends itself to successful team facilitation include observations of the following behaviours:

- Validating a team member's statement or position.
- Any indication of a change or modification in a team member's position on an issue.
- Restatement of the goal or mission of the team.
- Any summarization comments on the team's progress or discussions.
- When someone polls the rest of the team for consensus agreement.
- When there is a request for clarification of an opinion by another team member.
- The use of humour.
- When someone clarifies their position in greater detail.
- When someone suggests a procedure to help the team resolve an issue.
- When someone suggests celebrating the team's success at the conclusion of a decision or the implementation of a suggestion by the team.
- When someone reinforces someone else's opinion or when they give additional information that helps the team.
- When someone gives constructive feedback to another team member.

Negative feedback would include such observations as interrupting one another, biting or sarcastic humour, or when a team member is overly defensive about their position on an issue.

Defining Roles and Responsibilities

One of the key skills an executive facilitator must develop is their ability to clearly define the roles and responsibilities necessary for successful team problem solving. These roles would include that of the leader, the team facilitator, the team recorder, the team timekeeper and the responsibilities of each member of the team. There are specific duties required for each of these designated roles as each must focus on different aspects of the team process. Each team must go through a process of defining the responsibilities for each of these roles and clarify in writing what each role will be in the actual team process.

Our experience indicates that of approximately 40 per cent of the executive teams we have trained stated they did not need a designated team facilitator. Within ninety days after initiating their team process, 100 per cent of these executives asked us again what was the role of the facilitator because their teams were not working. It takes an exceptional executive to serve as both the team leader and the team facilitator because in one role he concentrates on the content of the agenda while in the other he must concentrate on the process by which the team is interacting.

It has also been our experience in the aluminum industry and in the computer board manufacturing industry that it is often more beneficial to create designated team facilitators who develop a career path that will require this skill for promotion. Of our clients who have developed this option, they estimate that it takes approximately 18 months of team facilitation to prepare them for a managerial position. One of our major clients went so far as to create a department of team facilitators which included 42 designated facilitators. They felt the managers with team facilitation experience made better business decisions as managers because they developed a broader perspective of the entire business and knew what impact their managerial decisions had on their employees.

The Successful Executive Team Facilitator

The idea of having designated facilitators is the perfect world. However, most organizations do not have the luxury of a dedicated facilitator and this role falls on the team leader or executive in charge of a corporate team. In order to develop their facilitator skills, some companies hold a pre-meeting including the team leader, the timekeeper, and the designated member of the team who serves as a facilitator. The same people meet after the meeting and discuss the role the leader played in the process. This requires the entire team to go through a team facilitator training process in order that all members on the team develop facilitation skills for the benefit of the organization.

If I were to list ten key behaviours correlated with successful executive team facilitation, I would include:

1. Don't do anything the team can do for itself.
2. Intervene to satisfy the team's needs, not your own.
3. Wait before intervening; give team members time to correct problems for themselves.
4. Start with validating the individual and end with validating the individual.
5. Avoid editing; let the team use its own methods and language.
6. Try to speak no longer than 30 seconds at a time.
7. When you hear the same thing for the third time, intervene.
8. When a team falls silent, that is your cue to keep silent.
9. Do more asking than telling; do more listening than talking.
10. Don't try to take over the team. (It always backfires.)

Conclusion

In conclusion, I would like to make few comments on the feedback we have received from team members concerning what they perceive to be the foremost critical skills of an executive facilitator. The first and foremost was that of authenticity, or how consistent were the verbal interventions by the executive and the executive's behaviours? Poor performing executives demonstrated striking evidence of contradictions between their verbal interventions and their actual behaviours during and after team meetings. Successful facilitators received feedback that all their interventions were consistent with their behaviours.

The second key factor was that of autonomy, or how well did the executive refrain from getting involved in the team's content issues? Some executives often intervened in the team's process with content related information while successful executives avoided contributing content related information and relied on team members for input on problem solving. It is our observation that this is the most difficult task for executives, that is, to refrain from telling the team what the executive wants them to do and how the executive wants them to do it. If teams do not feel they are granted autonomy by their executive leaders, they lapse into passive-aggressive behaviours and do not take responsibility for successful problem solving in team environments.

The third critical factor is directly related to the perceptive ability and listening skills of the executive. This is the perceived accuracy of the executive's interventions. This refers to the assessments by team members on how well the executive demonstrates an understanding of team dynamics and group processes. Unfortunately most executives do not take time to learn the dynamics of teams nor are they often presented with the opportunity to learn this kind of information. Low scoring executives appear to be unaware of most of the team's process characteristics while successful executives facilitate a team's process more accurately by responding to the team's full range of dynamics with appropriate intensity.

The fourth and final criteria for successful executive facilitation is that of acceptance. This is a team member's perception of how well the executive demonstrates his personal acceptance of all the team members. Too often executives show favouritism in team environments as demonstrated by their negative or nonverbal disregard for specific team members. The goal of the successful executive facilitator would be to be viewed as positively interacting with all the team members and not be perceived as demonstrating any negative behaviours toward a single member or group of members within a team .

CHAPTER 18

Organizing the External Business Perspective: The Role of the Country Coordinator in Action Learning Programmes

Patricia E. Levy

Introduction

THE continuum of the action learning experience is vast and diverse. Within this, the role of the country coordinator in an action learning programme is many-tiered and complex. The country coordinator is in essence the facilitator who must bring together all the diverse pieces of the project in order to actualize a specific programme in a selected country for the company's participants. To this end, the coordinator must be a person able to work on many different levels in different capacities all at the same time.

The views in this chapter are based on my experiences over the years as a country coordinator for action learning programmes in Europe and in Canada with some major corporate leaders in the field of action learning. While significant differences will arise in the approach to action learning within every company due to differences in corporate cultures and the needs and objectives of the company, I will try to extract some basic tenets which I believe may be useful in application to most corporate action learning scenarios.

In order to fully understand the role of the country coordinator in an action learning programme, we must examine a scenario of how the work could unfold. While details of programme design obviously vary dramatically from company to company, there are some general principles which will probably apply throughout.

What does an Action Learning based Executive Development Programme Look like?

Many corporations are now using action learning in the design and delivery of executive education programme tailored to their specific challenges, issues, industries and competitive strategies. The objectives of such programmes include: a positive impact on the company business; the personal development of participants; and the application of key learnings to other businesses within the company. The programme helps to draw upon the inherent strength of a company by having its executives solve problems in addition to outside consultants and in this way the company retains the process and knowledge to solve future problems in all businesses.

An action-learning based executive development educational programme essentially involves a method which uses actual strategic business issues and specific projects as the basis for investigation and project team work. The results include real value-added deliverables and final actionable recommendations to top executives. The experience gained by the participants themselves helps in the development of leadership and teamwork skills across boundaries along with the knowledge gained through the specific content of the course work itself.

Usually, a select group of company executives from around the world will participate in a programme. These are high impact, high potential individuals who are seen to be key contributors to the company and who have been nominated and selected by senior executives. This international group will be a global and diverse multi-functional and multi-discipline mix of participants from various parts or businesses of a company.

During the first phase of the programme they will take part in class sessions with academics as well as recognized business leaders. The participants will focus on a specific business interest for the company.

Following this intensive course learning, the participants will be grouped into teams to be deployed in different countries. Each learning team of participants will be placed in a country in order to concentrate on developing the business issue which has been given. They will participate in a comprehensive briefing on the country in which the team has been placed and the briefing will cover such areas as the economy, politics, employment, culture and of course, the subject area of the company's concentration in that country.

To help the class collect data and form its conclusions the executive development programme participants in each country conduct interviews during the next phase. These interviews are viewed as a key learning process for the participants and will also assist in familiarizing them with the rapidly changing marketplace and ideal business models. Interviews are conducted with best practice companies, current and potential customers, government officials, experts, distributors and company businesses.

During the final phase following the interviews in the field, the team works intensively to prepare a report. At the conclusion of the programme, the team presents their findings to the business leaders, company group chairmen, programme sponsor within the company, and perhaps as well as to the company's senior executive committee. The recommendations and conclusions of the reports may be implemented by the company in the short, medium, or long term. Alternatively, the company may decide not to act on the recommendations at all, either because there is a lack of agreement or for other business reasons.

Selection of the Country Coordinator

Once the business issue or business statement has been identified by the company the basic parameters of the project work must be established in terms of which countries will be selected, following which the country coordinator must be selected. There are several criteria by which the country coordinator should be selected. The skill set of the country coordinator should include very strong organizational skills with attention to detail. The country coordinator must be a good communicator, both oral and written. Strong interpersonal skills are required as the country coordinator must function well in many relationships during the project.

The coordinator must be well-connected and able to network effectively in the country for which they have been chosen to execute the project. The work requires the ability to shape a project moving back and forth from specificity to generality, from details to overall strategic thinking. The country coordinator must properly position the terms and goals of the project by communicating clearly with everyone from company support staff to company presidents and high-level government officials. Throughout the process, the country coordinator must be able to remain the consummate diplomat, representing the company's interests while being able to empathize with the needs and agendas of all the project participants.

The country coordinator's role is unique in that while it clearly involves being a consultant outside the company, at the same time the coordinator is constantly an ambassador for the company and must be careful to communicate the corporate values and objectives whenever needed. This means that the country coordinator must develop an integrated knowledge of the company and its values and a sensitivity to its business needs so that this is second nature as contacts and potential interview candidates are approached. At the same time, managing expectations is critical. This is of paramount importance because lack of clarity in communications with regard to the company's objectives in the action learning programme can lead to a negative outcome both for the programme and the company itself. It is up to the country coordinator, as a public voice representing the company during the project, to carefully manage outsiders' expectations.

Initial Meetings and Critical Relationships

Following the selection of the country coordinator, the company's executive education or management development leader will want to initiate a series of meetings whereby the process can be set on track for the actualization of the project. Meetings must be set up with the company executive education director, the country head, and the country coordinator. There should be a discussion about the project's business issue statement, critical issues facing each country and the roles and working relationship of company executives and country coordinators. The scope and timing of the project must be understood. An initial decision must be made as to the areas of the country and cities to be covered, subject to possible adjustments later if warranted by additional research or restrictions that become apparent.

In particular, there must be a relationship established between the country coordinator and the corporate executive education director (to whom the country coordinator reports) as well as a relationship established between the country coordinator and the corporate country head. Both of these must be good working relationships so that the country coordinator can take direction from the corporate executive education director and translate this into the country while working with the corporate country head.

The country head may or may not be amenable to working with the country coordinator depending on personalities and the individual's situation. A country head who is not feeling secure in a position may view the placement of a country coordinator as an intrusion, a threat to his or her autonomy within the company. There is a very large variable in the relationship between the county coordinator and the country head and this will have a direct impact on the work of the country coordinator. For example, where there is good cooperation between the two people, the country head may feel very comfortable working with the country coordinator in both the general and specific design of the programme and may be able to give many useful suggestions as to potential participants for the interview part of the programme. A perceptive country head will understand that the development of the action learning project is intensive and is best handled by someone outside the company who has been specifically selected for their expertise in structuring such programmes. Furthermore, it will be seen that it is of greater value to cooperate with the country coordinator than to create resistance to the coordinator and thereby to a programme which has been authorized by the company's senior executive. This also underlines in part why it is so essential that the action learning project must be fully supported at the highest levels of the company and the project sponsor must hold significant authority within the company.

The quality of this relationship will determine much of the degree of difficulty of the work for the country coordinator. It also can often lead the country coordinator directly into the realm of corporate politics. Throughout the project, the coordinator must ensure that open channels of communication are maintained with the corporate education director, to whom he/she is accountable, as there may very well arise a need for the director to intervene if the situation becomes fraught with difficulties and becomes unmanageable to the point where it will negatively impact upon the specific action learning programme.

Design and Planning of the Programme

With regard to the mechanics of the programme, the country coordinator needs initially to define the parameters of the programme so that a plan of attack can be swiftly and efficiently executed, given that there are critical time frames to meet for each programme. The country coordinator should set up a schedule with time lines and due dates for the completion of each of the following: creation of the initial contact list, verification of names and addresses, mailing of the information package, direct telephone contacts with potential interviewees, scheduling of interviews, reservation and confirmation of all logistical details including flights, hotels and transportation, special event planning and reservations, preparation of research and briefing material, presentation of country briefing. The entire process may require at least six to eight weeks, but interviews must be scheduled as early as possible as it becomes difficult to obtain good interviews at a late date since most busy people will have schedules which fill up early.

Initially, the country coordinator needs to map out the general categories of contacts that must be made for the establishment of an interview schedule. For example, those categories could include relevant best practices companies, government officials, current and potential customers and industry experts. As the setter of interviews, the country coordinator must ultimately decide who should be approached for interviews, but hopefully these decisions are made in close conjunction with the country head. The country coordinator will want to meet several times with the company head or contact in the country in order to jointly develop ideas for a list of organizations and people for the participants to interview. There could be a broad sweeping discussion or brainstorming of potential contacts for interviewee selection. The country coordinator should be prepared to defer to the country head's experience where appropriate and certainly be open to the many suggestions that the country head may have. Also, as the networking process unfolds, one contact may lead to another contact who could in fact be more appropriate for the actual interview. The country coordinator will have to carefully follow up on each such lead because it is key that the final interview in each case takes place with the best possible candidate.

Communications

In a sense, the country coordinator is the interpreter of the action learning programme who translates the business statement and objectives of the programme into reality. The country coordinator must convince others to participate in the programme by making the company, action learning concept and strategic business issues interesting to outsiders. The response of the outside world to contact by the country coordinator will depend primarily on the company's profile and history, but the country coordinator's ability and approach will play an important role. The skill of the country coordinator in clearly communicating the essence of the programme and the company to others will determine to a great degree the overall success rate in obtaining good interviews for the programme.

To this end, the country coordinator should first put together a concise package for mailing or distribution to potential contacts or interviewees. This information package should include an introductory letter (perhaps from the company itself), a programme description and a protocol so that whoever receives this material would understand immediately what the programme was about and what was being requested in the proposed interviews. The country coordinator will also want to consult with the company contact in the development of the form and protocol by which the interviews will be solicited. It is best if this package is vetted and approved by the company, either through the country head or corporate sponsor.

After deciding who should be approached for an interview or who should be initially contacted as a lead to finding out who should ultimately be contacted, the country coordinator will probably have an extensive mailing address list in hand. The mechanics of a mass mailing will need sufficient lead time, since it is best if the potential interviewees receive the material prior to being contacted directly by the country coordinator so they will already understand what the programme is about.

Following this phase, there will be constant communication between the country coordinator and the interviewees, the company, and the country head. Later, communications work with the team participants as they go through the interview process will be very important until the end of the programme.

Another valuable avenue of communication that should be maintained is between the various country coordinators in different countries who are all working on the same project. The country coordinators can share ideas and findings and methodologies as they progress with the project in this country. By networking with each other, the country coordinators can also assist each other with problems that are particular to their role and therefore understandable to each other.

Selection and Scheduling of Interviews

The interview selection and scheduling process is probably the most time-consuming part of the programme development for the country coordinator. The country coordinator will need to identify all the potential organizations and people that should be interviewed by the team. Relevant criteria are developed by the country coordinator in order to achieve the right selection of interviews, such as a benchmarking process in dealing with best practice companies. The country coordinator is then usually required to schedule and confirm a minimum number of interviews to include: experts, government officials, current and potential customers, distributors, best practice companies, company businesses.

Scheduling a programme such as this can be extremely complicated, given that it can involve many interviews per day, many participants and many cities. For example, as a minimum, there may be a group of eight company participants divided into four teams each having four interviews per day in different cities over the course of a week, so there may be a total of around 80 interviews in eight venues in five days. It is therefore best if there is a single gatekeeper of the schedule; that is, the country coordinator ultimately sets the interviews, subject of course to other needs and conflicts. This is helpful because the single tight control of the schedule by the country coordinator minimizes unnecessary scheduling conflicts and allows one person to do the constant juggling of scheduling conflicts that do arise and, as well, allows for a quick response where changes to the schedule must be made, even at the last minute.

The country coordinator must pay careful attention to scheduling a sufficient number of interviews for an effective programme without overloading the number of meetings. A perfect balance may be difficult to achieve, especially because different team participants may feel comfortable with different amounts of pressure from the programme. If there are not enough interviews, some teams may demand more at the last minute (which will be difficult to schedule) and if there are too many, some teams may react by not attending interviews which were scheduled. Neither result leaves a good impression of the company with outsiders.

In order to obtain an interview, the country coordinator will need to convince the potential interviewee of the value of participation in the programme. This is usually not self -evident and may require some time spent in first finding the right person in an organization and then in directly negotiating the interview with that person. Interviewees are not paid and yet are being asked to give an hour or more of their time to the programme, so the country coordinator must be sensitive enough to understand why the programme could possibly be of interest from the interviewee's point of view, given their own individual agenda of needs and already busy schedules. For example, one potential interviewee might decide to participate because the programme might be seen as a way of initiating negotiations with their own company, another person may want to get hired as a consultant to the company, and still another may want the company to join their association. There is often a *quid pro quo* in the interviewee's mind, even if it remains unsaid.

This is where the country coordinator must be skilful as a manager of expectations. In explaining the programme, the country coordinator must honestly portray it as an educational and developmental programme for the company participants as well as a business tool for the company, balancing both of these dynamic aspects to an action-learning executive development programme. Any misrepresentation could mislead the interviewees into believing that they may receive a direct benefit from participation which may or may not flow from the final outcome of the programme and this can have a negative impact on the perception of the company by others. On the other hand, it would be inaccurate to simply portray this type of executive development programme as merely educational for the participants and without possible business impact. For example, real synergies could arise between the team participants and the interviewees which could ultimately result in actual positive recommendations to be implemented by the company at some future date. Conversely, it is conceivable that knowlege could be gained in an interview which could ultimately have some sort of negative business impact on a participant's company.

The country coordinator will very often have to spend significant time and energy in giving pre-interview briefings to the interviewees in order to clarify the project and ensure that all relevant information is available to them. This will prepare the participants for the interviews and reduce any possible confusion about the interview process or inaccurate expectations about the project itself.

Logistical Planning

In some ways, the country coordinator must also be a logistics technician, accountable for the accuracy of every single detail in the planning of the programme. There is an enormous amount of logistical work and technical detail which must be precisely attended to by the country coordinator in the course of establishing an executive development action learning programme. All information about interview times, location and interviewees must be correct as mistakes can lead to embarrassment of the team participants and the company itself. The country coordinator must select and recommend hotels, restaurants, and special events to be used in each city during the programme. While it may not be necessary to actually provide the transportation between meetings, options must at least be made available to the team participants and the country coordinator should recommend and arrange local transportation to be used during the period of interviews and transportation to and from the airports to hotels. Travelling times between interviews should allow for the team participants to arrive punctually for their meetings. Flights and hotels must be carefully booked and re-confirmed.

It is very helpful to the company team participants if all the logistical and technical details can be put into a format which is readily understandable and accessible. For example, the participants will need their schedules, including the briefing day agenda and all interview meeting coordinates and details. They will also need to know flight and hotel and transportation arrangements, and any additional information that could be helpful such as restaurants or sights in the cities.

The country coordinator will probably coordinate, along with the company contact, a welcome dinner with other company managers. Depending on the programme and participants, there may be a need for the country coordinator to set up in advance some sort of cultural or entertainment event during the stay in the country which could serve the dual purpose of team building and relaxation during a hectic schedule. This could be anything from a special dinner with interesting guests, a tour, a theatre outing or sports event.

Interpreters

Given that the participants are often from other countries, there may be a need to use an interpreter for the interviews as language barriers within such meetings can lead to frustrations. The country coordinator must carefully select and recommend a professional interpreter who is able to handle the subject matter of the interviews while presenting a neutral and unbiased approach to both the team and the interviewee. All logistical details involving the interpreter must be arranged, such as the coordination of the interpreter at the interviews.

The selection of a good interpreter is very important to the programme. If an interpreter cannot handle the technical translation work the meetings will suffer. If an interpreter interferes in the flow of a meeting by giving subjective responses, the neutrality of the interview format will be affected and the objective research outcome may not be achieved.

The use of an interpreter to assist participants may increase the time required for each interview, and this will have to be factored into the scheduling.

Research and Readings

The country coordinator will want to provide research and readings to the participants to be distributed either in advance, during the first phase (more subject related) or to be reviewed during the in-country briefings. Copies of the country briefing, expert briefing and company briefing should be provided when the presentations are made.

As the interview phase proceeds, the team participants may collect research materials on their own. However, they may often need the country coordinator to assist in the collection of research materials during the interview week and later when they are actually preparing their final presentations and reports. While the country coordinator is not a research assistant *per se*, at the time there may be a real need for assistance in the collection and organization of materials, especially when they are working in another venue to put together their reports. Often it may not be necessary to actually get the material or information but hopefully the country coordinator will be able to guide the team to the information or find out how to get it. It may also be helpful to the team if the country coordinator can help to compile the material in a more usable form.

Country Briefing and Coordination of Expert and Company Briefings

After the arrival of the team participants in the host country and prior to the commencement of the interviews the country coordinator will have arranged for the team to receive a country briefing, a company briefing, an expert briefing, and any further initiation that is required. The most convenient way to cover all these presentations may be by having a specific briefing day set aside once the team participants arrive, but other arrangements can also be made.

The country coordinator must develop a country briefing to be presented to the team participants prior to the interview week and probably during a briefing day . The country briefing presentation should try to give an economic, political, historical, industrial and cultural framework for approaching the host country. While it is clearly not possible to cover all this material completely within a short presentation, the goal is to give the team some useful background on the country along with some cultural guidance so that they can begin their interviews with a sense of what the country is about and how country-specific issues will affect their search for answers in such a business environment..

The country coordinator will arrange for the company briefing and the expert briefing, helping in the development of the topics to be covered and reviewing the presentations in advance if necessary. The company briefing will give the company's country head the opportunity to set the stage and define the critical issues which the company faces in that country and the company activities which are ongoing. Finally, the country coordinator will arrange for an expert briefing in the subject matter of the company's field of business. The country head may help the country coordinator in the selection of the expert.

Interview Briefing and Debriefing

Where relevant, the country coordinator should provide the team with written materials about the interviews they will be conducting in a useful format. In addition, there should be a formalized time – perhaps during the briefing day – during which the country coordinator can fully brief all team participants about logistical and content information in preparation for each interview. The country coordinator will undoubtedly have a great deal of extra information which has been gleaned from pre-interview discussions with the interviewees and which can be shared with the team participants to make their interviews more focused. However, the country coordinator should attempt not to influence or bias the outcome of the interviews by giving a personal point of view about the interviews and issues to be discussed.

During the interview phase, it is probably extremely helpful for both the team participants and the country coordinator if there can be fairly regular or daily briefings before the interviews and debriefings after the interviews. This way, new information can be conveyed along with any problems that may have arisen or leads that must be followed-up during that time.

Finally, there should be some overall debriefing with the country coordinator after the team has completed their interviewing phase, and this can be done individually or as a group. A final debriefing will be of benefit to the country coordinator in trying to improve on similar work in the future as it may clarify what worked well and where there were problems in the programme. It also allows the team participants to continue their contribution to the overall programme, both in the present and for the future.

Guide, Intermediary and Troubleshooter for All Participants

By not being an actual stakeholder or part of the team, the country coordinator should be able to be an objective and nonbiased guide to the programme for all participants. The country coordinator should be a perceptive intermediary and contact point between the company, the team, and the interview participants throughout the programme so that any conflicts that arise can be sensitively and efficiently handled.

During the interview phase the country coordinator must be a fully available 'friendly helper' and guide to the programme in order to provide any back-up support to the participants as they conduct their interviews. While the interview schedule is finalized before the interview phase begins, there may arise an obvious need during that time to insert an additional meeting as a result of an interview or there may have to be last minute changes to the schedule due to unpredictable cancellations by interviewees. The country coordinator must ensure that all such changes occur smoothly and work out back-up plans where necessary. Similarly, the team participants may require extra help in any number of ways, be it for flight changes, communications with home or other team members, or to clear up a misunderstanding that arose in an interview. The country coordinator should be a patient troubleshooter providing a quick, flexible response to the problems and changing needs of others as they arise.

Finally, after the interview phase of the programme officially finishes, the country coordinator may have to follow-up certain issues or tie up loose ends for the company, team and interview participants. There will also be a need for the coordination of the company's 'thank you' letters and acknowledgements for the interviewees.

Knowledge management

It will be of benefit to the company if the country coordinator can in some way reference the planning work that has been done in the country so that the company can use it if need be in the future. Perhaps some of the interviewee information can be gathered together either in a binder or to be posted on the company's intranet or internal web site.

Throughout the interview setting process, the country coordinator will be interactively gaining knowledge about the company and the marketplace which can ultimately be of value to the company. The country coordinator will want to continually transfer this knowledge to the company where possible. For example, as the country coordinator discusses the programme and tries to set up interviews, a current customer may admit a dissatisfaction with the way the company has been operating or the president of a competitive company may note a weakness in the company's approach to the market or a government contact may suggest a regulatory aspect which the company could use to greater advantage. Debriefings with the team participants may also have revealed specific information which should be conveyed to the company but may not fit in as part of the final team presentation. All of this kind of business intelligence may be of use to the company and should be conveyed either to the country head or to the company executive education director.

Conclusion

It can be seen that the role of the country coordinator is complicated and multi-faceted and therefore demands strong organizational, interpersonal and business

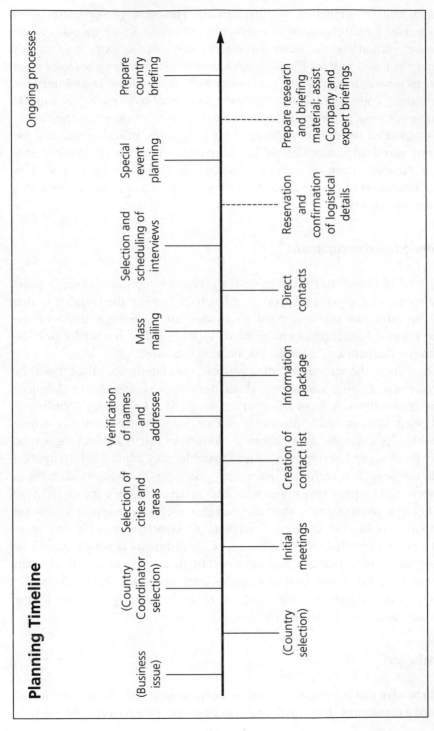

Figure 18.1 Role of the Country Coordinator – programme design (before in-country interviews)

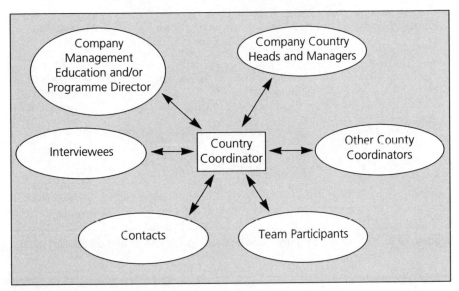

Figure 18.2 Role of the Country Coordinator – communications

skills. This is understandable, given that an executive development action learning programme is in itself complex in its dynamic combination of personal development for the executive team members and business development for the company.

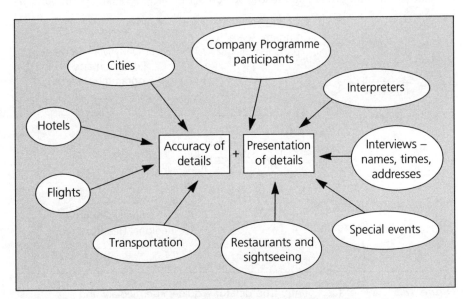

Figure 18.3 Role of the Country Coordinator – logistical planning

Identification	Selection	Scheduling Expectations	Managing
• Networking, brainstorming	• Find best interview candidate	• Single 'gatekeeper'	• Convince interviewees & understand their 'agenda'
• Relevant criteria	• Direct contact	• Optimum number	• Pre-interview briefings
	• Follow up leads		• Portray programme as educational/ business

Figure 18.4 Role of the Country Coordinator – identification and scheduling of interviews

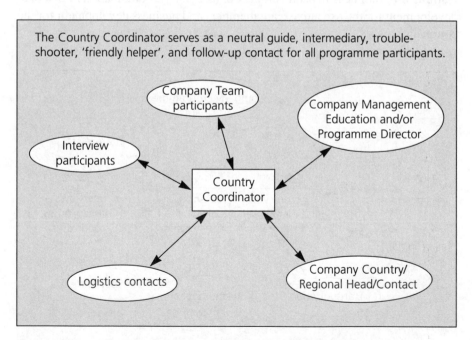

The Country Coordinator serves as a neutral guide, intermediary, trouble-shooter, 'friendly helper', and follow-up contact for all programme participants.

Company Team participants

Company Management Education and/or Programme Director

Interview participants

Country Coordinator

Logistics contacts

Company Country/ Regional Head/Contact

Figure 18.5 Role of the Country Coordinator – guide, intermediary and troubleshooter

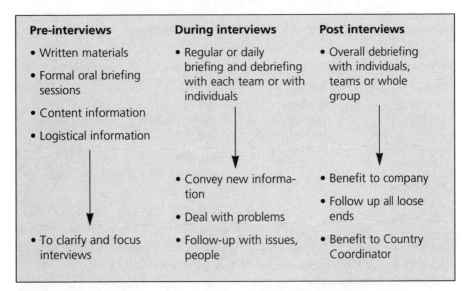

Figure 18.6 Role of the Country Coordinator – briefing participants

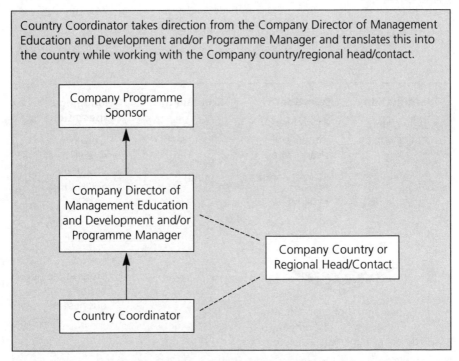

Figure 18.7 Working relationships of Company Executives and Country Coordinator (1)

Specific areas of cooperation between the Country Coordinator and Company Country/Regional Head/Contact

Meetings	Briefings	Special events	Interpreter
• Meet to jointly develop ideas for list of organizations and people to interview • Develop form and protocol to solicit interviews	• Arranging of briefings for team and company and on country and business issue(s)	• Welcome dinner with other company managers • Possible cultural event	• Country Coordinator recommends and contacts interpreter, in conjunction with company

Figure 18.8 Working relationships of Company Executives and Country Coordinator (2)

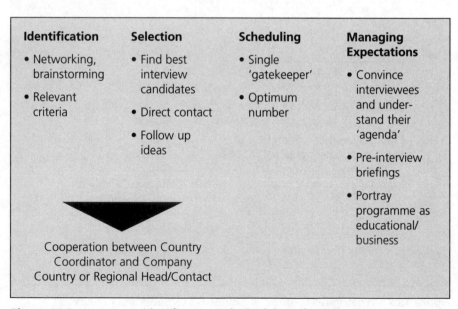

Identification	Selection	Scheduling	Managing Expectations
• Networking, brainstorming • Relevant criteria	• Find best interview candidates • Direct contact • Follow up ideas	• Single 'gatekeeper' • Optimum number	• Convince interviewees and understand their 'agenda' • Pre-interview briefings • Portray programme as educational/ business

Cooperation between Country Coordinator and Company Country or Regional Head/Contact

Figure 18.9 In-country: identification and scheduling of interviews

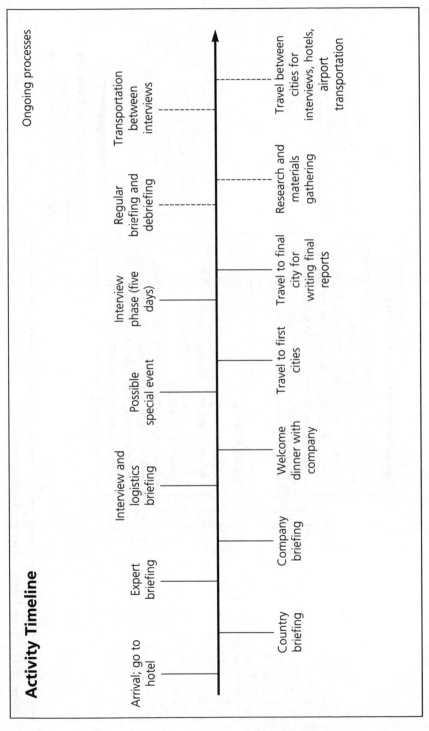

Figure 18.10 In-country: example of basic activities of team participants

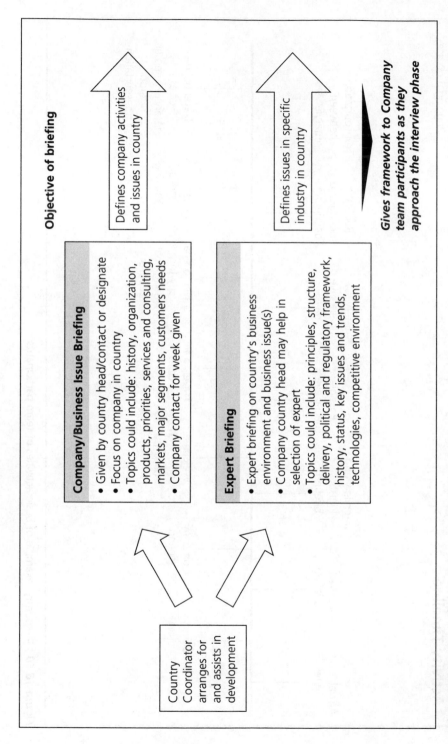

Objective of briefing

Defines company activities and issues in country

Defines issues in specific industry in country

Gives framework to Company team participants as they approach the interview phase

Company/Business Issue Briefing

- Given by country head/contact or designate
- Focus on company in country
- Topics could include: history, organization, products, priorities, services and consulting, markets, major segments, customers needs
- Company contact for week given

Expert Briefing

- Expert briefing on country's business environment and business issue(s)
- Company country head may help in selection of expert
- Topics could include: principles, structure, delivery, political and regulatory framework, history, status, key issues and trends, technologies, competitive environment

Country Coordinator arranges for and assists in development

Figure 18.11   Second week in-country: expert briefings

Interview Group	Interview Partner	Issues
Government	• Health Canada • Provincial Ministries of Health • Régie Régionale	• Status of health care system and environment • Future of heath care system and pace of change • Regulatory issues • Financing of health care system • Attracting the best and brightest people in the industry • Identification of consulting/services opportunities
Health Care Experts	• Doctors and Medical • Consultants • Associations • Universities	• Regulatory issues • View of government policies • Market segments to target for acquisitions and strategic partnerships • Understanding health care environment and pace of change • Role of information and information technology as an enabler for business and a source of revenue • Identification of consulting/services opportunities
Current and Potential Customers	• Hospitals • Regional Authorities • CLSC • Distributors and Suppliers	• Financing • Requirements and expectations of consulting/services • View of company's current consulting/services • Recent cost reduction efforts • View of company's consulting/ services vs. competitors • Identification of consulting/services opportunities • Impact on company's products businesses by consulting/services business • Identification of best organization and financial framework for consulting/services • Company's message or brand for consulting/services
Companies and Best Practice Companies	• Consultancy firms • Software • Related Companies • Pharmaceutical	• Marketing strategies • Best practices • Identification of possible synergies, acquisitions and strategic partnerships • Identification of best organization and financial framework for consulting/ services • Impact on company's products businesses by consulting/services business • Role of information and information technology as an enabler for business and a source of revenue • Attracting the best and brightest people in the industry • Identification of consulting/services opportunities

Figure 18.12 Example: Interviews – healthcare business issue

Team	Government	Experts	Customers	Companies	Total
Team 1	6	3	9	4	22
Team 2	2	5	9	8	24
Team 3	2	12	3	6	23
Team 4	5	2	13	13	21
Total	15	22	34	19	90

Figure 18.13   Example: Number of interviews by interview group

'Learning the Hard Way': Creating an Executive Development Opportunity for Learning and Reflection

Nigel Barrett

'So how was the business school programme, John? ... Oh, you know, I'm really grateful to the firm for letting me go. It was a great choice, pretty tough on the family but worth it nonetheless. I had a great time. It was a terrific experience and just the right programme for me. I learnt so much ... Great, what were the highlights in particular? Did you find the sessions on financial strategy as useful as we anticipated? ... Well yes they were useful as an update, but to be honest I guess we are as up to speed in what we are doing here. But you know I learnt far more from the other people on the programme than any of the faculty or the case studies they used, and what's more I guess I'll stay good friends with one or two of the other delegates for life. We really clicked on the same wavelength. Just having time to think away from the office was a real bonus too; it put so much of what we do into context'.

How often has this been the pattern of debrief discussions with high potential executives shortly after a major education programme, and not only with 'hi-po's' and not just experiences at leading business schools?

The truth is that the power of self-formulated networking, and the opportunity to reflect in a quasi-sabbatical environment with a peer group that holds mutual respect for each other, is a potentially powerful learning experience and highly motivational. The memory of such relationships endures way beyond the event, as it is timeless in its application.

With this very simple lesson from history the concept behind 'the executive programme for learning and reflection' was born, and the idea that was to become the acronym of the 'Explorer' Learning Network, created.

The environment and a little background

Research in NatWest in mid-1995 concluded that highly talented executives need business education but often do not feel that they want what is offered.

They, and their line masters, frequently expressed resentment at too much time being spent in intellectual debate away from the cutting edge of action. Time is too much of a premium, both emotionally and economically. Yet these self-same executives expressed a strong appetite to learn. They knew that they did not have all the answers and in many cases they looked back at their undergraduate university and postgraduate MBA or doctorate life as hugely important and formative parts of their education. However, they rarely attributed the same value to business education, particularly on open or company specific programmes. Although these programmes were usually seen as critical (by the employing corporation) to the future development of their key executives and future leaders, to truly talented executives it was the learning process itself, a sense of involvement, and direct relevance in application of the knowledge gained that ranked higher in their mind. The research included a survey of 250 25–33 year old executives, all seen to have significantly high potential. A remarkable 92 per cent responded to a paper questionnaire, demonstrating the need for and the importance attributed to the survey's objectives. Amongst the information gathered, 84 per cent indicated a preference for action based or reflection based learning compared to 42 per cent seeking short business school programmes and less than 15 per cent who thought further degree based education was important. A preference analysis ranked learning interventions by both personal interest and also perceived value to the corporation. They showed consistently that meeting individuals' aspirations was one of the most important features of gaining high engagement of executives in their personal development. Other learning instruments perceived as having high value included coaching and mentoring both as the receiver and the benefactor. The highest demand was for workplace based project learning on real issues on the company's strategic and tactical agendas.

The survey was undertaken as part of a comprehensive reappraisal of the education strategy of the corporation, itself a component of a fresh approach to executive development across the NatWest Group. In the strategy, emphasis was placed on clear differentiation between activities designed to create specific skill enrichment, short term development, strategic education or applied learning where outputs could be seen to add value at both the individual, team and organisational levels. This approach was a derivative of the Balanced Business Scorecard approach and could be seen as a Balanced Learning Scorecard. The historical focus was observed to have been dominated by spend and activity in the skill and development quadrants , whereas the higher added value education and learning components had been neglected.

The necessity to identify and develop the future leaders of organisations is well understood, but too often HR systems and processes have been too inflexible to meet the needs of rapidly changing organisations and ever more complex business challenges. This chapter does not discuss the strategy in total, suffice to say that for each part of the Group, pragmatic, yet robust identification and development of the next generation of leaders was put in place. For those identified as 'corporate property' the length of the preferred supply list of open business school programmes was significantly reduced but the spend held at the same levels. The philosophy was one of fewer but deeper relationships.

There remained a significant conundrum that had to be resolved. The business directors and the high potential executives were demanding education but with an apparent paradox of conflicting pressures and priorities. Education was constructively seen as an essential investment and not a cost without value.

The Need

The learning intervention required was endorsed by the Group's CEO and all his executive directors. They decreed that it must have the following characteristics:

- Be economic and demonstrably add value.
- Have minimal time away from the job.
- Be multicultural.
- Be international.
- Be strategic.
- Be 'out of the box' in originality.
- Be multifunctional.
- Be intellectually stretching and stimulating.
- Offer individual learning with no taught answers.
- Be an enduring experience.
- Be applicable to the everyday jobs of participants.

The delegates when researched added a few other key demands:

- It should be fun.
- It should recognise individual preferences.
- It should be novel.
- It must involve other companies.

Traditionally many of these challenges have been seen in the specifications for education consortia programmes. These programmes have significant advantages over open enrolment programmes. The benefits are well documented and written about elsewhere in this book. Similarly their weaknesses are well known and the challenges were to prove to be no less in establishing a learning network. The vulnerability to personality changes in the sponsors is a traditional major challenge. Equally, other weaknesses like the fine tuning of programme specification in the search for consensus, the agreement on the delegate profile (and its subsequent delivery), cost sharing, steering group management, agreement on suppliers and partners and built-in inflexibility over time had got to be avoided wherever possible.

An Experiment and some Good Fortune

As is sometimes the case the opportunity to create an experiment in learning arose from an existing OD initiative. Since 1994, along with others, NatWest was a funding member of the initiative led by Peter Senge's team at MIT undertaking research into innovative organisations for the 21st Century. The executive of the project were meeting in June 1996 at Heythrop Park, the NatWest Group's Learning Centre near Oxford in the UK and at the author's invitation three of the MIT faculty were invited to stay after the business meetings and join in a networking learning experiment. Some 15 executives, five each from three international companies were invited to a workshop to explore the 'Implications of Technology for Leadership into the 21st Century'. It is worth noting that all the executives were of very high potential within their own companies, clearly capable of being seen in the highest positions within a few years in any of the industries present; namely global telecommunications, global consultancy and global financial services. They were a quite exceptional group. Drawing upon the emerging research from MIT the executives were able to share their experiences, ignorance, fears, emotions, and knowledge of the subject with some of the world's greatest thinkers in the field. Costs were nominal as MIT entered into the spirit of the experiment. For everyone present this was a true learning opportunity. With minimal facilitation, and an almost total absence of structure in the shape of a formal timetable, the conversation over two days was stimulating and surprising.

The lack of structure was a surprise to delegates and faculty alike, but as soon as this new rule became the rule, the need for traditional signposts and landmarks, normally defined in a training programme, became irrelevant. The first discovery had already taken place, namely there was no prescribed nor any expected output. The learning opportunity, and indeed the individual learning and subconscious peer group benchmarking, were becoming the outputs themselves. The fact that the companies present were at the same time competitors, suppliers and partners seemed to enhance the opportunities to learn and experiment. It was after all a totally risk free environment.

A highly significant event occurred early on the second day. After several accumulated hours on the topic of the agenda, as in all good learning events, the delegates took control of the occasion. One executive, interested in technology and its application, but not a technophile, bluntly suggested to the group that they avoid mention of the Internet for a period of one hour. He wondered 'how the millions in the slums of Sao Paulo who had yet to make a telephone call, had no electricity or running water would react to the conversation they were all indulging themselves in'. Clearly articulating a passionate challenge to the group, the executive was equally demonstrating the talent perceived by his corporate high potential label. What followed was a debate for two hours, revisited more than once, about the ethical dilemmas for leaders. Instead of talking about the inevitable challenges for technology, the social conscience of the future captains of industry was being put to the test. From technology to ethics the conversation moved to putting these challenges to the global political framework, global financial paradigms and even at one point the concept of global tax regimes to equalise the distribution of wealth. Almost in the same breath the economics of Marx and Silicon Valley entrepreneurs were meeting with the realities of the virtual technology industry and the poverty of the Third World. All this from a group of highly educated high earning executives from three multinational, but primarily Western, corporations. Just what had we discovered?

One thing was for certain, no programme designed to achieve such a range of debate, would have achieved the same goals in 36 hours. The basis of the learning network had been discovered and, without trying, piloted successfully.

The learning points were so simple. Let talented people talk together in a low risk, task-free environment with subtle facilitation and the self-learning takes over. The need to put the conversation in context was taking place without any need for syndicate breakouts or structure, the learning was coming from the peer group's mutual respect for each other. But if this was the discovery, how could it be harnessed to be of greater benefit to the sponsoring companies? The temptation to believe that there had been some great discovery had to be tempered, after all we knew that the learning processes articulated by these very people had asked for this kind of intervention. Like all good customers they asked for, they received and they were delighted. Equally, to believe that a new model for learning for broad scale application was in place would have been folly. The experience was intensive, capitalised on the intellect of the delegates, exploited their willingness and appetite to learn and was fun and flattering. That said it was of such a powerful experience to those involved that it felt appropriate to harness the concept. But how?

Building the Case for the Network

After a period of reflection and many informal soundings from business executives, target high potential executives and HR professionals, a group of interested companies started to agree on the outline of a new learning network. What would be different from more conventional networks? How could it be established for such a small target population? Who would run it? What were the economics of such a venture; surely a network of this nature already existed so why not just buy in to someone else's network?

In discussion with companies it was quickly apparent that the learning needs articulated above were universal across the globe, across industry sectors and seemed to have rarely been addressed by such informal learning vehicles. No immediate comparators were identified. The oxymoron was that by creating a network, was the very structure of the network going to impede its free spirit, the very fuel of the learning process?

Similar to consortia programmes, if the learning process seemed to be quite magical then would the person specification, costs, suppliers etc. all end up heading into the same logistical and political quagmire? A loose collective of 13 companies was formed, they were all blue-chip names such as GlaxoWellcome, BP, Philips, British Airways, Seagrams and IBM amongst others. One by one informal conversations brought together representatives from the pharmaceutical, airline, oil, chemical and automotive industries, telecommunications, drinks, confectionery, food and fast moving consumer goods sectors, in addition to financial services, computer manufacturing, software and systems, electronics, and the media. The group comprised head to head competitors and suppliers who could as easily be competitors as partners. The global headquarters of the companies were distributed widely with six headquartered in the UK, two in Germany, one in the Netherlands, another from Canada, and three in the USA. Their combined employment exceeded 1.7 million and together represented an economy of a medium sized country. One was in the public sector. Almost all had or were experiencing consolidation in their industry, responding to new global pressures, fighting for survival by tight cost management or applying new innovations to add shareholder value. The absence of a high street retailer was a serious omission but as a starting point this represented a diverse if not completely comprehensive network. The geographical spread could have been broader but a start had been made.

The Network Comes to Life

NatWest volunteered to build upon the experience of the pilot programme and hosted a full workshop in June 1998, fully two years after the pilot programme.

In itself this illustrates the complexity of the early establishment phase. The logistics alone of getting 13 international companies together to agree the format and take shared ownership, had to be added to the essential debate on the necessary business cases and securing the necessary steps of faith. It was at times tediously time consuming, but it was vital that the critical preparation for the network was established on the right footing. Eleven of the founder companies took part with 38 delegates and faculty. The topic, appropriately, was 'Complexity and Ambiguity – the Challenge for Leadership'.

The topic was critical, not only for its context, but as a flagship issue to set the standard for future meetings. It had to be stretching and relevant, but transferable across the globe and across industries and functions. It was important in the first instance to avoid having delegate class experts in the workshop. A keynote input from an international academic, an economist and anthropologist, was the key catalyst. NatWest's Group CEO had agreed to host a dinner for delegates and sponsors from member companies, and shared his personal thoughts on the topic from both a professional and private viewpoint in a distinctly candid and 'off the record' manner. Two case studies from the members' own companies were used as illustrations of real issues, these being supported, and put in academic context, by two Ph.D. research fellows at a leading international business school sponsored by one of the member companies. An external guest speaker from Switzerland led a discussion on a recent mega-merger to stimulate debate on the uncertainty aspects of the topic. As with the pilot, the delegates rapidly assumed responsibility for the content of the workshop, the notional timetable was kept in the back of the mind rather than dominating the event, and feedback was extremely positive.

Outputs were essentially personal and their relevance depended on the context of the individual's role and their company's strategic agenda. The normal action plan output of education events was replaced with a series of sound-bites which were seen to allow the delegates a personal prompt to remember the experience and the learning. It also became a vehicle for sharing the emotion of the learning rather than the specific 'ah ha' factors with their sponsoring companies. Experience has subsequently suggested the need for more detail to enable the transfer of learning in the company and make it less of a selfish experience.

Feedback

The following are quotes from sponsoring companies:

- 'It was seen as a help in creating catalysts for change'.
- 'It encouraged external focus'.
- 'It made our people realise that there is complexity beyond our own challenges'.

Some of the delegates' feedback was equally encouraging:

- 'What a great reminder to challenge my own mindset'.
- 'I recognised that I need to move my organisation form a mechanical view of life to a brain view, why didn't I always know this?'
- 'In a world of management by numbers I guess you can't quantify complexity, or can you?'
- 'I was amazed at the instant respect we all had for each other, total strangers becoming close friends within a day'.

Not everyone was happy, a minority opinion was:

- 'I didn't get a great deal out of it, but then I'm probably the loser'.

Inevitably, and by design, the outputs were highly individualized but the corporate benefits whilst intangible were seen universally as positive. That is not to say there were no critics. For some delegates there was insufficient personal networking time, for others too much. For some the topic was too abstract, to others the escape from daily short-term pressures was an opportunity to put work in context. The total costs were seen as low and high added value. The chargeout rate was less than £600 plus travel per delegate.

What did we learn?

So what were some of the learnings? Was it really learning the hard way? Administratively it was a logistical nightmare. These executives were all critical people to their own corporations and the last minute cancellations could have presented an imbalance. The idea of some members that networks are self-actualising was tested to the limit. The need for a logistical hub was discovered to be critical. Was the academic balance too strong? Did all the companies match the person profile expected? Too many HR people came to 'try it out'. Some companies sent four delegates, some just one which was going to create a problem going forward as embedding the philosophy takes time and several cohorts are needed to drive the benefits home. The members decided themselves that they wanted to take the topic forward and establish an ongoing relationship.

A key factor was to be the appetite of the HR or Learning Director in the company and in particular their ability to influence their CEO or sponsoring business partners. Time was to show that where this was weak the network was potentially vulnerable to losing those participants. The network was to demonstrate clearly that in different ways the key to success was to be above all in three critical areas. Firstly, the ability of the HRD function to deliver executive commitment and hence the modest funds required. Secondly the vision to see that a learning network could present a unique extension to even the best developed hierarchy of learning interventions and education programmes, and thirdly the proximity of the HRD team to their very high potential executives. Could they deliver delegates on a 'trust me' basis rather than the conventional needs and solution analysis approach.

Another vital ingredient was to be the patience and tenacity in keeping the network together. Whilst the intellectual purity of a self-managed network was desirable, it was to prove critical that the energy of the NatWest team and the vision of one or two individuals would be required to sustain the momentum. A core membership of companies began to emerge and this was to be critical in the next phase and subsequent development beyond NatWest sponsorship and into a commercial network.

Adapting and Reflecting on the Experiences

So the model had stood the test of a full workshop. The businesses all continued to give support and the feedback encouraged the network to have another go. As a structural 'rule' it was decided that some of the delegates from each company would roll forward to the next event and others would join so creating a continuous learning experience. This was getting closer to a true network whilst allowing the concept and learning opportunity to be experienced by a greater number.

In November 1998 another workshop was held. Co-designed by three companies, organised by one of them, accommodation provided by a second and the third providing a case study. The numbers were kept smaller, 23 delegates. No academics were used but as before, the topic was approached from a non-conventional viewpoint. The subject was again of universal interest: 'Brands'. Four cases were used to examine the topic. One company had good experience of building the employee proposition as part of the brand, another taking a public sector brand into a global commercial market, another the pure advertising creation of a new brand. Finally 'Greenpeace' was used as an example of a brand being used for social pressure and its impact on changing commercial strategy and attitudes from outside the corporation or the customer/ supplier relationship. Additionally, on this occasion the design allowed time for delegates to bring their own 'Brand' problems to the group for mini brainstorms for action, drawing upon the diverse experiences of volunteer helpers to help new colleagues solve problems. The high profile business dinner host again proved to be a valuable reinforcement.

Where Now?

As companies have established more confidence in the network there have been a few key observable trends. The degree of passion for the network varies across the group and no doubt in time there will be some that drop off the listing and others will contribute a disproportionate amount of energy to sustain its life. The network needs a hub. The intellectually satisfying model of a self driven format has proven to lack the necessary commitment from all partners and the challenge will now be to formalize and fund the essential facilitation and focal point to ensure the momentum is not lost.

The next stage is a more structured Steering Group to formalize the commercial relationships, agree the agenda and ensure hosts for future events. The agenda already in the pipeline will embrace other key generic issues such as, 'Speed to market', 'Innovation and Entrepreneurship', 'New competitors', 'Electronic Commerce', 'Global financial strategy', 'The impact of new regulators' and so forth.

Already members of the Network have seen and taken opportunities as a direct result of the relationships established at the workshops. The 'keep in touch' end of course comment has for many become a reality as individuals have followed through the networking principle to help with personal challenges. This form of indirect mentoring is proving particularly popular. Individuals faced with challenges in their roles have frequently entered into e-mail debates to solve problems from the experience of new friends in different environments.

One member in the Network has agreed work assignments as part of their own internal action learning programme for senior managers to diversify their thinking with other Network members. The same executives will in due course reconnect with future Network activities thus sustaining the learning longer. Another member has used placements in non-competitor environments for similar action learning experiences. One oil company made an 'open house' invitation to all network companies to have them join other companies to experience a programme on innovation skills.

Other companies are examining the possibility of graduate exchanges, another creating a parallel HR Directors network, another is considering if the vehicle will adapt on an in-company basis, recognising that the diversity of its own group of companies creates a learning and development opportunity with a very similar challenge.

Inevitably there will be changes to the membership of the network. Strategic priorities will wax and wane. Personalities will change. It is most likely that the original 13 companies will reduce and be regrown with new members. The transfer from a free ride to a commercially funded hub will test the commitment from some, not only for straight financial reasons but also as such funding requires more formal budgetary commitment, albeit that the sums of money are small. That said, there is no shortage of international organizations that see the network as attractive and in turn they will bring new riches to the learning. Arguably it is critical that membership must change. The network needs committed members and new ideas and challenges. Complacency and apathy are its worst enemies and the membership has to be ruthless in the discard of any partners who fail to meet their collective responsibilities.

Hard Lessons in the Learning Process

Whilst the underpinning rationale for the network is very simple, the difficulties in bringing it into life were formidable and potentially are its downfall. It is unusual in failing to match the packaged solution and not easily meeting normal business evaluation criteria. After all the inputs are hard to define, the delegates are unknown to most, briefing is managed through a multitude of voices, many companies are willing to take part but a smaller number are able or willing to be active in their involvement for such a small population. The key has proven to be that where the most senior line executives and their learning teams are very close to each other, this initiative carries support without question. In the high sponsorship environments costs are not seen as an impediment, rather a high added value intervention. Time is made available for visible support and resources are more readily made available.

Choosing the right delegates is critical. They must be 'the very best of the very best' and want to learn. Delegates with the approach of going to learn how to do something better may well be disappointed. Nothing is taught, only learning is acquired. The group will not tolerate observers, so a high degree of personal contribution is not only essential but correlates directly with the enjoyment and personal learning gains from the experience. Self awareness in a peer group is a powerful experience but can also be quite threatening to those who find that when inside their organization they are invariably seen as Crown Princes or Princesses but when put with peers from other companies are ordinary foot soldiers.

The strength of the network rests in an implicit trust and belief that executives add value to themselves at the same time as they contribute value to others. It also assumes an implicit trust in the relationship of the companies and the need to respect privileged information.

Who can tell where networks of this nature will go in the future? Will it survive? The most important experience is doing it and recognising the learning on the journey is more valuable than the trophy at the end of the trip.

The network has also created a magic of its own. Ask the participants who have been on more than one event and would wish to have a resident season ticket! Where does the magic come from? The answer is the concept and the delegates.

Notes to Chapters in Part II

16 Facilitating High Performance Teamwork and Leadership

1   J. William Pfeiffer, and John E. Jones (eds.), *A Handbook of Structured Experiences for Human Relations Training*. San Diego: Pfeiffer & Co.,1981.

2   Geert Hofstede, *Cultures and Organizations: Software of the Mind – Intercultural Cooperation and Its Importance for Survival*. New York: McGraw-Hill, 1997; *Cultures Consequences: International Differences in Work-Related Values*. London: Sage, 1984; Kurt Lewin, *Resolving Social Conflicts: Field Theory in Social Science*. New York: American Psychological Association, 1997. Alfons Trompenaars, and Charles Hampden-Turner, *Riding the Waves of Culture: Understanding Cultural Diversity in Global Business*. London: Irwin, 1998. Charles Hampden-Turner and Alfons Trompenaars, *The Seven Cultures of Capitalism: Value Systems for Creating Wealth in the United States, Japan, Germany, France, Britain, Sweden and The Netherlands*. New York: Doubleday; 1993.

3   Roger W. Birkman, *True Colors: Get to Know Yourself and Others Better with the Highly Acclaimed Birkman Method*. Nashville: T. Nelson, 1995.

4   Meredith Belbin, *Changing the Way We Work*. London: Butterworth-Heinemann; 1997; *Managment Teams: Why They Succeed or Fail*. London: Butterworth-Heinemann; 1996; *Team Roles at Work*. London: Butterworth-Heinemann; 1996.

5   Isabel Briggs Myers, *Introduction to Type: A Guide to Understanding Your Results on the Myers-Briggs Type Indicator*. Palo Alto: Consulting Psychological Press, 1993; Isabel Briggs Myers, and Peter B. Myers, *Gifts Differing: Understanding Personality Type*. Consulting Psychologists Press; 1995.

6 Jon R. Katzenbach, and Douglas K. Smith, *The Wisdom of Teams: Creating the High-Performance Organization*. Boston, MA: Harvard Business School Press, 1992.

7 Irving L. Janis, *Groupthink: Psychological Studies of Policy Decisions and Fiascoes*. Boston, MA: Houghton Mifflin, 1982.

17 Executive Team Facilitation: Some Observations

* Chris Argyris, *Interpersonal Competence and Organizational Effectiveness*. Homewood, IL: Dorsey Press, 1962.

* Robert Blake, Studying Group Interaction. In: L. P. Bradford, K. Benne and J. Gibb, (eds.) *T-Group Theory and Laboratory Method*. New York: Wiley, 1963.

* Donna Deeprose, *Recharge Your Team: Keep Them Going and Going*. New York: AMCOM, 1998; *The Team Coach: Vital Skills for Supervisors and Managers*. New York: AMCOM, 1995.

* Thomas Ollerman, *Facilitator Intervention Profile*. Meza, Arizona: Innova, 1999.

* W. B. Reddy, *Intervention Skills: Process Consultation for Small Groups and Teams*. San Diego: Pfeiffer and Co., 1994.

* R. M. Schwartz, *The Practical Facilitator: Practical Wisdom for Developing Effective Groups*. San Francisco: Jossey-Bass, 1994.

* Irwin D. Yalom. *The Theory and Practice of Group Psychotherapy*. New York: Basic Books, 1995.

Recommended and Referenced Sources

This is not an exhaustive list of sources on action learning. It is meant as a convenient road map to the recent literature.

The sources are divided into five subject areas or themes :

Action Learning: Company Experiences.
Action Learning: Varieties in Approach and Philosophy.
Action Learning, Action Research and Organizational Learning.
Action Learning: (Multicultural) Team and Individual Development, Coaching and Facilitation.
Action Learning; Executive Learning and Development: Issues and Trends.

Action Learning: Company Experiences

Adams, Doris and Dixon, Nancy M. Action Learning at Digital Equipment. In: Mike Pedler (ed.) *Action Learning in Practice*. Aldershot, UK: Gower Press, 1997.

Auteri, Enrico. Fiat revs up the engines of change. *Personnel Journal*. 1994, 73 (5), pp. 107–13.

Balog, J. Kevin. Chief Executive Peer Groups: A Case Study in Action Learning. Ph.D. dissertation, Department of Leadership and Educational Policy Studies, Northern Illinois University, Dekalb, IL; 1993.

Barham, Kevin and Heimer, Claudia. *ABB The Dancing Giant: Creating the Globally Connected Corporation*. London: Financial Times and Pitman, 1998.

Bolt, J. F. Achieving the CEO's agenda: education for executives. *Management Review*. May 1993, pp. 44–8.

Boshyk, Yury. Beyond Knowledge Management: how companies mobilise experience. *The Financial Times*. 8 Feb. 1999, Mastering Management; pp. 12–13.

Casey, David and Pearce, David (eds.) *More than Management Development: Action Learning at GEC*. Farnborough, UK: Gower Press, 1977.

Corona, Paul L. Custom programs of executive education: a case study of the Indiana University School of Business – Whirlpool Corporation Partnership for Excellence – Manager Development Program. Ph.D. dissertation, Faculty of Education, Indiana University, 1998.

Dotlich, David and Noel, James L. *Action Learning: How the World's Top Companies Are Re-Creating Their Leaders and Themselves*. San Francisco: Jossey-Bass, 1998.

Foy, Nancy. Action Learning comes to industry. *Harvard Business Review*. April 1977, 55(5), pp. 158–68.

Freedman, Nigel J. Operation Centurion: managing transformation at Philips. *Long Range Planning*. 1996; 29(5), pp. 607–15.

Galvin, Robert W. Knowledge makes the difference at Motorola. *Strategy and Leadership*. March–April 1996, 24(2), pp. 42–43.

Gordon, Jack. My leader, myself: Faux freethinkers and the new cult of the CEO. *Training*. Nov. 1998, pp. 54–62.

Graves, Jacqueline M. Bye-bye Smarties? Corporate employees learn by solving real-life problems rather than being trained by consultants. *Fortune*, 22 August 1994, 130(4), p. 18.

Howard, Robert (ed.) *The Learning Imperative: Managing People for Continuous Innovation*. Boston, MA: Harvard Business Review Books, 1993.

Inglis, Scott. *Making the Most of Action Learning*. Aldershot, UK: Gower, 1994.

Kelly, Kevin. Motorola: training for the millennium. *Business Week*. 28 March 1994, pp. 158–163.

Noel, James L. and Charan, Ram. Leadership development at GE's Crotonville. *Human Resource Management*. 1988, 27(4), pp. 434–47.

Panni, Aziz. Centurion defends Philips. *International Management* July–August 1994, 49(6), pp. 22–5.

Ready, Douglas A. Educating the survivors. *Journal of Business Strategy*. March–April 1995, 16(2), pp. 28–37.

Sadler, Philip (ed.). *International Executive Development Programmes*. London: Kogan Page, 1998.

Santhanaraj, Stephen. The Philips' approach to management and organisation development. *Journal of Management Development*. 1990, 9(5), pp. 16–28.

Sattelberger, Thomas and Westerbarkey, Peter. HR initiates strategic culture change. In: Sadler, Philip (ed.). *International Executive Development Programmes*. London: Kogan Page, 1998.

Sellers, Patricia. Pepsico's new generation. *Fortune*, 1 April 1996; 133(6) pp. 44–49; European edition, pp. 110–18.

Sherman, Stratford. How tomorrow's best leaders are learning their stuff.

Fortune, 27 November 1995; 132(11), pp. 64–70; European edition, pp. 90–102.

Stewart, Thomas. GE keeps those ideas coming: it wrote the book on Management. now Jack Welch is rewriting it – to tap employees' brainpower. *Fortune*, 12 August 1991; 124(4), p. 40.

Stuart, Peggy. Global outlook brings good things to GE Medical. *Personnel Journal*. June 1992; 71(6), p.138.

Tichy, Noel and DeRose, Christopher. Roger Enrico's master class. *Fortune*, 27 November 1995; 132(11), pp. 71–2; European edition, pp. 105–6.

Ulrich, Burkhard and van Berk, Dr. Shaping the future: international management development at Volkswagen. In: Sadler, Philip (ed.), *International Executive Development Programmes*. London: Kogan Page, 1998.

Ultimatum at Philips. *Business Week*, 17 November 1997, pp. 30–1.

Walter, G. M. *Corporate Practices in Management Development*. New York: The Conference Board; 1996; no. 1158-96-RR.

Wiggenhorn, William. Motorola U: when training becomes an education. In: Robert Howard, (ed.), *The Learning Imperative: Managing People for Continuous Innovation*. Boston, MA: Harvard Business Review Books, 1993.

Yeung, A. K. and Ready, Douglas A. Developing leadership capabilities of global corporations: a comparative study in eight nations. *Human Resource Management*, 1995; 34(4), pp. 529–47.

Action Learning: Variations in Approach and Philosophy

The Traditonalist or 'Classical' Reg Revans School of Action Learning

Alan Mumford (in Pedler, 1997) provides a very good overview of the various approaches to action learning within what I have called the traditionalist or classical school of action learning, influenced by Reg Revans and his writing. It should be read first by anyone trying to navigate through the variations of action learning. Also instructive is the article by Nancy Dixon (in Pedler 1997) outlining some of the differences, as she sees it, between the US and UK approches to action learning.

Cusins, Peter. Action Learning revisited. *Industrial and Commercial Training*. 1995; 27(4), pp. 3–10.

Dixon, Nancy, M. More than just a task force. In: Mike Pedler (ed.), *Action Learning in Practice*. Aldershot, UK: Gower Press, 1997.

International Foundation for Action Learning. Newsletter.

Marquardt, Michael J. *Action Learning in Action: Transforming Problems and People for World-Class Organizational Learning*. Palo Alto: Davies-Black, 1999.

McGill, Ian and Beaty, Liz. *Action Learning: A Guide for Professional, Management and Educational Development*. London: Kogan Page, 1996.

McLaughlin, Hugh and Thorpe, Richard. Action Learning – a paradigm in emergence: the problems facing a challenge to traditional management education and development. *British Journal of Management*, March 1993; 4(1), pp. 19–27.

Morris, John. Action Learning: reflections on a process. *Journal of Management Development*. 1987; 6(2), pp. 57–70.

Mumford, Alan. How managers can become developers. *Personnel Management*. 1993; 25(6), pp. 42–5.

Mumford, Alan. *How Managers Can Develop Managers*. Aldershot, UK: Gower Press, 1998.

Mumford, Alan. Making the most of Action Learning. *Journal of European Industrial Training*, 1995; 19(5).

Mumford, Alan. Managers developing others through Action Learning. *Industrial and Commercial Training*. 1995; 27(2), pp. 19–27.

Mumford, Alan. A review of the literature. In: Mike Pedler (ed.), *Action Learning in Practice*. Aldershot, UK: Gower Press, 1997.

Mumford, Alan (ed.). *Action Learning at Work*. Aldershot, UK: Gower Press, 1997.

Pedler, Mike. *Action Learning for Managers*. London: Lemos & Crane, 1996.

Pedler, Mike. Interpreting Action Learning. In: John Burgoyne and Michael Reynolds (eds.), *Management Learning: Integrating Perspectives in Theory and Practice*. London: Sage, 1997.

Pedler, Mike (ed.). *Action Learning in Practice*, 3rd edn. Aldershot, UK: Gower Press, 1997.

Revans, Reginald W. *The ABC of Action Learning*. London: Lemos & Crane, 1998.

Revans, Reginald W. *Action Learning*. London: Blond & Briggs, 1979.

Revans, Reginald W. *The Origins and Growth of Action Learning*. Bromley, UK: Krieger [Chartwell-Bratt], 1982.

Revans, Reginald W. *The Theory of Practice in Management*. London: Macdonald, 1966.

Smith, Bryan and Dodds, Bod. *Developing Managers through Project-Based Learning*. Aldershot, UK: Gower Press, 1997.

Weinstein, Krystyna. *Action Learning: A Practical Guide*. Aldershot, UK: Gower Press, 1998.

Action Reflection Learning

Marsick, Victoria. Experience-based learning: executive learning outside the classroom. *Journal of Management Development*, 9(4), pp. 50–60.

Marsick, Victoria J.; Cederholm, Lars; Turner, Ernie and Pearson, Tony. Action-Reflection Learning. *Training and Development*. August 1992, pp. 63-6.

Marsick, Victoria J. (ed.), *Learning in the Workplace: Theory and Practice*. Beckenham, UK: Croom-Helm, 1987.

MiL Institute International Newsletter. Lund: Sweden

O'Oneil, Judy; Marsick, Victoria; Yorks, Lyle; Nilson, Glenn and Kolodny, Robert. Life on the seesaw: tensions in Action Reflection Learning™. In: Mike Pedler (ed.). *Action Learning in Practice*. Aldershot, UK: Gower Press, 1997.

Rohlin, Lennart; Skarvad, Per-Hugo; and Nilsson, Sven Ake. *Strategic Leadership in the Learning Society*. Lund: MiL Publishers, 1998.

See also the contributions on 'Reflection-in-Action'

Schön, D. *The Reflective Practitioner*. New York: Basic Books, 1983.

Seibert, Kent. Reflection-in-action: tools for cultivating on-the-job learning conditions. *Organizational Dynamics*. Winter 1999, pp. 54–65.

Seibert, Kent and Daudelin, Marilyn W. *The Role of Reflection in Managerial Learning: Theory, Research, and Practice*. New York: Quorum Books, 1999.

Business Driven Action Learning

See Boshyk; Dotlich and Noel; articles on Motorola and General Electric above.

Nixon, Bruce. Real time management development: a case study offering lessons for successful transformation. *International Journal of Business Transformation*. 1998; 1(4), pp. 222–28.

Rothwell, William J. *The Action Learning Guidebook: A Real-Time Strategy for Problem Solving Traning Design, and Employee Development*. San Francisco: Jossey-Bass, 1999.

Action Learning, Action Research and Organizational Learning

Argyris, Chris. *Knowledge for Action: A Guide to Overcoming Barriers to Organizational Change*. San Francisco: Jossey-Bass, 1993.

Argyris, Chris. *On Organizational Learning*. Oxford: Blackwell, 1992.

Argyris, Chris and Schön, Donald A. *Organizational Learning II: Theory, Method, and Practice*. Reading, MA: Addison-Wesley, 1996.

De Geus, Arie. *The Living Company*. Boston, MA: Harvard Business School Press, 1997.

Davenport, Thomas and Prusak, Laurence. *Working Knowledge: How Organizations Manage What They Know*. Boston, MA: Harvard Business School Press, 1998.

Dixon, Nancy M. *The Organizational Learning Cycle: How We Can Learn Collectively*. New York: McGraw-Hill, 1995.

Garrett, Robert. Learning is the core of organisational survival: Action Learning is the key integrating process. *Journal of Management Development*. 1987; 6(2), pp. 38–44.

Kleiner, Art and Roth, George. How to make experience your company's best teacher. *Harvard Business Review*, September 1997.

Kolb, D. *Experiential Learning*. Englewood Cliffs, NJ: Prentice-Hall, 1984.

Papows, Jeff. *Enterprise.com: Market Leadership in the Information Age*. London: Nicholas Brealey, 1999.

Pedler, Mike; Burgoyne, John and Boydell, Tom. *The Learning Company: A Strategy for Sustainable Development*. London: McGraw-Hill, 1997.

Senge, Peter. *The Fifth Discipline: The Art and Practice of the Learning Organization*. New York: Doubleday, 1990.

Starkey, Ken (ed.). *How Organizations Learn*. London: International Thomson Business Press, 1996.

Watkins, Karen E. and Marsick, Victoria J. *Sculpting the Learning Organization: Lessons in the Art and Science of Systemic Change*. San Francisco: Jossey-Bass, 1993.

Action Learning – (Multicultural) Team and Individual Development, Coaching and Facilitation

Argyris, Chris. *Interpersonal Competence and Organizational Effectiveness*. Homewood, IL: Dorsey Press, 1962.

Beaty, Liz; Bourner, Tom and Frost, Paul. Action Learning: reflections on becoming a set member. *Management Education and Development*. 1993; 24(4), pp. 350–67.

Belbin, Meredith. *Changing the Way We Work*. London: Butterworth-Heinemann, 1997.

Belbin, Meredith. *Management Teams: Why They Succeed or Fail*. London: Butterworth-Heinemann, 1996.

Belbin, Meredith. *Team Roles at Work*. London: Butterworth-Heinemann, 1996.

Birkman, Roger W. *True Colors: Get to Know Yourself and Others Better with the Highly Acclaimed Birkman Method*. Nashvile, TN: T. Nelson, 1995.

Blake, Robert. Studying group interaction. In: Bradford, L. P., Benne K. and Gibb J., (eds.), *T-Group Theory and Laboratory Method*. New York: Wiley, 1963.

Briggs Myers, Isabel. *Introduction to Type: A Guide to Understanding Your Results on the Myers-Briggs Type Indicator*. Palo Alto: Consulting Psychologists Press, 1993.

Briggs Myers, Isabel and Myers, Peter B. *Gifts Differing: Understanding Personality Type*. Palo Alto: Consulting Psychologists Press, 1995.

Deeprose, Donna. *Recharge Your Team: Keep Them Going and Going*. New York: AMCOM, 1998.

Deeprose, Donna. *The Team Coach: Vital Skills for Supervisors and Managers*. New York: AMCOM, 1995.

Dotlich, David and Cairo, Peter C. *Action Coaching: How to Leverage Individual Performance for Company Success*. San Francisco: Jossey-Bass, 1999.

Hall, Douglas T. Otazo, Karen L. and Hollenbeck, George P. Behind closed doors: what really happens in executive coaching. *Organizational Dynamics*. Winter 1999, pp. 39–53.

Hampden-Turner, Charles and Trompenaars, Alfons. *The Seven Cultures of Capitalism: Value Systems for Creating Wealth in the United States, Japan, Germany, France, Britain, Sweden and The Netherlands*. New York: Doubleday, 1993.

Hofstede, Geert. *Cultures Consequences: International Differences in Work-Related Values*. London: Sage, 1984.

Janis, Irving L. *Groupthink: Psychological Studies of Policy Decisions and Fiascos*. Boston, MA: Houghton Mifflin, 1982.

Katzenbach, Jon R. and Smith, Douglas K. *The Wisdom of Teams: Creating the High-Performance Organization*. Boston, MA: Harvard Business School Press, 1992.

Lewin, Kurt. *Resolving Social Conflicts: Field Theory in Social Science*. New York: American Psychological Association, 1997.

Liebowitz, S. Jay and Holden, Kevin T. Are self-managing teams worthwhile? A tale of two companies. *SAM Advanced Management Journal*. 1995; 60(2), pp. 11–17.

McCauley, Cynthia D.; Moxley, Russ S. and Van Velsor, Ellen (eds.), *The Center for Creative Leadership Handbook of Leadership Development*. San Francisco: Jossey-Bass, 1998.

Ollerman, Thomas. *Facilitator Intervention Profile*. Meza, AZ: Innova, 1999.

Pfeiffer, J. William and Jones, John E. (eds.), *A Handbook of Structured Experiences for Human Relations Training*. San Diego, CA: Pfeiffer, 1981.

Reddy, W. B. *Intervention Skills: Process Consultation for Small Groups and Teams*. San Diego, CA: Pfeiffer, 1994.

Schwartz, R. M. *The Practical Facilitator: Practical Wisdom for Developing Effective Groups*. San Francisco: Jossey-Bass, 1994.

Tornow, Walter W. (ed.). *Maximizing the Value of 360-Degree Feedback: A Process for Successful Individual and Organizational Development*. San Francisco: Jossey-Bass, 1998.

Trompenaars, Alfons and Hampden-Turner, Charles. *Riding the Waves of Culture: Understanding Cultural Diversity in Global Business*. London: Irwin, 1998.

Vallely, Ian. Grow your people to grow your business. *Works Management*. 1993; 46(8), pp. 24–25.

Versteeg, Anna. Self-directed work teams yield long-term benefits. *Journal of Business Strategy*, 1990; 11(6), pp. 9–12.

Vince, Russ and Martin, Linda. Inside Action Learning: an exploration of the psychology and politics of the Action Learning model. *Management Education and Development*, 1993; 24(3), pp. 205–215.

Yalom. Irwin D. *The Theory and Practice of Group Psychotherapy*. New York: Basic Books, 1995.

Action Learning; Executive Learning and Development: Issues and Trends

Argyris, Chris. The executive mind and double-loop learning. *Organizational Dynamics*. Autumn 1992, pp. 5–22.

Argyris, Chris. Good communication that blocks learning. *Harvard Business Review*. July–August 1994; pp. 77–86.

Argyris, Chris. *Interpersonal Competence and Organizational Effectiveness*. Homewood, IL: Dorsey Press, 1962.

Argyris, Chris. Kurt Lewin Award Lecture, 1997: Field theory as a basis for scholarly consulting. *Journal of Social Issues*, 53(4), pp. 811–27.

Argyris, Chris. Teaching smart people how to learn. In: Robert Howard, (ed.), *The Learning Imperative: Managing People for Continuous Innovation*. Boston, MA: Harvard Business Review Books; 1993.

Bolt, J. F. Tailor executive development to strategy. *Harvard Business Review*, November 1986; 63(6), pp. 168–76.

Bolt, J. F. Ten years of change in executive education. *Training and Development*, August 1993, pp. 43–4.

Bongiorno, Lori. Corporate America's new lesson plan. *Business Week*, October 1993, pp. 102–4.

Boshyk, Yury. Trends in executive learning. *Japan Trends '99*. January 1999, p. 55.

Bradshaw, Della. Schools turn their attention to star qualities: growth is being fuelled by a distinct shift in demand from open enrolment programmes to customised programmes. *Financial Times*. London; 11 October 1999; *Financial Times Survey*: Business Education: I.

Cramer, Stuart and Dearlove, Des. *Gravy Training: Inside the World's Top Business Schools*. Oxford: Capstone, 1998.

Garratt, Robert. *The Learning Organization and the Need for Directors Who Think*. Aldershot: Gower, 1987.

Majors, Gail and Sinclair, Mary-Jane. Measure results for program success. *HR Magazine* 1994; 39(11), pp. 57–61.

Miller, P. A strategic look at management development. *Personnel Management*. August 1991, 23, pp. 45–48.

Mumford, Alan. New ideas on Action Learning. In *Approaches to Action Learning: Papers Delivered at a Private Seminar in London*. Keele, UK: Mercia Publications, University of Keele, 1992.

Otala, Leenamaija. *European Approaches to Lifelong Learning: Trends in Industry Practices and Industry – University Cooperation in Adult Education and Training*. Geneva: European University-Industry Forum (CRE-ERT: Standing Conference of Rectors, Presidents and Vice-Chancellors of the European Universities, and The European Round Table of Industrialists), 1992.

Plompen, Martine (ed.). *Unleashing the Power of Learning: Executive Education and Development in Europe*. Brussels: European Foundation for Management Development, 1999.

PriceWaterhouse Change Integration Team. *The Paradox Principles: How High-Performance Companies Manage Chaos, Complexity and Contradiction to Achieve Superior Results*. Chicago: Irwin, 1996.

Reading, writing, and enrichment: private money is pouring into American education – and transforming it. *The Economist*, London; 16 January 1999, pp. 57–8.

Ready, D. A., Vicere A. A. and White, A. F. Linking executive education to strategic imperatives. *Management Learning*. 1994; 25(4), pp. 563–78.

Seibert, Kent; Hall. D. T. and Kram, E. K. Strengthening the weak link in strategic executive development: integrating individual development and global business strategy. *Human Resource Management*. 1995, 34(4), pp. 549–67.

Teare, Richard; Davies, David and Sanderlands, Eric. *The Virtual University: An Action Paradigm and Process for WorkPlace Learning*. New York: Continuum, 1999.

Vallely, Ian. Grow your people to grow your business. *Works Management*. 1993; 46(8), pp. 24–25.

Versteeg, Anna. Self-directed work teams yield long-term benefits. *Journal of Business Strategy*. 1990; 11(6), pp. 9–12.

Vicere, A. A. and Fulmer, R. M. *Crafting Competitiveness: Developing Leaders in the Shadow Pyramid*. Oxford: Capstone, 1996.

Vicere, Albert A. and Fulmer, Robert M. *Leadership by Design: How Benchmark Companies Sustain Success through Investment in Continuous Learning*. Boston, MA: Harvard Business School Press, 1999.

About the Contributors

Nigel Barrett

nbarrett@dircon.co.uk

Managing Director of Balanced Learning, a specialist human resource consultancy. He holds a Visiting Fellowship in the field of Executive Development at Cranfield School of Management, and is an Affiliate Professor of HR Strategy at the Theseus Institute. After graduating from Churchill College, Cambridge, Nigel had an extensive career in the railway industry for 12 years and then moved to the banking and financial services sector, holding several senior HR positions across the Midland Group and then for the HSBC Group across Europe, following the merger with Midland in 1992. In 1994 Nigel joined the NatWest Group where he led the Group's Executive and Organizational Development strategy.

Matthias Bellmann

Matthias.Bellmann@ZP.SIEMENS.DE

Recently appointed Group Vice President, Personnel, Information and Communication Products, and formerly Executive Director Corporate Human Resources at Siemens AG with responsibilities for HR Development, Management Learning and the Siemens International Leadership Center Feldafing, Germany. Before then he was with Asea Brown Boveri and Nixdorf Computer and was engaged with Training, Management Development, Change Management and Business Consulting. He studied psychology and pedagogy and specializes in adult education and human resources management.

Yury Boshyk

Yury.Boshyk@global exec-learning.com *and* boshyk@theseus.fr

Founder and Director of Global Executive and Business Driven Action Learning; involved in designing, teaching and organizing business driven action learning programmes for over ten years with General Electric, Johnson &

Johnson and other multinationals. Professor of Strategy and International Business, Theseus International Management Institute, Adjunct Professor, Ivey School of Business, University of Western Ontario, and formerly with IMD in Switzerland, University of Toronto, and Harvard. He is also a consultant and author. He received his doctorate from the University of Oxford and his M.Sc. from the London School of Economics.

Ron Bossert rbosser@corus.jnj.com

Director, Education and Development at Johnson & Johnson World Headquarters in New Brunswick, where he is responsible for Executive Development. Prior to joining Johnson & Johnson in 1989, he held a number of managerial positions in management education at Mack Trucks, and various administrative and teaching positions in the Illinois and Pennsylvania State College and University Systems, and Cedar Crest College. He has also consulted and conducted management development programmes for several multinational organizations. Dr. Bossert's educational background includes a Doctorate in Higher Education Administration from Pennsylvania State University.

Wolfgang Braun w.braun@metagroup.com

Managing Director and Partner in the firm META Mergers & Acquisitions. Until 1998, Wolfgang Braun was Vice President Corporate Executive Development and International Management Programs in the Daimler Chrysler Corporate University. Prior to this assignment, he was the Director for Business Development and Senior Manager Corporate Strategy at the Systemhaus of Daimler-Benz Inter Services. Wolfgang Braun has worked as IT-Manager for the Chief Information Officer of Robert Bosch and as a Business Consultant for Digital Equipment. He was a Product Manager for Computer Products and developed and launched three software products as an entrepreneur at Hewlett-Packard. He earned a Master of Science degree under the Fulbright scholarship program and received a Diplom Ingenieur degree from the Fachhochschule in Furtwangen.

Nigel J. Freedman Nigel.Freedman@theseus.fr

Professor of Strategy at Theseus International Management Institute and Adjunct Professor at The Peter Drucker School of Management at Claremont Graduate University, California. Before then he was at Philips Headquarters in The Netherlands where he was a member of the Corporate Strategy Group for ten years, with special interests in the development of strategic management and in new business activities, and later became Deputy Director of Management Training & Development. He is a Founder Member of the Strategic Management Society, past member of the Editorial Board of Strategic Management Journal and editor of the book 'Strategic Management in Major Multinational Companies'.

Mary Rose Greville

Greville@theseus.fr

Professor of Organizational Behaviour at the Theseus Institute, formerly with IMD in Switzerland and currently also a member of the academic staff at the School of Business Studies, Trinity College, University of Dublin. She specializes in leadership in changing and ambiguous situations, building high performance teams, and changing corporate cultures. Professor Greville has acted as consultant to numerous corporations and organizations. Professor Greville is Irish and graduated with first class honours in social sciences at University College, Dublin. She has a diploma in European Studies from the College of Europe, Bruges, and a M.Phil in sociology from the University of Kent at Canterbury, UK.

Pierre Guillon

pguillon@dow.com

A member of the Global Human Resources Development (HRD) Strategic Center for The Dow Chemical Company, he is in charge of benchmarking activities and leads the HRD team on the Strategic Growth Initiative. He joined Dow in France in 1978 as Account Manager and later chose to work in the Human Resources management group, often in line assignments, in Spain, Switzerland, Benelux and for all Europe. On the global level he led the Measurement team, focusing on client satisfaction, employee surveys, corporate scorecards and benchmarking activities. Pierre holds a B.A. in International Law and Economics from the University of Paris. Perhaps because he has sailed around the world, he is located in a virtual office in Normandy, France.

Ken Hansen

A10278@Namerica.mot.com

As Vice President and General Manager of Motorola University, he has responsibility for the University's operations in Europe, the Middle East, Africa and Asia Pacific regions. In this capacity, he oversees a diverse organization of 220 professional training associates in 22 countries around the world. The operations staff consists of instructional technology professionals, and functional experts on delivery functions. Ken joined Motorola in 1992 from Xerox Corporation where he was Director of Corporate Education and Training. Ken served on the Board of Directors of Lake Forest Graduate School of Management, and is a past member of the Board of Directors of the American Society for Training and Development.

Colin Hasting   colinhastings@btconnect.com

A consultant, author, teacher and speaker, he spent ten years in management and then nine years on the faculty of Ashridge Management College. In 1988 he co-founded New Organization Consulting, which focuses on the management of change, in particular the project way of working, cross boundary and international teamworking, and new organization forms. Colin is co-author of two books, 'Superteams' and 'Project Leadership', recently released in a new expanded second edition. He has also published 'The New Organization: Growing the Culture of Organizational Networking'.

Ron Hosta   Ron.Hosta@theseus.fr Ron.Hosta@theseus.fr

Joined IBM as a financial analyst in May 1968 and held several management positions in the area of supply/demand planning. In 1993 he accepted a position in the Latin American Headquarters as manager of Leadership and Executive Development and then returned to headquarters to take responsibility for the Global Executive Program and the New External Hire Executive Orientation Program at a time when IBM was under the newly apponted CEO Louis V. Gerstner, Jr. Ron retired from IBM recently after a thirty year career. Ron has a B.Sc. in accounting and finance from the University of Vermont and an MBA from the State University of New York at Albany. He is currently associated with the Theseus Institute as executive-in-residence.

Robert Kasprzyk   RKASPRZYK@dow.com

Global Director of Employee Development for the Dow Chemical Company, responsible for the design of the ongoing learning resources and employee development process, and leads a team of professionals focused on improving individual development and effectiveness. Before then he was the Director of Executive Education for the Dow Chemical Company. He was responsible for the design of the ongoing worldwide leadership development network activities focused on the senior executives of the Dow Chemical Company. He also led the Executive Education for Future Leaders process and was involved in the design of, and renewed interest in, 360 degree feedback and employee data gathering.

Wolfgang Kissel

wolfgang.kissel@roche.com

Vice President, International Human Resources and Management Development at Hoffman La Roche, Diagnostics Division responsible for supporting the integration process of Roche and Boehringer Mannheim, and for the Top 300 people. Before the acquisition he was Vice President Management Development at Boehringer Mannheim. He joined the company after graduating with a doctoral degree from the Institute of Toxicology, University of Mainz in Germany.

Gordon L. Lackie

lackie@hetnet.nl

Although fully qualified as a Chartered Mechanical Engineer, he has mainly worked as a Management Consultant. In 1978, he emigrated to The Netherlands, and joined a client company (Ballast Nedam NV). In recent years, he has concentrated upon Management Development. He achieved most personal satisfaction from working with Ballast Nedam's 'young potentials', by implementing the company's 'Initial Management (Training) Programme', and from organizing its first company-wide Management Game. He has been actively involved in the BOSNO Consortium action learning programme since 1986. He has a Dutch wife, holds both British and Dutch nationalities but values, most of all, his Scottish origins.

Victoria M. LeGros

Victoria.M.LeGros@usa.dupont.com

While she is still working in DuPont's Photopolymer & Electronic Materials Business, she is currently 'on loan' to corporate Human Resources where she is responsible for the design, development and delivery of the Leadership for Growth (LFG) action learning programme. LFG has been recognized as a 'best practice' by the American Society of Training and Development. Vickie started her DuPont career in 1979 as salesperson for the former Medical Products Department. In subsequent years she had various business management, marketing and operations assignments in DuPont's Electronic Imaging and Printing & Publishing businesses.

Patricia Levy

p.levy@sympatico.ca

A Canadian lawyer and private consultant who has acted as country coordinator in executive development action learning programmes in the USA, Canada, the Czech Republic and Slovakia for several mutinationals. She held legal and policy positions in the Government of Ontario, and helped establish an independent legal and business advisory consulting firm which represents multinational Swiss and North American companies within the Czech Republic and Europe. She received an Honours Bachelor of Arts degree from the University of Toronto and a Bachelor of Laws degree from Osgoode Hall Law School in Toronto. She holds Canadian and Swiss citizenships and presently has offices in Toronto and Prague.

Stephen Mercer   stephen.r.mercer@boeing.com

Since 1998 Vice President, Learning and Leadership Development, The Boeing Company where he is responsible for leading the team tasked with creating the Boeing Leadership Center – including a new educational campus and learning centre in St. Louis and integrating the leadership development curriculum. Before then Steve was with the General Electric Company for thirty years. After several other assignments throughout the corporation, he was appointed to the GE Management Development Institute in Crotonville. For many years he was director of GE's executive level action learning programmes. He and his team led action learning programmes in over 50 countries on five continents. His team also delivered the Crotonville Core Leadership Development curriculum, as well as special customer Executive Programs for GE's global customers in such areas as China, Southeast Asia, and Russia. He holds a mechanical engineering degree from City College and an MBA from Xavier University.

Guy Mollet   gs.mollett@village.uunet.be

Holds a MSc. Degree in Civil Engineering from the Rijksuniversiteit Gent, in Belgium and for two years he was an assistant professor at the same University. After his military service he worked for ten years in Paris and in Brussels as a consultant for the French Consulting group AndrÈ Vidal & Paul Planus. In 1978 he joined the Volkswagen Group as Personnel Director of Volkswagen Brussels SA. Between 1998 and 1992 he was VP-HR of Volkswagen of America and later of the VW-North American Region (USA, Canada & Mexico). In 1993, as programme director, he created and conceived the VW-Group Management Development Department. Since 1995 Guy Mollet has been appointed Director of HR-Research and Benchmarking for the VW-Group worldwide. He now works as an independent consultant.

Tom Ollerman   tom@innovainc.com

President of INNOVA, Inc., an international consulting firm specializing in organizational creativity and innovation, located in Mesa, Arizona. He has been

Director of Behavioral Medicine in a large medical teaching hospital, an international seminar leader and consultant for twenty one years, as well as holding graduate teaching positions on three university faculties. He is a licenced Psychologist and an Associate Member of the American Psychological Association and the American Management Association. He holds a Ph.D. in Counseling Psychology and completed a NIGH Postdoctoral Fellowship in Community Psychology at Johns Hopkins Medical School, Department of Psychiatry, Baltimore, Maryland. He enjoys white water rafting and training guide dogs for visually impaired children.

Jeannine Sorge
jsorge@dow.com

Manages global Human Resources communications for The Dow Chemical Company where she provides expert communications counsel to her clients in the areas of compensation, benefits, human resource development, and workforce planning. Most recently, she has provided communications expertise in the implementation of the Six Sigma process within Dow. Upon receiving her Master's degree in Public Relations from Michigan State University, Jeannine joined Merck & Co., Inc., in Marketing Communications, where she provided writing, editing, and design expertise in support of animal health and agricultural products, as well as human health pharmaceuticals.

Paula S. Topolosky
Paula.s.Topolosky@usa.dupont.com

Paula has worked for the DuPont Company for 23 years and is currently a Business & Organizational Consultant in the Global Services Business, an internal shared services group that supports all of the Strategic Business Units in the company. During her tenure with DuPont, Paula has led various groups including Instructional Design, Technical Publications and Printed Communications. Currently, she specializes in leadership development, particularly at the first line and middle management levels, and assists the businesses manage large-scale organizational change. In 1998, she completed her doctorate and is planning to publish her dissertation entitled 'A Historical Study Investigating the Relationship Between Employee Satisfaction and Business Results'.

Miko Weidemanis
miko.weidemanis@hq.scancem.com

Senior Vice President Human Resources and Board Member, Scancem AB, a leading material producer in Scandinavia with headquarters in Malmo Sweden and with large subsidiaries in the USA, UK, Germany, Africa and in Asia. He has had numerous international assignments and for several companies such as the Nitro Nobel Group, the Tarkett Group and others. He continues to play an active role on many boards both in Scandinavia and abroad. He holds an MBA from the Gothenburg School of Economics.

Index

259